The World of the Roosevelts

Published in cooperation with the Franklin and Eleanor Roosevelt Institute
Hyde Park, New York

General Editors:
William E. Leuchtenburg, William vanden Heuvel,
Douglas Brinkley, and David B. Woolner

FDR AND HIS CONTEMPORARIES
Foreign Perceptions of an American
President
Edited by Cornelis A. van Minnen and
John F. Sears

NATO: THE FOUNDING OF
THE ATLANTIC ALLIANCE AND
THE INTEGRATION OF EUROPE
Edited by Francis H. Heller and John R.
Gillingham

AMERICA UNBOUND
World War II and the Making of a
Superpower
Edited by Warren F. Kimball

THE ORIGINS OF U.S. NUCLEAR
STRATEGY, 1945–1953
Samuel R. Williamson, Jr. and Steven L.
Rearden

AMERICAN DIPLOMATS IN THE
NETHERLANDS, 1815–50
Cornelis A. van Minnen

EISENHOWER, KENNEDY, AND
THE UNITED STATES OF EUROPE
Pascaline Winand

ALLIES AT WAR
The Soviet, American, and British
Experience, 1939–1945
Edited by David Reynolds, Warren F.
Kimball, and A. O. Chubarian

THE ATLANTIC CHARTER
Edited by Douglas Brinkley and David R.
Facey-Crowther

PEARL HARBOR REVISITED
Edited by Robert W. Love, Jr.

FDR AND THE HOLOCAUST
Edited by Verne W. Newton

THE UNITED STATES AND THE
INTEGRATION OF EUROPE
Legacies of the Postwar Era
Edited by Francis H. Heller and
John R. Gillingham

ADENAUER AND KENNEDY
A Study in German-American Relations
Frank A. Mayer

THEODORE ROOSEVELT AND
THE BRITISH EMPIRE
A Study in Presidential Statecraft
William N. Tilchin

TARIFFS, TRADE AND EUROPEAN
INTEGRATION, 1947–1957
From Study Group to Common Market
Wendy Asbeek Brusse

SUMNER WELLES
FDR's Global Strategist
A Biography by Benjamin Welles

THE NEW DEAL AND PUBLIC
POLICY
Edited by Byron W. Daynes,
William D. Pederson, and
Michael P. Riccards

WORLD WAR II IN EUROPE
Edited by Charles F. Brower

FDR AND THE U.S. NAVY
Edward J. Marolda

THE SECOND QUEBEC
CONFERENCE REVISITED
Edited by David B. Woolner

Eleanor Roosevelt and Adlai Stevenson

Richard Henry

macmillan

First published in hardcover in 2010 by PALGRAVE MACMILLAN® in the United States—a division of St. Martin's Press LLC, 175 Fifth Avenue, New York, NY 10010.

Where this book is distributed in the UK, Europe and the rest of the world, this is by Palgrave Macmillan, a division of Macmillan Publishers Limited, registered in England, company number 785998, of Houndmills, Basingstoke, Hampshire RG21 6XS.

Palgrave Macmillan is the global academic imprint of the above companies and has companies and representatives throughout the world.

Palgrave® and Macmillan® are registered trademarks in the United States, the United Kingdom, Europe and other countries.

ISBN: 978–1–137–27032–0

The Library of Congress has cataloged the hardcover edition as follows:

Henry, Richard, 1921–
    Eleanor Roosevelt and Adlai Stevenson / by Richard Henry.
        p. cm.—(The world of the Roosevelts series)
    Includes bibliographical references and index.
    ISBN 978–0–230–61826–8
        1. Roosevelt, Eleanor, 1884–1962. 2. Stevenson, Adlai E. (Adlai Ewing), 1900–1965. 3. Roosevelt, Eleanor, 1884–1962—Political and social views. 4. Stevenson, Adlai E. (Adlai Ewing), 1900–1965—Political and social views. 5. Presidents' spouses—United States—Biography. 6. Statesmen—United States—Biography. 7. Friendship—United States—Case studies. 8. United States—Politics and government—1945–1989. 9. African Americans—Civil rights—History—20th century. I. Title.

E807.1.R48H45 2010
973.9—dc22   2010000109

A catalogue record of the book is available from the British Library.

Design by Newgen Imaging Systems (P) Ltd., Chennai, India.

First PALGRAVE MACMILLAN paperback edition: October 2012

10 9 8 7 6 5 4 3 2 1

Printed in the United States of America.

CONTENTS

PART I

CHAPTER 1

THE UNITED NATIONS, CRUCIBLE OF THE ALLIANCE

IN JANUARY 1941, immediately following his inauguration for a third term, President Roosevelt turned his prodigious energies to securing passage of H.R, 1776, the so-called "lend-lease bill." The measure authorized the president to transfer any supplies, including munitions, "to the government of any country whose defense the President deems vital to the defense of the U.S." It was a rather thinly disguised device—seen as such by much of the nation's media—for circumventing the widespread isolationist sentiment of the populace; many predicted an extended and bitter debate in Congress.

But Roosevelt, master tactician that he was, had prepared to capture the initiative from congressmen and senators who still thought the United States could stay out of "Europe's war."[1] In January he had sent Harry Hopkins, his trusted White House advisor, on a secret mission to ascertain from the U.K. prime minister the nature and extent of England's needs for American assistance. The prime minister was preparing a major speech that would be broadcast on worldwide radio networks. At Roosevelt's request, according to Doris Kearns Goodwin,

> Hopkins asked Churchill to skew the speech to American public opinion by promising that lend-lease was the best means to keep the Americans out of the war. A month later Wendell Willkie, Republican candidate for President who had run a strong race against Roosevelt the previous year, had carried a personal message from FDR to Churchill, containing a verse from Longfellow's *The Building of the Ship:*
>
> Sail On, O Ship of State, Sail On, O Union Strong and great! Humanity with all its fears, With all the hopes of future years, Is hanging breathless on thy fate!

Churchill had used those lines in his February 9 speech, adding: "We do not need the gallant armies which are forming throughout the American Union.... Put your confidence in us.... We shall not fail or falter.... Give us the tools and we will finish the job."

On his return to the United States, Willkie went immediately to the Hill to support the bill, saying, "If the Republican party makes a blind opposition to the bill and allows itself to be presented to the American people as the isolationist party, it will never again gain control of the American government."[2]

The bill sailed through both houses with substantial majorities, and at ten minutes of four on the afternoon of March 11, a smiling Roosevelt signed lend-lease into law. Three hours later, the president declared the defense of Britain vital to the U.S. and authorized the navy to turn over to Britain thousands of naval guns and ammunition, three thousand charges for bombs, and two dozen PT boats. Full of confidence, the president told reporters he had already begun work on a supplemental request of $7 billion to implement lend-lease.[3]

That summer the 16,000 workers at the Federal Ship-building and Dry Dock Corporation in Kearney, New Jersey voted to strike. The company had refused to accept National Defense Mediation Board recommendations, and secretary of the navy Frank Knox decided to take over the entire plant. A presidential executive order authorizing such a move would be required. On August 9, Secretary Knox decided to send his new assistant, Adlai Stevenson, to carry the necessary papers to the president for his signature. The next day, shortly before Stevenson departed from his Navy Department office, Secretary Knox confided that there was a second reason for the mission: He had just learned from Admiral Chester Nimitz that "a heretofore reliable source" had just reported that Stalin and Hitler had begun secret negotiations "You are to deliver this message to the President, and to no one else," said the admiral.

Roosevelt, it developed, was aboard the heavy cruiser *Augusta* steaming toward Rockland, Maine from a secret meeting off the Newfoundland shore with Prime Minister Churchill. The two leaders had just completed what came to be known as the " Atlantic Charter," setting forth the war aims of the Allies. Here Walter Johnson, editor of the eight-volume *The Papers of Adlai E. Stevenson*, takes up the story:[4]

What took place on his trip to see the President, Stevenson enjoyed telling in immense detail.... Weather prevented Stevenson's airplane from taking off. When the plane finally reached Rockland, the President's ship had already docked.

Stevenson persuaded the pilot to land in a primitive grass field, then flagged a car down and asked the driver to take him into town. But as Stevenson reached the station, the train was departing. He had the pilot fly him to Portland.

After several hours watching a motion picture until the President's train reached Portland, Stevenson found the platform blocked by a huge crowd of people. Portland police were unimpressed when he told them he had an important message for Roosevelt. Finally Senator Claude Pepper of Florida appeared and Stevenson explained the urgency of his mission. Pepper went aboard the train and after some fifteen minutes a presidential aide, Edwin M. Watson, emerged and asked Stevenson for his papers. After Stevenson refused, Watson returned to the train. Five minutes later, Watson appeared again and said the President would see him

Roosevelt was at dinner with Mrs. Roosevelt, Harry Hopkins, Grace Tully—the President's personal secretary—and presidential aide Marvin McIntyre as Stevenson entered the car.

"Well, Adlai," said Roosevelt smiling. "I'm glad to see you again. Glad to hear you're working for Frank Knox."

According to Stevenson, he mumbled something incoherent and said he had some emergency papers for the President to sign.

"Let's have a look at them," Roosevelt said.

Stevenson's own written account of what occurred follows.

I opened up my brief case clumsily and fished out the Kearney shipyard papers. I explained the intricate situation as best I could, as the President's dinner got colder and the others more restive, and pointed out where he was supposed to sign the order. He looked it over for a minute and then said:

"Well now, Adlai, you just leave all these papers in your folder with me, and I'll read them over tonight. We'll have a meeting at the White House in the morning. You fly back to Washington and arrange it. Tell Secretary Knox I'd also like to see him and Myron Taylor and the Attorney General at nine o'clock—and you be there, too."

"But Mr. President," I said, "this executive order is supposed to be signed right now!"

"I think it will work out all right this way," said the President.

"Well," I said, "if you say so I guess it will be O.K!" I marvel that I could have talked like such a fool but I was so nervous I hardly knew what I was saying—mostly, I suppose, because I hadn't yet said the really important thing—the message—and I didn't know how to deliver it with all those people sitting around. I could see he was waiting for me to leave, and I had to come out with something. The talk went about like this:

"I have something else to tell you, Mr. President."

"Do you, Adlai? What is it?"

"Well, Mr. President, it's a message from Admiral Nimitz. He said to tell you...alone."

"Oh, I think you can tell me here, Adlai."

"No, I can't." I had a feeling that everyone was doing his best to keep from laughing! I had an idea, just in time. "Can I write it down, sir?"

"Why, certainly."

I took the menu and I wrote on the back of it, "Admiral Nimitz has heard from a heretofore reliable source that Stalin has started negotiations with Hitler."

Then I gave him back the menu. He read it carefully and then looked up at me.

"Adlai," he said, "do you believe this?"

That was too much! I didn't know what I thought. "Why, I don't know, Mr. President," I stammered.

"I don't believe it," said F.D.R. "I'm not worried at all. Are you worried, Adlai?"

I said I guessed I wasn't so much worried after all. Then, mission completed after a fashion, I took my departure, and in my embarrassed confusion, I wheeled around and crashed right into a closed door, thus bending my crooked nose some more. I flew back to Washington, woke Secretary Knox to tell him about the meeting at the White House, and we all went over there at nine o'clock. My crowning mortification was that the President hadn't even opened the envelope containing my precious Kearney shipyard papers. He pulled them out and settled the whole business in fifteen minutes and signed the Executive Order. As for the negotiations between Stalin and Hitler, the President was, of course, right, and the Admiral's source was unreliable, that time."

The two principals of this memoir had been formally introduced (rather awkwardly from Stevenson's point of view) but he and Eleanor Roosevelt would not become personally acquainted for another four years—in London.

* * *

Navy Secretary Frank Knox died suddenly in the spring of 1944, and Stevenson resigned from the Navy Department shortly thereafter to return to his Chicago law practice. (A year later he would receive the Navy's Distinguished Civilian Service Award for "outstanding service to the United States Navy...from June 30, 1941 to June 13, 1944.") Three months later he joined his friend George Ball in London as a member of the U.S. Strategic Bombing Survey, a special presidential mission to assess the effects of Allied bombing in Germany. "He did a hell of a job," Ball reported, "worked very hard, interviewed everybody. When he undertook any job like that he was absolutely tireless."[5] Before leaving to take up his new responsibilities, Stevenson had been offered the directorship of the newly created Foreign Economic Administration, whose function would be to "assure proper distribution of surplus property abroad and the settlement of claims in other countries." Almost simultaneously the

Office of War Information had asked him to head all its overseas operations. He refused both positions but was clearly now well on the road to the international role he had long wished for.

In February 1945, as World War II was nearing its end, Stevenson went again to Washington, this time as assistant to Archibald MacLeish, special assistant secretary of state in charge of Public and Cultural Relations. Occasionally he also worked directly for MacLeish's boss, Secretary of State Edward R. Stettinius. On April 12, President Roosevelt died at Warm Springs, Georgia of a massive cerebral hemorrhage. In May, following a plan he had conceived with Churchill and Stalin, delegates from fifty nations convened at San Francisco to draw up the United Nations Charter. Twenty-five hundred media representatives descended on a conference whose official delegates totaled little more than half that number. There was much infighting among reporters vying for inside stories about the fledgling organization; some of it on occasion approached physical violence. Stevenson was appointed official intermediary between the delegates and the media. As such, he assumed the mantle of "official leaker."

> It became standard operating procedure [he later told the Commonwealth Club of Chicago] for Stettinius once a week to read me a burning lecture somewhere on the essential importance of absolute secrecy about delegation and Big Five meetings in the famous penthouse on top of the Fairmont. But these admonitions were always reserved for the presence of certain U.S. delegates and afterward we went into his bedroom for a drink and a review of "Operation Titanic" as it was called—whether I needed more help, what such and such a section of the press was saying and could I get out a little more in this direction or that.[6]

The *New York Times*' "Scotty" Reston later wrote, "This was one of the few conferences where the press was handled really well." After two months of grueling labor, consensus was achieved among all parties and the conference adjourned. In June Stevenson returned to Libertyville, Illinois, ostensibly to resume work with his Chicago law firm.

On June 28 he addressed the annual meeting of the Chicago Bar Association, giving a detailed explanation of the emergent organization's objectives and the means for achieving international security and peace as envisioned by the Charter. Summing up, he said,

> The reason they met was because in a period of 30 years some forty million human beings have been killed by the oldest and worst plague we know. The purpose for which they met was to write a constitution for an organization through which the nations of the world might work together in their common hope for peace.

Amid the confusion, the Babel of tongues, and the complexity of it all, a cynic could well say that the remarkable thing was not that they wrote a better charter than anyone had a right to expect, but that they succeeded in writing a charter at all! They succeeded because it was the common and equal determination of all those who participated in its labors that the Conference must reach agreement; that a charter must be written—not a charter, but the best possible charter on which all could agree.... It was an achievement about which history will have much to say, and perhaps it could only have been done in the course of a great war by a generation which has suffered frightfully, and by nations many of whom have lost the best of two succeeding generations.[7]

The San Francisco meeting had decided that a preparatory commission should meet in London prior to the convening of the General Assembly's first session. Delegates would formulate the foundational structure of the new agency. Stevenson was eager to be part of the birthing of this new agency on whose success he felt the prospects for a peaceful world might well depend. To that end, following the UN Charter conference, he had ghost-written a letter for Under-Secretary Joseph Grew to be forwarded to James F. Byrnes, President Truman's recently appointed secretary of state: the letter stated that Stevenson was "on his farm at Libertyville, Illinois, telephone—233-J and does not intend to resume his business in Chicago immediately in any event." It was a clear bid for his participation in the next stage of the fledgling UN organization. Without waiting for a response, Stevenson returned to Washington to lobby for a position on that commission. By fall he had won appointment as both alternate delegate and "first deputy" for former secretary of state Stettinius. He would have the personal rank of minister.

*   *   *

On September 4, 1945 Adlai Stevenson, Secretary of State James F. Byrnes, and the other members of the U.S. delegation to the London meetings boarded the *Queen Elizabeth* in New York. Still configured as a troop ship, the vessel had landed 15,000 soldiers at the pier just three days before. Stevenson was billeted in a cabin with Norman Padelford, expert on waterways and professor at Massachusetts Institute of Technology. "Our fellow passengers," Stevenson noted in his diary, "are some 2000 assorted Europeans going home after the long refuge, Red Cross girls, soldiers and civilians— going to Germany. There are twelve little iron bunks for Padelford and me to sleep in." Charles ("Chip") Bohlen, State Department Russian expert who had served as Roosevelt's translator at both the Yalta and Potsdam conferences of the "Big Three" and later as President Eisenhower's ambassador to

Moscow, joined the pair half-way through the journey, perhaps to assess Adlai's degree of sophistication about the Soviets.

It was the first time Bohlen had met Stevenson and, as Bohlen reports in his diary, the two of them had many conversations during the voyage, mostly about U.S.-Soviet relations. Stevenson impressed Bohlen with "the freshness and sensitivity of his mind and his civilized approach to world problems." One aspect of his thinking, though, Bohlen found "particularly striking and disturbing." Although not denying "the seriousness of the task we faced," Bohlen noted, Stevenson seemed "less concerned with the realities of the problem than with its effect on the American mentality. He feared that the rise of strong anti-Communist sentiment would inhibit genuine liberals." Bohlen agreed that Stevenson had a point (as evidenced by the subsequent McCarthy era), "but one of the inevitable consequences of his view was to play down the gravity of the problem of our relations with the Soviets."[8]

Stevenson was not entirely comfortable about his prospects. Writing his law partner James F. Oates, Jr. the day of the sailing, he confessed it would be "a new field for me...international negotiations....It will be slow and tedious at best and I'm destined to learn something about patience in 3 languages!"

Docking at Southampton on September 10, he was met by Secretary of State Stettinius's representative and whisked by limousine to London. The Preparatory Commission's Executive Committee—composed of representatives from nine nations in addition to the Big Five: Edward Stettinius (the United States), Philip Noel-Baker (the United Kingdom), Dr. Wellington Koo (China), Andrei Gromyko (U.S.S.R.), and René Massigli (France)— wasted no time getting down to work. The very next morning Stevenson met with Secretary Stettinius and the State Department staff; other meetings continued into the evening. His prediction about the need for patience was confirmed from the start. On September 13 Wilder Foote, a Stettinius assistant, wrote his wife: "Adlai is discouraged at the amount of talking that seems to be necessary before anything gets done in the committees. It is certainly a slow process. The least point is discussed and since every speech has to be translated from English to French or French to English, the time drags horribly."

His responsibilities doubled on October 16 when Secretary Stettinius took ill and had to fly to New York for gall bladder surgery. As the secretary's deputy, Stevenson assumed the chairmanship for the remainder of the session. After eight weeks of day and night labor the executive committee completed its work, producing a 200-page report to the full preparatory commission whose first session would convene on November 23. The report described the issues that would have to be definitively decided by the

General Assembly at its first meeting in January. Those included the recommended organizational structures and rules of procedure for each of the constituent UN agencies: the General Assembly itself, the Security Council, the Food and Agricultural Organization, the World Bank and International Monetary Fund, UNESCO, the Economic and Social Council, the UN Relief and Rehabilitation Agency, the Civil Aviation Conference, the International Court of Justice, and others. In Stevenson's words, the commission had "put the flesh on the bare bones of the San Francisco Charter."

The preparatory commission's second session—the first of the full commission—convened in the Main Conference Room of the Methodist Church House at 10 a.m., November 24. (The facility served throughout the war as Parliament's temporary quarters on the assumption that the Parliament buildings themselves would be a prime target for the Germans' V-2 rockets.) Sir Philip P.J. Noel-Baker, head of the British delegation, presided. He began by expressing the wish "that this hall...were perhaps a little more adequate to the [commission's] task. But at least this place has what Mr. Churchill calls 'the great advantage of being too small for the purpose for which it is designed.' As he explained it," Sir Philip continued, "it is only when you have a place that is much too small that you get the right atmosphere for deliberative assemblies.'"[9]

From the first, the Soviet delegates proved difficult but Stevenson, whose "grace, eloquence, and humor," according to one observer,[10] "lightened many a heavy debate," had secured their eventual collaboration. In a prescient and somewhat sobering assessment, he summarized for a British audience the grueling and inevitably dull tasks they had just completed: "I venture to say that 90% of the recommendations were adopted unanimously and considering the wide disparity of viewpoint, tradition and experience...among the governments represented, it was almost spectacular. But the disagreements, the hot words and the Russian stubbornness always made the news and will always do so, I suppose...on and on into the future which will not make it any easier to enlist the enlightened public opinion of the world."

When the sessions ended, Philip Noel-Baker wrote Stevenson: "The full onslaught of the Soviet campaign fell on you, and I wish we had been able to share it better. But at least it makes it easier for me to congratulate you on the fair and public-spirited work you did, and on the amazing patience and skill you showed. None could have done it better."[11] Edward Stettinius wrote him on November 28 saying: "I hear nothing but praise for the way in which you have not only completed the work of the Executive Committee, but also the way in which you have taken hold in the Preparatory Commission itself." Stevenson's well-honed diplomatic skills proved as invaluable in the Preparatory Commission as they had been in the Executive Committee. On December 11, 1945 Dean Acheson, then under-secretary of state, wrote

Stevenson: "I want you to know how much all of us in the Department appreciate the magnificent job you have been doing in London on the Preparatory Commission. We are most fortunate to have had you there throughout the work of the Executive Committee and the Preparatory Commission, and we would have been in bad shape without you.... I have heard from many sources nothing but the highest praise for the tact and effectiveness with which you have directed the work of the United States during these last few weeks." By December 23 the commission had completed its work and members could return home for a well-earned rest. The General Assembly would hold its very first session on January 10, 1946.

* * *

Since catching her first glimpse of Stevenson in that Gilbert-and-Sullivan scene on a railroad dining car in Maine, Eleanor Roosevelt had led her characteristically brim-full life as First Lady: playing hostess to the never-ending list of White House guests—among them was Prime Minister Churchill, a rather frequent (and difficult) visitor; serving briefly as Fiorello LaGuardia's deputy at the Office of Civil Defense; paying visits to the troops in the Pacific theater (a 25,000-mile journey) and taking an almost equally arduous tour (13,000 miles) throughout the Caribbean. "On my return," she said, "I had letters to write to hundreds of people because during the trip[s] many other boys I met asked me to write to their families back home." Reflecting later on the period from 1941 to 1945, she wrote: "I think I lived those years very impersonally. It was almost as if I had erected someone outside myself who was the President's wife. I was lost somewhere deep down inside myself. That is the way I felt until I left the White House."[12]

When her husband died at Warm Springs in April 1945, Eleanor thought (for a moment) that she would retire to her Val-Kill cottage at Hyde Park, New York, and lead a somewhat quiet life. She would continue writing her *McCall* magazine and *My Day* columns, reacquaint herself with her family and enjoy her wide circle of friends. Harper & Company had secured her promise to write her autobiography. She also wanted to travel, a trip to the Soviet Union standing at the top of her list.

But she hadn't spent her entire adult life in public service in order now at age sixty-one to renounce that world altogether. Thus when Harry S. Truman, the new president, invited her to join the U.S. delegation to the first meeting of the United Nations General Assembly, Eleanor Roosevelt overcame her initial hesitancy—("How could I be a delegate to help organize the United Nations when I have no background or experience in international meetings?")—and accepted. Her acquiescence was the first step on the path she would follow throughout the remaining seventeen years of her life.

Truman knew that Franklin D. Roosevelt had cherished as his greatest and most durable potential legacy the establishment of a world body in which international problems could be collaboratively addressed and international disputes diffused before they collapsed into all-out wars. *New York Times* reporter Anne O'Hare McCormick wrote that "Roosevelt. was looking to the inauguration of the San Francisco Conference as the crowning act of his career. This was his project. He proposed it, set the time and place of the meeting, speeded up the preparations in the belief that it was supremely urgent."[13]

Roosevelt had planned to address the opening session of the conference and had commissioned Archibald MacLeish to write that speech for him[14] but died just thirteen days before it convened.

There is little question that Eleanor Roosevelt herself had had a major hand in helping the president frame and own that vision.[15] Emblematic of an attitude she had long held was her response to reporters' questions at the press conference that she held on the day her husband died. "We will have to get over the habit of saying what we as a single nation will do," she said. "When we say 'we' on international questions in the future, we will mean all the people who have an interest in the question. A United Nations organization is for the very purpose of making it possible that all the world's opinion will have a clearing place."[16]

With the other members of the U.S. delegation,[17] she went aboard the *Queen Elizabeth* on December 31, 1945 bound for England. She was skeptical at first about what she could bring to this momentous gathering, but her hesitation was salted with a new-found exhilaration: "For the first time in my life," she told the press a bit giddily, but insisting that they treat her comment as off-the-record, "I can say just what I want. For your information, it is wonderful to feel free."

Her *My Day* column on December 21 had enumerated the strengths she felt her presence would represent in the new world body:

> Some things I can take to the first meeting: A sincere desire to understand the problems of the rest of the world and our relationship to them; a real goodwill for people throughout the world; a hope that I shall be able to build a sense of personal trust and friendship with my co-workers, for without that understanding our work would be doubly difficult.

She had been giving much thought on her daily shipboard walks to her impending responsibilities:

> It is evident to all of us that this desire among the peoples of the world [for no more wars] must express itself to their leaders in no uncertain terms, for

difficulties are bound to arise among nations as controversies do among individuals. There will be times when solutions to knotty problems will seem well-nigh impossible. It will be the determination of the people in the various nations, prodding their representatives to find compromises if not ultimate solutions, and to set up methods which can be tried on a temporary basis, which will keep the organization going.[18]

She found a concern growing in her mind as her acquaintance with the other delegation members deepened:

> The old fears, the old type of diplomatic and political thinking will have to be changed, but they will not change overnight. The old type of economic thinking which has often led to certain types of political action, will also have to be changed and subordinate itself to the main objective before us-peace and a better life for the peoples of the world as a whole.

It would be the *peoples'* responsibility to see that such change occurred; the average citizen would have to see the United Nations and its constituent bodies as indispensable to the maintenance of peace and the winning of a better life for all. This would be a theme that, like the opening bar of Beethoven's Fifth Symphony, would resound throughout her writings over her entire lifetime:

> This cannot happen...without the necessary vigor on the part of the people in every nation to make their desires known, nor can it happen unless the difficulties can be brought out in the open and discussed. The people may not feel they understand the details of a situation...[but they] can insist on the ultimate objectives which they wish to attain.
>
> The little people are the ones who fight the wars, they are the ones who work their hearts out in production, they are the ones who suffer the most during the wars and afterward.

At Adlai Stevenson's suggestion Mrs. Roosevelt had been appointed by the State Department to Committee Three where social, humanitarian, and cultural issues would be considered. It was an assignment the experienced members of the delegation considered innocuous enough. Later she wrote: "I could just see the gentlemen of our delegation puzzling over the list [of committees] and saying, 'Ah, here's the safe spot for her—Committee Three. She can't do much harm there!' "[19] As matters developed, Committee Three under her guidance became the source of one of the United Nations' greatest achievements: the Universal Declaration of Human Rights.

On January 6, the day after landing on British soil, she wrote Joe and Trude Lash: "Tonight I dine with Mr. and Mrs. Adlai Stevenson. He has headed our work on the temporary [Preparatory] commission since Mr. Stettinius had to go home and I hope to learn something about the people on the other delegations who are still not even names with which I am familiar." That evening—"ER" reported it was a "late" one—began a friendship that would last till Eleanor Roosevelt's death sixteen years later. Dorothy Fosdick was also there. She had served as aide to Secretary General Alger Hiss during the San Francisco conference and later would hold a similar post with Secretary of State James F. Byrnes. Stevenson, who held her in high regard, commented later on "the splendid background and paper work done by the State Department in preparation for this Assembly. In all aspects of the work it is superb and evidently...Dorothy Fosdick *et al* are entitled to the major share of the credit."[20]

Committee Three held its first meeting on January 8, 1946 in Church House. Though she made no mention of the fact in either her personal diary or her *My Day* column, Eleanor Roosevelt was promptly chosen chair of the committee and continued in that role until it concluded its work.

It is worth speculating on why she was chosen over other members of a distinguished group of mostly men—she had early commented publicly on the paucity of women delegates to the meetings. Some of the more obvious reasons come readily to mind: She bore the magical Roosevelt name, and most of the several hundred people who had come to London for these meetings recognized how much the new organization owed to this woman's husband. (A smaller, more knowledgeable group rightly credited her with having kept his and the world's eyes on the single cause for which the recent terrible war had been fought: the UN itself.) Her travels and years in the White House had provided her a wide acquaintance with numerous world leaders. In preliminary discussions of the committee's work she had demonstrated a sophisticated appreciation of the complexity of the issues it would be asked to resolve. She also spoke fluent French and competent Italian. (On one occasion after Professor Cassin had been speaking for twenty minutes, she queried the committee whether they had understood the good professor's comments. Responded to in the negative, she forthwith provided a competent summary.)

But there were more subtle, human reasons that made her the natural choice as committee chair. As Durward Sandifer, her State Department adviser, noted, Eleanor Roosevelt had the capacity for "pulling out of other people, what they had to offer. She could get people from all walks of life to talk and to communicate to her their thinking and their ideas." She would then incorporate these ideas and use them in her own formulations. Equally important, she projected her own personality so that "people felt she was their friend." Furthermore she was "practical, pragmatic and realistic, and quite prepared to find the best way of saying anything to meet different points of view." [21]

Deaf in one ear, she was a very careful listener. Photographs of her at committee and assembly meetings at this period show an uncommonly attentive woman, frequently with head cocked and brow knit, as if to assure herself that she wasn't missing anything. The other members of Committee Three soon recognized that these qualities, along with her other abilities, made her the natural choice to guide the committee in its work.

By far the most urgent problem confronting Committee Three was the problem of refugees "Nansen passport" holders,[22] and other "displaced persons." A background paper furnished by the State Department estimated that by the middle of 1946—even with mass repatriation operations following the war—the number of non-repatriables would range as high as 1,250,000–1,500,000 people "for whose permanent establishment some long-term concerted international effort will presumably have to be made."[23]

From the start the Soviet Union and its satellites argued strenuously that all persons displaced by the war should naturally wish to return to their home countries, and that those who felt otherwise should be regarded as "quislings, traitors, Fascists and undemocratic elements"; there was no need for an international agency to supervise such repatriation; bilateral negotiations between the countries concerned could resolve all cases. Another group of nations that included the United States, the United Kingdom, Panama, Belgium, and South Africa held that human considerations should trump political ones: the right of conscience in individual circumstances should be honored. They offered a resolution, reading "No refugees or displaced persons...shall be compelled to return to their country of origin." The debate waxed and waned for an entire month.

On January 29, she wrote in her diary:

> The papers should not be pessimistic, progress is being made. Vandenberg and Dulles are largely responsible for pessimism, I think. These representatives of ours don't build friendship for us. They have no confidence so they are rude and arrogant and create suspicion. Honesty with friendliness goes down but they haven't the technique. Jimmy Byrnes' over cordiality isn't right either. Why can't we be natural and feel right inside and just let it come out?

Another revealing diary entry reads,

> 9:30 to midnight listening to speeches on UNRRA [the United Nations Relief and Rehabilitation Agency, charged with the physical restoration of the devastation caused by the war.] Everyone agreed with [U.S. delegate] Sol Bloom, praised his speech and patted him on the back and he was as pleased as a little boy and went off today to board the ship tonight and sail for home feeling a

hero.... He is able but so many foibles! All these important people have them, however. I'm so glad I never _feel_ important, it does complicate life.

By February 2, the constant talking required by the negotiations was beginning to take its toll on Mrs. Roosevelt; a diary entry on that day reads,

> For two days I've had no voice. No cold, just no voice. I hope it returns by Monday night when I have to speak at a dinner.[24]

The climax in the refugee debate finally came when Mrs. Roosevelt was charged with arguing the case for the group of nations that wanted the right of conscience recognized as superior to that of governments. The speech she delivered ad lib in opposition to Soviet representative Andrei Vishinsky, who had been chief prosecutor at Stalin's 1936 show trials, was called by Durward Sandifer, her State Department adviser, "the most important speech ever given by an American delegate without a prepared text." Summing up, she said it was the United Nations' task "to frame things which...will consider first the rights of man, which will consider what makes man more free, not governments, but man!"[25] On February 7, her position won the full committee's unanimous approval. This, however, did not deter the Soviets. As the Annual Report of the UN for 1946–47 recorded, "When the report of the Third Committee came before the General Assembly at the 29th plenary meeting on February 12, 1946, the representative of the U.S.S.R. reintroduced the amendments previously rejected in the Committee. After considerable debate all amendments were rejected and the General Assembly...adopted the text as presented by the Third Committee." An International Refugee Organization was born, at last.

On February 6, a week before the session adjourned, Mrs. Roosevelt noted an insight that came to her from hearing delegates from other nations speak of their anxieties as well as their hopes for the new organization. The meetings, she wrote, were

> a liberal education in backgrounds and personalities but one thing stands out. Since the Civil War we have had no political or religious refugees fleeing our country and we forget to take it into account. No European or South American forgets it for a minute. Next, it seems to take years of stability to make you look beyond your own situation and consider that there are human rights that operate for those who think in a way that you think wrong!

It had been an arduous, demanding six weeks during which Eleanor Roosevelt emerged from near obscurity to a position of respect and admiration in the world's eyes. Doubting members of the U.S. delegation—notably Vandenberg and Dulles—accustomed to the rough and tumble of political maneuvering that she had mastered in no time, acknowledged their surprise and pleasure. "Mrs. Roosevelt is doing a splendid job," Senator Vandenberg told a group of colleagues during the debates. "She has made a fine impression on all the other delegations. I want to say that I take back everything I ever said about her, and believe me it's been plenty."[26] And John Foster Dulles, in an uncharacteristic moment of humility, confessed on leaving: "I feel I must tell you that when you were appointed I thought it terrible and now I think your work here has been fine."[27] By February 10, she was anticipating the end of the General Assembly sessions and looking forward—with some trepidation—to visiting refugee camps in Germany before flying home, a gesture in response to a U.S. Army request. That evening she had invited the Stevensons as well as Alger Hiss (acting UN secretary general) and his wife to dinner, her only diary comment about the evening: "They are all nice."

On the 11th she wrote, "I don't look forward to seeing Europe. I am afraid it will be a haunting horror." (The possibility that Stevenson might accompany the Connallys and herself had made the prospect seem somewhat less daunting, but that plan fell through.)

From the time she landed at Southampton to her departure for the United States, she and Adlai Stevenson had seen each other in a comparatively relaxed setting only three times; each had been leading a frenetic life. In addition to shouldering her Committee Three and General Assembly responsibilities, Eleanor had received a steady stream of guests who were friends from her early youth at Madame Souvestre's school as well as from her much later visit to London in 1941. Women's groups, cultural societies, members of Parliament, diplomats, soldiers and sailors, and international aid workers sought her out, frequently with invitations to speak to their organizations. Added to these pressures on her "off duty" time was a practice that early turned into a habit of inviting the wives of delegation members from other countries, delegates themselves, and UN staff members for tea at her apartment. "I discovered that in such informal sessions we sometimes made more progress in reaching an understanding on some question before the United Nations than we had been able to achieve in the formal work of our committees," she wrote.[28] There was also, of course, her daily column to write and the diary to keep up ("I am seeing all the deposed Kings this week. Greece and Yugoslavia the same afternoon!"), and no day felt complete without a half dozen or more personal letters dispatched to various friends. She rarely slept before 11 p.m.

Stevenson's schedule was similarly hectic. When the General Assembly sessions adjourned in mid-February 1946, he had been in London five months. As a member of the Preparatory Commission's Executive Committee, he had proven himself an accomplished mediator, a disciplined conceptual thinker, and an affable colleague. He had assumed Secretary of State Stettinius's chairmanship for the commission's work when the secretary was forced to return to New York for a gall bladder operation, serving in that position from November 24 to December 23, 1945. He had played a critical role in the preparation of its 200-page report to the full commission. Under-Secretary-General Brian Urquhart credited him with doing "most of the work" of Secretary Stettinius. Stevenson's "grace, eloquence and humor," he reported, "lightened many a heavy debate."[29] Finally, when James F. Byrnes had succeeded Stettinius as secretary of state, he had left Stevenson in charge of the political negotiations over appointments to General Assembly president, vice presidents, chairs, and members of UN agencies and committees. As Stevenson reported later to Chicago's Commercial Club, "We elected five out of six of our slate on the Security Council, seventeen out of eighteen on the Economic and Social Council, and twelve out of fifteen members of the International Court of Justice."[30] Saville R. Davis, managing editor of the *Christian Science Monitor*, called Stevenson "the hero of the elections," noting that "he drafted with great patience and skill a list which represented not what the United States wanted but, nearly as possible, what all delegations and groups wanted. The result was a phenomenal electoral success."[31]

Despite the limited opportunities for becoming personally acquainted, each would later remark on the indelible impression the other had made. In a presidential campaign speech on Stevenson's behalf delivered at Charleston, West Virginia in 1956, Eleanor Roosevelt described the real beginnings of their friendship. Referring to the very first session of the General Assembly that met on January 10, 1946, she said,

> I went to the first meeting to organize the UN and that is where I really came to know Adlai Stevenson. I had seen him before, but never really knew him as a person....At that first meeting Adlai Stevenson did all the preparatory work since the meeting in San Francisco up to the London meeting. Every country had a group of people working in the Preparation Committee, he headed ours and did wonderful work. He knew all the other people and told us when we came who they were and what they did. I was worried as I was the only woman and felt I was looked on not as "one of the crowd." Mr. [John Foster] Dulles and Mr. [Senator Arthur] Vandenberg [R.- Michigan] were not happy that I was along, so I worked with great care and read all the time on the steamer about the State Department position papers. Adlai Stevenson told us about the people in the other delegations. He really made a study of the people we would deal with, and what the setup would be and much background information. This made all the difference in our ability to work with others. I watched Adlai Stevenson from then on, and he worked on several of the Committees. Some people gain respect and others lose respect when you are working with them. Adlai Stevenson gained....

Stevenson, during the October 2 Meeting of the General Assembly, noted in his diary,

> Delegation meeting in the morning.... Listened to speeches all afternoon while all the other delegates—except Mrs. Roosevelt—whose fidelity, as at London, is a marvel—drifted away. Drove back with her afterward and she explained that she felt it was only polite to stay and listen to the speeches of other countries.... Discussed politics, languages and education. Everything confirms conviction that she is one of the few really great people I have known.[32]

Amply evident in both these observations is a mutual respect for the other's intellectual grasp of the complexities involved in the work they were doing, the interpersonal skills each brought to that work, and the personal integrity and sense of *noblesse oblige* with which they approached it. But it was still a somewhat arm's-length admiration. The seed of genuine friendship was clearly present as possibility, but it would take some time before it flowered.

The UN's various working committees completed their initial assignments by the end of the last London session of the General Assembly on February 14, 1946. Eleanor's Committee Three had described and approved a comprehensive structure for dealing with the refugee and displaced persons problems through a proposed Constitution for the International Refugee Organization. Senator Vandenberg pronounced this organizational phase of the agency's life "a phenomenal success and a vigorous omen of hope for the tolerant cooperations [*sic*] which are the lifeblood of this adventure." News and governmental media globally concurred in his judgment.

Eleanor Roosevelt, courtesy of the United States' army and air force, completed with the Connallys a tour of the war's devastation in Germany. As though to confirm in her own mind the results of the efforts she had led over the preceding months, she met at two camps near Frankfurt with Baltic states refugees whose futures were still hanging in the balance while they awaited word of lost relatives or permission to emigrate. She then went on to Berlin where hardly a building had escaped the Allies' carpet bombing. The tour over, she flew home for a respite at her beloved Val-Kill retreat in Hyde Park. Adlai Stevenson boarded the *Queen Mary* at Southampton on February 24, spent a few days in Washington D.C.—where he declined Secretary of State Byrnes's offer of an ambassadorship to either Argentina or Brazil[33]—and returned to his old law firm in Chicago.

They were given little time to recoup their energies before both were recalled to continue their work with the organization to whose firm foundation they had both contributed so much. About a month after her return,

Mrs. Roosevelt received notice that the Economic and Social Council of the UN had appointed her to the "Nuclear Commission on Human Rights." Its function would be to formulate recommendations for the projected United Nations Human Rights Commission. Almost simultaneously President Truman requested that she again serve as a member of the U.S. delegation, this time to the second part of the first session of the General Assembly. She would be active in the agency for the next seven years.

Stevenson spent much of his first months back in the United States speaking to civic and political organizations about the aims of the newly created institution and the functions of its constituent agencies. Then in July President Truman appointed him an alternate delegate to the UN's upcoming General Assembly meeting. He would be responsible "for the coordination of the activities of the eight political liaison officers" headed by the U.S. ambassador to Uruguay "and trouble-shooting for [Ambassador and Chief of Delegation Warren] Austin generally." This latter responsibility involved writing speeches for the ambassador; facilitating consensus among delegation members on policy issues such as the importance of maintaining the Security Council's veto provision (the linchpin guarantee of both U.S. and U.S.S.R. participation), the nature and amount of U.S. economic assistance for Europe's recovery, and the percentage of the total UN budget to be paid by the United States; securing exposure in the media for the agency; and a myriad of other matters. He was not pleased, he noted in his diary on October 22, when, "while out of the room for a few minutes...Vandenberg asked to be relieved of first responsibility for Committee 2 [Economic and Financial] and suggested that I take his place on that Committee. When I returned, I protested but Austin insisted and I am stuck! It is apparent that they have cut out more work—Committee 2, Headquarters and political liaison—than I can properly handle."[34] But "stuck" he was. Throughout his UN career he would nightly retire to his bed close to exhaustion.

The General Assembly's first sessions in New York State—technically "the second session of the First General Assembly"—met in the former Sperry Gyroscope Company's plant at Lake Success,[35] a small village on Long Island and a forty-minute journey from mid-Manhattan; Mrs. Roosevelt's Nuclear Commission meetings were held in the oak-paneled library at Hunter College[36] in the Bronx. Under her skillful chairmanship the commission in three weeks had drawn up recommendations to the Economic and Social Council on the framing of an international bill of rights and on procedures for naming the full eighteen-nation Commission on Human Rights.

Again, given their respective obligations, she and Stevenson saw relatively little of each other, though both participated in exploratory field trips and related deliberations on the future headquarters site for the UN, and occasionally they did manage to go back to Manhattan together from

Lake Success. (He had a suite at the Pennsylvania Hotel, which was the delegation's operating headquarters; she had purchased an apartment on Washington Square.) The General Assembly reconvened on October 23, while the new Human Rights Commission would not hold its first meeting until January 1947.

Roughly 1 million of the original 10 million refugees who had been made homeless and/or stateless by World War II were still in legal and political limbo. "How to support them; how to get them back to their own countries or how to get them resettled elsewhere?" were, in Stevenson's words, questions the General Assembly's new session faced. Following the London sessions, there had been an international conference on those questions in July, and correspondingly extended debate in the Economic and Social Council. Now came six weeks of continuous debate in the assembly during which the Soviet Union and the Eastern Bloc nations offered seventy-nine amendments to the I.R.O. constitution, all of them designed to compel the repatriation of political dissidents whose fear was grounded in solid evidentiary conviction, all of them previously dismissed by Committee Three action. They were likewise dismissed, one by one, by the General Assembly that finally adopted the I.R.O.'s constitution as it had been approved by Mrs. Roosevelt's Committee Three.

In January 1947 Stevenson was asked by UN Secretary General Trygvie Lie to accept a position as his deputy secretary general. A diary entry of January 6 reads,

> Lie offered me $24,300 tax exempt & the "guest house" at Lake Success. Long interview followed by talks with [William H.] Stoneman [personal assistant to Trygvie Lie] and [Assistant Secretary General A.D.K.] Owens....Can't make decision so quick. Tempted...but I must stay at home now & get family situation straightened out. Also might as well try out political situation there.

This last comment was in all likelihood prompted at least in part by discussions Stevenson had been having with Mrs. Roosevelt. She had never been enthusiastic about President Truman and considered him a weak chief executive and a man in too many ways out of sympathy with her husband's political program. "The President is well meaning," she wrote to David Gurewitsch, "but such a little man!"[37] Given her growing admiration of Stevenson's leadership role in helping shape the emerging United Nations and her undoubted concern that most of the domestic agenda of her husband's "New Deal" vision was regarded by those at the highest levels of power in the Democratic Party as either unobtainable or undesirable, she had begun to think that this urbane, articulate statesman possessed many of the qualities, the insight, and the political philosophy that had made her husband such a successful political leader. She encouraged Stevenson to try his hand at domestic politics when he returned to his Illinois farm.

By mid-January he was back in Chicago, testing the political waters. He had friends and acquaintances in all the right circles from which to launch a political career. Soon a small group of mainly independent Democrats and Republicans was scheming to secure party support for a Stevenson bid for the U.S. Senate seat held by Republican Senator C. Wayland ["Curly"] Brooks. The new reform leader of the Cook County Democratic Party, Jacob M. Arvey, however, had a different idea: He persuaded the Democratic Central Committee to tap Professor Paul H. Douglas for that position, feeling Douglas' war record would make him a stronger competitor against Brooks. Arvey suggested that Stevenson run for governor of Illinois. Though he protested that all his experience and interest pointed to his being a better fit for the Senate spot, Stevenson finally consented to campaign for the gubernatorial position. In the next six months he would give speeches before the Council for Democracy, the Northwest University Law School, the Commonwealth Club, the Chicago Council on Foreign Relations, the Commercial Club of Chicago, and the Chicago Board of Trade, to name but a few of many, as well as across the breadth of downstate Illinois.

Evidence that the Central Committee's enthusiasm for Stevenson had not yet filtered down to workers at the ward level was driven home to an aspiring Stevenson volunteer, Abner Mikva, who tells this story:

> It was 1948, and I was a law student at the University of Chicago. Adlai Stevenson was running for Governor of Illinois. .I stopped in to the 8th Ward Regular Democratic Headquarters on my way home from school and said that I wanted to volunteer for Stevenson. "Who sent ya?" asked the quintessential Chicago ward committeeman, cigar in hand. "Nobody" I responded. He put the cigar firmly in his mouth and said "We don't want nobody nobody sent." That was my introduction to Chicago politics.[38]

Stevenson meanwhile was wondering why he had refused the post offered by Trygvie Lie:

> Have been worrying about declining that job at U.N.—equivalent to $75,000 salary before taxes. Why don't I do what I want to do and like to do and is worth doing? The questions others ask sometimes hard to answer.

On his birthday, February 5, the same *angst* haunted his self-examination:

> Am 47 today—still restless, dissatisfied with myself. What's the matter? Have everything. Wife, children, money, success—but not in law profession. Too much ambition for public recognition; too scattered in interests; how

can I reconcile life in Chicago as lawyer with consuming interest in foreign affairs—desire for recognition and position in that field? Prospect of Senate nomination sustains & at same time troubles, even frightens me. Wish I could at least get tranquil and make Ellen happy and do go[od] humble job at law.

He decided that a speech by Mrs. Roosevelt before the Chicago Council on Foreign Relations could earn him useful local attention, especially if he were given the role of her introducer. He issued the invitation on March 3, 1947, achieving thereby that distinguished lady's first appearance in Illinois on behalf not only of the United Nations but also of Adlai Stevenson himself. Introducing her, he said there was nothing he would presume he could tell his listeners about their honored guest:

> I can't help recall the plight of the world traveler and professional lecturer who was deploring the fact that there was always someone in the front row who knew more about the place he was talking about or what he was talking about than he did. My luck is so bad that if I talked about life among the lamaseries of Tibet, Marco Polo would be in the audience—or Mrs. Roosevelt.
>
> No, there are too many Marco Polos in the audience. There is nothing I can tell you about Mrs. Roosevelt, much as I should like to try.

Whereupon he went on to tell them a good deal of which they were either only dimly aware or, more likely, entirely ignorant:

> I do want to say, because I am very proud of it, that I have had the invigorating experience of serving with her for long, relentless nights, weeks and months, in the formative period of the United Nations, first at the General Assembly in London a year ago and then at the General Assembly in New York this [past] fall. At both she was assigned the most difficult tasks as a senior member of the United States Delegation.
>
> I have seen with my own eyes what many have said—that day in and day out she carries a heavier schedule than most any man.
>
> I have seen her conduct with patience, firmness, eloquence and dignity the long, long fight for the International Refugee Organization—the fight for the cherished right of political sanctuary for the thousands of refugees and displaced persons from northern and eastern Europe who do not wish to return to their native lands. And I have seen her win that exasperating battle against the bitter, implacable opposition of the Soviet Union, and emerge with even greater respect among the Russians and the eastern bloc. ...
>
> I have seen personal mail delivered to her in baskets—mostly asking for help.
>
> I have seen her work from early morning to midnight day after day, and then go home with the next day's documents and come back early in the morning better prepared than anyone with half her load.

I have seen the faces of the crowds along the streets waiting for her to pass by.

But I have never seen her impatient, undignified, thoughtless. I have never seen her too busy for courtesy, or for someone who needed her.

With goodness an American woman has won the respect, the confidence and the love of more people, great and small, at home and abroad, than, I venture to say, any living person.

It is better to light candles than to curse the darkness.

Mrs. Roosevelt, United States member of the all-important Commission on Human Rights of the United Nations.

It was an effusive introduction, bordering on the adulatory, that may have caused the self-effacing Mrs. Roosevelt to blanch a bit. Her generous response was characteristically restrained:

I was very glad when I saw Mr. Stevenson again at the second meeting of the First Assembly in New York. Mr. Stevenson was an alternate, but in all but name he was a full delegate, and certainly carried out not only the work of the alternate, but all the work of a delegate. So we became accustomed, I think, to feel that he carries his full share of all the burdens whenever he is around, and that was very comforting to other members of the delegation.[39]

There was little communication between them over the ensuing year. Mrs. Roosevelt was managing the excruciating parliamentary passage for what would ultimately become the United Nations' Universal Declaration of Human Rights. The effort would require another nineteen months before consensus would be reached. Stevenson, meanwhile, was barnstorming Illinois in his campaign for the governorship. He did make one try for a return engagement for Mrs. Roosevelt, writing her on March 24, 1948 that the Democratic State Organization was most anxious to have her come to Illinois "for the last lap of the state campaign with a bang-up mass meeting here [in Chicago]—and you are the best 'bang' in the Party." Mrs. Roosevelt declined the invitation, saying that as long as she was at the UN she felt it inappropriate to engage in U.S. partisan politics.

But the health and vitality of American democracy was a lifelong concern and, as she had demonstrated in her *My Day* columns on numerous occasions, encouragement of her readers' backing strong, liberal candidates for public office was never far from her mind. By late summer President Truman was significantly down in the polls and the media were predicting the likelihood of a landslide victory for the Republicans that November. Undaunted, Mrs. Roosevelt's September 11, 1948 column called attention to several emerging young political leaders whose futures she thought promising. Chester Bowles, governor of Connecticut, was a candidate for the U.S. Senate (he would later be appointed ambassador to India). Hubert H. Humphrey, mayor of Minneapolis, also sought a U.S. Senate seat (He would later become a vice presidential, then presidential candidate). She thought highly of Chet Holifield and Helen Gahagan Douglas in California, both of whom would subsequently serve with distinction in the Congress (in Mrs. Douglas's case, as a member of the U.S. delegation to the United Nations). Paul Douglas, running for Congress, and Adlai Stevenson, candidate for governor, were Illinois liberals her column singled out for commendation. Of Stevenson she wrote:

> Mr. Stevenson has a very long and unique experience in preparing for the first United Nations General Assembly meeting in London. He learned what negotiation with other nations meant, and it certainly will help him in the national scene, where patience and the art of negotiation must be practiced much as it is practiced in the international field.

In the meantime her patience with the Soviets' tactics of delay and obfuscation was growing thin. She described how she waited for her chance as Dr. Pavlov, "an orator of great power," "seemed likely to go on forever, but I watched him closely until he had to pause for breath. Then I banged the gavel so hard that the other delegates jumped in surprise: 'We are here,' I said, 'to devise ways of safeguarding human rights. We are not here to attack each other's governments, and I hope when we return on Monday the delegate of the Soviet Union will remember that!' I banged the gavel again. 'Meeting adjourned!' "[40] Simultaneously she was lobbying U.S. officialdom from the president on down to endorse the UN's two-state solution to the Palestinian-Israeli stand-off. The United States seemed incapable of developing a cohesive policy and sticking by it, changing its stance periodically, she felt, in order to frustrate the latest stance taken by the U.S.S.R.

Even without her help Stevenson was elected with a plurality of 572,000 votes over his Republican opponent. No other governor in Illinois history had won by such a margin. More than a half million citizens crossed party lines to vote for Stevenson. There was even speculation that the impact of his campaign had won Illinois—and, therefore, perhaps the nation—for Truman, who edged out Thomas E. Dewey by only 33,612 votes. The "Stevenson phenomenon" drew national media attention: clearly here was a man who, if he could prove himself a capable governor, might become a significant figure in Democratic Party politics at the national level. Mrs. Roosevelt cabled from Paris her congratulations on his victory. As in his introduction at the Chicago Council on Foreign Relations meeting, his reply reveals that he still felt more deferential toward her than would be the case a few years hence: "Nothing has pleased me and flattered me as much as your cable of congratulations. Your thoughtfulness and consideration have always been beyond my understanding, and now I have an eloquent personal example of it. I only hope I can do half as well in my so-called 'public life.'"

He appended a postscript: "P.S.—It's all your fault! You told me last fall to go ahead and have a try at it, and I have profited enormously from the experience quite aside from the amazing victory. So I am grateful to you on still another count!"

*   *   *

Save for the occasional invitation to address this conference or that rally, to lend one's name to this or that new organizational effort on behalf of a worthy cause, it would be another four years before their paths crossed again. In the interim Adlai Stevenson's time and attention were almost entirely absorbed by his gubernatorial responsibilities while Mrs. Roosevelt's energies were focused upon seeing the Universal Declaration of Human Rights through to final adoption by the United Nations. That triumphal moment came at 3 a.m. on December 10, 1948 at the Palais de Chaillot (subsequently called the Palais des Nations) in Paris when forty-eight nations cast their votes for the Declaration while eight abstained. Two small nations' representatives were absent.

According to James Hendrick, her State Department adviser at the time, the final session had been especially rancorous, the U.S.S.R.'s representatives realizing full well that the other Commission members were ready to approve the draft declaration they had been working on since April 1946. As the other delegates' limousines departed the Palais' parking lot, a weary quartet—Mrs. Roosevelt, Hendrick, the Russian representative Alexander Bogomolov and his wife—paused where the corridor opened onto the spacious entry hall. "There was a wonderful childlike element in Mrs. Roosevelt," Hendrick told Joe Lash, "which occasionally popped out. You know those wonderful marble floors in the Palais des Nations. 'I'd love to slide on those floors,' said Mrs. Roosevelt. 'I'm very tired, while you look fresh as a daisy,' I said as we walked away. 'Now you can slide on those marble floors'—with which she took two enormous slides."[41]

Next day Dr. Herbert V. Evatt of Australia, then president of the General Assembly, declared that this was "the first occasion on which the organized community of nations has made a declaration of human rights and fundamental freedoms," adding that "It is particularly fitting that here tonight should be the person who has been the leader in this movement, assisted though she has been by many others—the person who has raised to even greater honor so great a name.... I refer, of course, to Mrs. Roosevelt, the delegate of the United States." The assembly stood for an ovation that lasted several minutes. Secretary General U Thant called the Declaration "the Magna Carta of Mankind."

During his "citizen" campaign Stevenson had refused to be intimidated by Democratic Party bosses or to pander to special interests. The consequence was that he could begin his administration of a state widely known for its entrenched corruption by addressing the major issues he had outlined in the campaign. Over his four years in office, admirers said, he rid Illinois of a multimillion-dollar cigarette-tax counterfeiting racket; brought the formerly patronage-indebted state police under civil service; eliminated political shakedowns for state jobs by appointing prominent business executives to handle public contracts; secured $10 million a year from the state gasoline tax for construction of new rural roads to help farmers get their produce to market; enforced an industrial safety program that made 1951 the best safety year in Illinois history; doubled the state budget for schools, public aid, and welfare by $330 million; took public utilities regulation out of politics by making the Illinois Commerce Commission completely independent; fired 1,300 state employees from useless jobs; brought the state's mental hospital system from near the bottom nationally to what the eminent psychiatrist Karl Menninger called "one of the country's best."[42]

He also fought hard for a state Fair Employment Practices bill, but the Republican Senate defeated his bill. He proved himself politically fearless by vetoing the Broyles Bill that would have instituted a state loyalty oath—it was introduced at the height of the McCarthy "Red scare" about Communists in government—famously concluding his veto message with the terse comment "We must not burn down the house to kill the rats." (In a notable speech to the American Legion in August 1952 he would use the same words to describe the character assassination tactics of Joseph McCarthy and his congressional allies.) He also proved that he could maintain his irrepressible sense of humor even under the pressures of running a state of 8.5 million citizens; an example was his veto message of a bill that had been introduced by a group of bird lovers who wanted cats restrained the way dogs were. His message concluded:

> The problem of cat versus bird is as old as time. If we attempt to resolve it by legislation who knows but what we may be called upon to take sides as well in the age old problems of dog versus cat, bird versus bird, or even bird versus worm. In my opinion, the State of Illinois and its local governing bodies already have enough to do without trying to control feline delinquency.

Though she rarely saw or corresponded with him during Stevenson's years as Illinois governor, Stevenson's rising star in the political firmament did not entirely escape Mrs. Roosevelt's notice. Apart from an occasional request for the governor's investigation of a correspondent's retirement benefits or disability claim, her duties at the United Nations, both as U.S. delegate to the General Assembly and as chair of the Human Rights Commission, required her almost undivided attention for nearly seven years until president-elect Dwight D. Eisenhower curtly accepted her resignation in late December 1952.

Mrs. Roosevelt wrote in her *Autobiography*: "After the Declaration was accepted, it seemed to me that the United States had held the chairmanship of the Human Rights Commission long enough. So at the 1951 meeting of the Commission in Geneva I nominated Mr. Charles Malik of Lebanon, with the consent of my government." He was duly elected and from then till February of the next year she was "just a member but a most interested member." She also continued as a member of the U.S. General Assembly delegation. When General Assembly meetings adjourned in February, she arranged a whirlwind trip "the long way home": Lebanon, Israel, India, Pakistan, Burma, Indonesia. On her return congressional members of the House and Senate, the secretaries of state and defense, and the director of the CIA all requested private debriefing sessions on her trip. She had clearly become accepted among Washington's powerful as her country's leading unofficial goodwill ambassador.

Adlai Stevenson meanwhile was weighing the options that were before him as the last of his four years as Illinois governor was coming to an end. His administration had laid the foundation for significant improvements in education, transportation, civil service, and fiscal responsibility (although critics were frustrated by his "penny-pinching" fiscal policies). He had also considerably refined his political skills, though he would always feel better suited for the world of international diplomacy than that of domestic politics. Another four years, he thought, could assure the permanence of many of the measures he had been able to introduce. He would run for a second term, hoping to consolidate some of the reforms he had initiated and to introduce others he thought might receive support.

In the months leading up to the 1952 Democratic Party's National Convention, two issues dominated party dialogue: Who could mount the strongest campaign against General Dwight D. Eisenhower, the Republican Party's presumed presidential candidate, and how could Democrats frame their position on the explosive issue of civil rights in terms that would be acceptable to liberals and increasingly militant African Americans without alienating the Southern wing of the party.

Over the next eight years Mrs. Roosevelt and Adlai Stevenson's differing convictions on questions of civil rights would cast a slight shadow over their friendship, but as the year began her enthusiasm for the renewal Stevenson could bring to the Democratic Party and to the world was increasing by the week.

PART II

CHAPTER 1

THE 1952 CAMPAIGN

THE YEAR 1952 WAS HARRY S. TRUMAN'S FINAL YEAR of a second term as U.S. president and he would not run again. Ever since 1948 professional pols, pundits, media moguls, and Harry Truman himself had been eying Stevenson as his potential successor. By early 1952 "Stevenson-for-President" committees were forming throughout the country. President Truman had asked Stevenson in January to become a candidate, reiterating that request in March. On both occasions Stevenson declined the invitation. Truman concluded that Stevenson's refusal betrayed "indecisiveness." (The charge was emphatically denied by Carol Evans, his personal secretary, who said, "I never once knew him to be indecisive in matters having to do with public affairs or with public interest. He was decisive and he was honest. The very few times I saw him to be indecisive were when he was required to make decisions about himself." Carl McGowan, his closest personal adviser, wrote, "He was quick and decisive on the issues that came before him. Occasionally he would drive us up the wall [about personal matters], but if a public matter arose, it was handled with dispatch. We never had any trouble getting him to face hard choices or make bad decisions."[1] Porter McKeever wrote, "There is not a single person who worked with him closely as governor or as candidate who will tolerate the suggestion that he was indecisive."

On March 13, he wrote Alicia Patterson:

> I just don't want to go out for it; I wouldn't be honest with myself if I did and I attach importance to the inconsistency of being a candidate for Gov. of Ill. and publicly or even privately running for Pres....I will...concentrate on being and *running* for Gov. unless the Democratic convention should nominate me which would seem very unlikely.[2]

It was an admission that, whatever scruples he may have had, if party forces would, indeed, engineer a draft he would feel obliged to accede to their demand. He would resist their overtures as long as he felt able to do so, but the final decision, he knew, would be out of his hands.

On April 17, the New York State Democratic Committee was giving a dinner for Averell Harriman and asked Stevenson to speak. He had decided not to attend, but when party officials urged that his absence would be misinterpreted, he relented. As a defensive measure, on April 16 he issued a statement designed to quash the burgeoning movement for a presidential draft. It said in part,

> Before I was ever considered for the Presidency, I announced that I would seek re-election as Governor of Illinois. Last week I was nominated in the Democratic primary....I have repeatedly said that I was a candidate for Governor of Illinois and had no other ambition. To this I must now add that...I could not accept the nomination for any other office this summer.
>
> Better state government is the only solid foundation for our Federal system, and I am proud and content to stand on my commitment to ask the people of Illinois to allow me to continue for another four years in my present post.

In his remarks to 2,500 of the party faithful at the Harriman dinner, as if to underscore the decision set out in his statement of the previous day, he resorted to the inimitable Stevenson wit:

> I am told that I am here at the head table by misrepresentation and fraud, that you invited a candidate for President but got a candidate for Governor instead....I think I have the answer to all of our perplexities here tonight. I found this letter on my desk just before I left Springfield, Illinois this afternoon:
>
> HONORABLE GOVERNOR STEVENSON,
>   Sir, You should marry Mrs. Franklin D. Roosevelt and you should run for the Presidential nomination and put Mrs. Roosevelt on the ticket for Vice-President and you will go over big.
>
> Now I propose to send this message to Mrs. Roosevelt with the respectful comment that I think it an excellent idea, but after all this is leap year.[3]

Yet the more insistent the voices became urging him to run, the more intense his struggle with himself, and the more ambivalent he became. On the one hand, his reverence for the office of the presidency was such that no one, he thought, should feel qualified to occupy it. On the other hand, how could he ignore the gathering groundswell of support that kept building for his presidential candidacy? Following the Harriman dinner, *New York Times* political columnist Arthur Krock told Stevenson: "I think you may face the prospect of one of the true drafts in our political history."[4] Nonetheless, as late as July 12, final day of the Republican Convention, his press secretary, William Flanagan, issued a statement declaring, "He is a candidate for re-election as Governor of Illinois, and as he has often said, wants no other office. He will ask the Illinois delegation to respect his wishes and he hopes all of the delegates will do likewise." It sounded like a definitive and final dismissal of party hopes. The following day, however—opening day of the Democratic Convention—Stevenson's speech welcoming the delegates to Chicago and Illinois completely turned the tables on any plans he may have had for returning to Springfield. It has been called one of the greatest speeches of the twentieth century.

> Here, on the prairies of Illinois and the Middle West, we can see a long way in all directions. We look to east, to wast, to north and south. Our commerce, our ideas, come and go in all directions. Here there are no barriers, no defenses, to ideas and aspirations. We want none; we want no shackles on the mind or the spirit, no rigid patterns of thought, no iron conformity. [an unmistakable reference to the McCarthyite hysteria of the hour.] We want only the faith and conviction that triumph in free and fair contest.
>
> As a Democrat perhaps you will permit me to remind you that until four years ago the people of Illinois had chosen but three Democratic governors in a hundred years. One was John Peter Altgeld, a German immigrant whom the great Illinois poet, Vachel Lindsay, called the Eagle Forgotten; one was Edward F. Dunne, whose parents came here from Ireland; and the last was Henry Horner, but one generation removed from Germany. Altgeld was a Protestant, Dunne was a Catholic, and Horner was a Jew. That, my friends, is the American story, written by the Democratic Party, here on the prairies of Illinois, in the heartland of the nation.

After reviewing the Democratic Party's record during the preceding twenty years, acknowledging that mistakes and errors in judgment had been made, he turned his hearers to the future:

> It is a very solemn hour, indeed, freighted with the hopes and fears of millions of mankind who see in us, the Democratic Party, sober understanding of the breadth and depth of the revolutionary currents in the world.... They see in us relentless determination to stand fast against the barbarians at the gate, to cultivate allies with a decent respect for the opinions of others, to patiently explore every misty path to peace and security.
>
> What counts now is not just what we are against, but what we are for. And who leads us is less important than what leads us—what convictions, what courage, what faith—win or lose. A man does not save a country, or a civilization, but a militant party wedded to a principle can.

The speech was greeted with thunderous applause. It also provided added momentum to the draft campaign that in preceding weeks had already picked up considerable steam. Four days later Stevenson found himself his Party's Presidential nominee.

His acceptance speech on July 26 was a demonstration not only of his eloquence but also of his humility.

> I have not sought the honor you have done me, [he began]. I *could* not seek it because I aspired to another office, which was the full measure of my ambition. One does not treat the highest office within the gift of the people of Illinois as an alternative or as a consolation prize....
>
> That I have not sought this nomination, that I could not seek it in good conscience, that I would not seek it in honest self-appraisal, is not to say that I value it the less. Rather it is that I revere the office of the Presidency of the United States....
>
> I hope and pray that we Democrats, win or lose, can campaign not as a crusade to exterminate the opposing party, as our opponents seem to prefer, but as a great opportunity to educate and elevate a people whose destiny is leadership, not alone of a rich and prosperous, contented country as in the past, but of a world in ferment....
>
> More important than winning the election is governing the nation. That is the test,...the acid, final test....Sacrifice, patience, understanding and implacable purpose may be our lot for years to come. Let's face it. Let's talk sense to the American people....
>
> Rather we lose the election than mislead the people; and better we lose than misgovern the people. Help me to do the job in this autumn of conflict and of campaign; help me to do the job in these years of darkness, doubt and of crisis which stretch beyond the horizon of tonight's happy vision, and we will justify our glorious past and the loyalty of silent millions who look to us for compassion, for understanding and for honest purpose. Thus we will serve our great tradition greatly.

Newspaper, radio, and television commentators nationwide were nearly unanimous in their recognition that here was a powerful new voice that, as Richard Goodwin would write over a decade later, "changed the face of American politics, enriching the democracy, providing a base on which talent could aspire to power, opening a gateway to public life through which many who never heard his voice will some day enter."[5]

The next four months would be the most harrowing as well as exhilarating of Adlai Stevenson's life thus far.

*   *   *

For her part, Mrs. Roosevelt, having fulfilled her obligations at the United Nations, now felt freed, for the first time since becoming an international civil servant, to renew her interest in domestic politics. Invited to address the

Democratic National Convention, she recalled that it was twenty years earlier "almost to the day" that her husband had stood "on this same platform" to outline the case for electing him president of the United States. Astutely drawing a parallel between the circumstances under which her husband and Stevenson had both marched onto the national stage, she said,

> In 1932 Franklin Roosevelt was a relatively unknown voice on the national political scene. He was running against a man who had been President for four years and who prior to assuming that high office had won a world-wide reputation for his great work in Europe. But the people nevertheless listened to my husband's voice and as you know the Democratic Party won that election.
>
> Today, twenty years later there is a new voice of democracy in our land—the voice of our Democratic candidate for the President of the United States. It is a voice that says the same thing in Virginia as it does in Harlem. It is a voice that talks sense to the American people. The Republicans claim that Governor Stevenson is talking over the heads of the people and his reply is, "The people are wiser than the Republicans think...." We will support him with our prayers and our work and God willing he will lead us well.

Returning home, she wired the new nominee: "My warm good wishes and hopes that you will win and bring us the kind of administration that will help our country and the world to peace."

He replied,

> Nothing has pleased me more than your thoughtful and encouraging wire. I had hoped I might see you while you were in Chicago, but I did have an opportunity to listen to your speech. I shall do the best I can with my limited experience and talents, and your good will will be a constant encouragement.

It was clear that she saw Stevenson as the sole figure on the political scene in 1952 who would try to solidify her husband's—and her own—domestic and international programs. She also felt that that conviction obliged her to share advice and counsel with him as events unfolded in the course of the campaign. Thus, on August 6, she sent Stevenson a letter suggesting that he "ask, as soon as possible," for a meeting with Bernard Baruch, financier and advisor of presidents from Wilson to Eisenhower.

> This may seem to you a waste of time and of course, if you feel it is, I do not want you to consider this suggestion. However, over the years Mr. Baruch gave some good financial advice to my husband and he has had long experience in organizing materials in two wars.
>
> Unfortunately, President Truman is so annoyed because Mr. Baruch could not give up his old rule of not coming out openly for a candidate[6] and heading

a financial committee for him that they exchanged unfortunate letters and President Truman felt that his information could be of no use to him.

You may feel exactly the same way but I have always found that while it took a little tact and some flattery to get on with the old gentleman I got enough information with valuable experience back of it to make it worth while. He is not always a liberal and you will not always agree with him but fundamentally he is sound and I think it is valuable to have some contacts with him, particularly unofficial ones.

She ended her letter: "With warm good wishes and appreciation of the fact that I am just adding one more headache to the many you probably have, believe me, Very cordially yours."[7] This was the first of what, over the next eight years, would grow into a body of advisory opinions on resources, strategies, principles, and issues "her" candidate—and friend—must not lose sight of.

Stevenson replied that he was "much impressed in what you said about Mr. Baruch" and assured her that he "planned to see him in New York when I am there. You have never added a 'headache' and you never will. I hope you will give me any suggestions you can as the campaign progresses."

Years later, writing in her *Autobiography*, Mrs. Roosevelt said,

> In 1952 it was my opinion that Governor Stevenson would probably make one of the best Presidents we ever had, but I also believed that it was practically impossible for the Democrats to win the election because of the hero worship surrounding General Eisenhower. I did make a speech on the United Nations at the Democratic National Convention that year at the request of President Truman, and I came out for Governor Stevenson, but I did not intend to be active in that campaign and I was not.[8]

Writing this paragraph at several years' remove from the event, she had evidently forgotten just how involved she was during her candidate's first try for the presidency. Although she did not speak as widely on his behalf as she would in 1956, she was active rallying the Stevenson forces and issuing statements that provided the rationale for electing Stevenson rather than Eisenhower. An example was her statement to Students for Stevenson: "I suppose [he] has a better world understanding than almost any other man in this country, and more important, he actually knows men who have been in their governments in practically every country in the world.... It seems to me that thoughtful people will be glad to have a candidate with such background and preparation."[9]

On September 9, she dropped in at Stevenson's New York headquarters to jolly up the staff. Special effort should be made, she said, to secure the support of Republicans and independents and promised to provide names as they occurred to her. Subsequently she expressed her alarm at the disorganized condition of the New York State campaign organization. That evening she wrote her daughter, Anna, that it seemed that the Stevenson volunteers were doing all the campaign heavy lifting while the party regulars were sitting on their hands. As late as September 30, matters had still not improved; on that date Stevenson himself reported to Wilson Wyatt, his personal campaign manager:

> I talked with Mrs. Roosevelt and she said she is willing to speak anywhere, any time and under any sponsorship, and also to make TV appearances or broadcasts. The only request she has received is from Lloyd Garrison for a 12-minute recording which she is doing shortly, and also to appear on Sunday at a political rally in Harlem. ...
>
> She volunteered that she thought the regular organization in New York is woefully weak, ineffective and inactive, and was also distressed by a report that the regulars "had requested the volunteers to keep out of upstate New York, "where she thought they would be more valuable than the regulars."[10]

Limited as Mrs. Roosevelt considered her role to have been, it was inevitable that their collaboration in the campaign should have changed the quality of their relationship. What had till then been a relatively arm's length "mutual admiration society" began slowly to become a more personal one. Her enthusiasm for Stevenson, however, had certainly not dulled the clarity of her political judgment. By September she had begun worrying about his ability to connect with voters. She decided to share with readers of her *My Day* column her evaluation of his campaigning style, voicing a concern that subsequently turned out to be widely shared among the public. On September 4, she wrote,

> He is making a very good impression in all of his major speeches. He has wit and humor, charm, restraint and intelligence.
>
> But these things alone will not win the presidential election for the Illinois governor. He must find out how to have the people feel that he is talking to them individually and that they must listen or they will miss something that really affects their daily lives. This is a gift that can be cultivated, and the candidate who achieves this close relationship with most of the people in his audience probably will win on Election Day.

In her September 13 column, she returned to this same concern about Stevenson's inability to connect with his hearers in a personal way:

> Occasionally the Governor is a little academic. Please remember, Mr. Governor, we are usually sitting down after a long day's work to listen

to you in our living rooms. We want to feel that you are visiting us, that you have something that you want us to know about in order that we may help you. We don't want to be talked down to, we just want you to tell us very simply what your problems are and what you face in the great task you are asking us to help you meet by voting for you in November.

She had put her finger on what ultimately may have been an important reason for Stevenson's failure to win the presidency.

By October, though throughout their friendship until just before she died he addressed her with very few exceptions as "Mrs. Roosevelt," she had begun using—on rare occasions—his given name. A handwritten letter to her (that has apparently been lost) prompted such a response:

> Dear Adlai [it read] What a lovely letter from you, and how wonderfully kind of you to take the time to write me in longhand. Unfortunately my handwriting is so bad these days that nobody can read it.
>
> My summer has been a most miserable one but now that the fever is routed I hope I will get back on my feet quickly. At the moment I expect to be home by next week and just as soon as I am able to have visitors I hope you will be among the first.

It was signed: "With my love to you, Affectionately."

The seed of friendship had broken its husk of formality and flowered. Thus, when later that month Stevenson managed a visit to Val-Kill while on a campaign swing through northern New York State, his sister Buffie could comment,

> It was such a gay, easy half-hour. We knew that John Roosevelt had come out for Ike, and Mrs. Roosevelt told Adlai that one evening when John and his wife were out, neighbors went in and filled their whole house with Stevenson banners and buttons! Seeing my brother and Mrs. Roosevelt together, I had a strong sense of their mutual respect and appreciation. Over breakfast our hostess and Adlai were exchanging funny stories about the rigors and rush of campaigning. A few days later, when she introduced him at a luncheon in New York...she referred to that, and my brother asked her if she could please tell him how a candidate ever found time to get his hair cut.[11]

This, as Stevenson biographer John Bartlow Martin wrote, became the dominant tone of the entire campaign of 1952,

> the tone that made those who were directly involved in it and millions who watched it remember it so fondly. There was a gaiety, a spontaneity, a freshness, an insouciance about it that was extraordinarily appealing to countless people weary of pompous politicians. It endeared [Stevenson] to the reporters

who crisscrossed the nation with him that fall, and some of them lost their objectivity and, though they worked for Republican newspapers, ardently wanted him to win. It attracted to his cause, too, great numbers of intellectuals. It made him seem an extraordinarily appealing civilized human being—which he was[12].

A sampling from a speech to the State Committee of the Liberal Party in New York City, August 28, 1952:

> I have, of course, read about you in the published writings of certain columnists and I am fully aware that you are very dangerous characters. I'm informed that attacks on you from the right are equaled in violence only in denunciations in the communist press.
>
> Well, I know how that is. In my very brief political career I've sometimes wondered if I had any friends left. And then they suddenly nominated me for President, and I wondered if I hadn't too many friends. But if I have, by any chance, too many friends, I am sure time will take care of that! You know how it is in an election year—they pick a President and then for four years they pick on him.
>
> I am running on the Democratic platform. I am for it, and I'll fight for it and I expect to win on it. No platform, of course, can resolve all of our dilemmas. As vital, it seems to me, as the written word is the spirit and the resolution of those who embrace the written word. The real question is whether a platform represents the clicking of a ghost's typewriter, if I may put it that way, or the beating of a human heart.
>
> Our opponents also have a platform. In modern times they've honored us Democrats by borrowing many phrases from past Democratic platforms. Now because of the timing of the conventions, this inevitably leaves them four years behind. But I suppose plagiarism must, nevertheless, be considered a form of progress.

A favorite anecdote from the campaign trail concerned the middle-aged woman who came gushing up to him in the crowd following a speech: "Oh, Mr. Stevenson, your speech was positively superfluous." To which he replied, "Thank you, madam. I've been thinking about having it published posthumously."

"Oh, that will be nice. The sooner the better."

*   *   *

It is not the purpose of this study to evaluate the shortcomings and the achievements of Adlai Stevenson's political campaigns.[13] Rather it is to acquaint the reader with the perspectives, the convictions, the style, and the spirit that he and Mrs. Roosevelt brought to the calling of public service, both in this country and on the international stage, and to probe the nature of the friendship they shared. Numerous experts have remarked that the campaign of 1952 was a high watermark in this nation's political discourse, George Ball, for example, writing, "He lighted up the sky like a flaming arrow, lifting political discussion to a level of literacy and eloquence, candor and humor, that tapped unsuspected responses in the American electorate."[14]

It does seem worth noting the enormous impact that technology exerted on the conduct of the 1952 presidential campaign, as it would on every such campaign thereafter. For it was in 1952 that "the medium," as Marshal McLuhan brilliantly saw, became "the message." In 1948 only 340,000 American homes had television sets. By 1952, there were 17 million TV's and politics was moving from a deliberative process to the world of "focus groups" and candidate "handlers," the sound-bite and the three-second quip. Adlai Stevenson was disdainful of this new phenomenon, he found it demeaning and fraudulent. "What do the Republicans think the White House is, a box of cornflakes?" "The lights, cameras and make-up annoyed him," says Porter McKeever, "they smacked of show biz, artificiality, manipulation, and seemed to block him off from rather than link him to the people he was trying to reach."[15] Further complicating his campaign was his inability to conform to television's strict time requirements. On too many occasions the purchased time slot would be spent before he had finished his speech, so audiences were left in mid-thought.

His impatience with the superficiality and trivialization of the political process led him, following the 1956 campaign, to propose a major change in the way presidential contests are conducted. Testifying before the Federal Communications Commission, he made a radical proposal:

> Suppose that every Monday evening at peak viewing time, for an hour and a half, from Labor Day until election eve, the two candidates aired their views...on public questions. The time should not cost them or their parties anything.

The result, he thought, would bring to campaigns the dignity and substance they deserved.

> It would end the tendency to reduce everything to assertions and slogans. It would diminish the temptation of politicians to entertain, to please and to evade the unpleasant realities.[16]

As with many of his proposals, this one was leagues ahead of its time.

On November 4, the electorate chose a military hero over a statesman as the nation's thirty-fourth president. Stevenson received only 89 votes in the Electoral College to Eisenhower's 442. The popular vote was closer: Eisenhower 33,936,234, Stevenson 27,314,992 votes. It was a landslide.

Back at the governor's mansion in Springfield, Stevenson was working in his office till after midnight, having decided an hour earlier that Eisenhower had won. At 12:40 a.m. he went to the Leland Hotel to deliver his concession speech, famously ending with a story:

> Someone asked me as I came in, down on the street, how I felt, and I was reminded of a story that a fellow townsman of ours used to tell—Abraham Lincoln. They asked him how he felt once after an unsuccessful election. He said he felt like a little boy who had stubbed his toe in the dark. He said that he was too old to cry, but it hurt too much to laugh.

He returned to the mansion for a few brief toasts to his inner circle of supporters before turning in. One woman present said: "Governor, you educated the country with your great campaign," prompting Stevenson's reply: "But a lot of people flunked the course." John Bartlow Martin tells us: "Fran Martin, to whom he offered the first glass, had won the election pool; she gave the money to Stevenson, telling him it was an early contribution to the 1956 campaign fund. He said, 'I take it shamelessly.'"[17]

Two days later Mrs. Roosevelt wrote Stevenson:

> Needless to say I am concerned and distressed for the country that you are not to lead us in the next four years. Nevertheless I think perhaps I should congratulate you very warmly for the problems will be so great perhaps no one could cope with them successfully. It will mean, however, that you will be free to do many things in the international field and I am sure that is where you can be most useful. I hope you are not completely exhausted by the campaign but I noticed you and Mrs. Ives look as fresh as possible. With every good wish and hoping to see both of you soon.

Replying a few days later, Stevenson wrote,

> You were, as always, more than good to write me so promptly. I have no regrets about the campaign except the disappointments of many friends. On the contrary, I feel a profound sense of gratitude for the experience and to countless friends who gave me help and encouragement. You are at the front of the list and I shall never be able to thank you properly. With my utmost respect and affection, I am faithfully yours, Adlai.

He spent the next month winding up his gubernatorial responsibilities in Springfield, strategizing with Democratic Party leaders about ways to redefine the party's role in national and world affairs, and responding to some of the nearly 100,000 letters that poured into his office lamenting the results of the election.

Writing to Mrs. Roosevelt on December 10, after alluding to these dull matters, he said,

> I hope we can make the [Democratic National] Committee something really useful during this interval in which we will have no access to the resources of the Executive Departments and no patronage. After twenty years it will be quite a new concept and enterprise.
>
> If I were to write you a dozen letters I could not hope to succeed in thanking you for your help, morally and actually, during my late ordeal. But some time soon I hope to have a chance to try in person!

On December 13, he addressed the Gridiron Club in Washington D.C.[18] There was not the slightest hint in the speech of his physical state of near-exhaustion. It was a vintage Stevenson performance:

> Perhaps I should begin by apologizing to those of you who work for a living and who thought I was out front, somewhere beside Mississippi, Britain and France. The fact was, of course, that the General was so far ahead we never saw him.
>
> I was happy to hear that I had even placed second. ...
>
> But I wonder if I'm not entitled to some kind of a record. Did anyone starting from scratch ever *enter* our public life with such widespread approval, and then *leave* with such widespread approval—all in the space of four years? Frankly, I think the chroniclers of our times have overlooked the meteoric beauty and brevity of my political career.

For nearly forty minutes he kept his audience of newspaper and other media people laughing till their sides ached. More than once during the campaign he had decried the fact of ours being a "two-party country with a one-party press." Now he shared the thought he hoped his hearers would carry home:

> Every lesson of history is that democracy flourishes best when speech is freest. No issue is more important—and more troublesome—in this time of conflict with massive repression than the preservation of our right, even to bore each other...Never was the responsibility of the majority press greater to make clear that it is concerned about the freedom of all Americans, and not merely about its own liberty to agree with itself. Your typewriter is a public trust. Its sound may be the most beautiful noise you know, but it has meaning and justification only if it is part of the glorious discordant symphony of a free society.

CHAPTER 2

ON THE WORLD STAGE

IN THE SUMMER OF 1952, soon after he won his party's nomination, Adlai Stevenson had decided "if elected" to travel to Asia "to meet the people with whom I would have to deal, and to give the best possible evidence of our profound concern for the Orient." When the electorate chose Dwight D. Eisenhower rather than himself, the soon-to-be-retired Illinois governor decided to take such a trip anyway. The excuse he gave the press was probably a bit disingenuous: "I can see no political significance in the trip," he said, but "It will obviously enhance what authority I might have for writing in the future." More to the point, one suspects that he was remembering the gathering at the Governor's Mansion in Springfield on election night and Fran Martin's "early contribution to the 1956 campaign fund." His eye was still on the prize.

The center of gravity in world affairs, Stevenson observed, was shifting eastward to the countries of the Pacific Rim. There Communism appeared to be making its greatest inroads among the common people from the Philippines to China. It seemed obvious that from there would come the greatest challenges for whoever, following Eisenhower, might occupy the White House. Yet with his sights clearly set on a career on the world stage, Stevenson had visited none of these emerging nations. How better to shift mental-emotional gears and educate himself at the same time?

Shortly after Christmas he had received a letter from his friend Chester Bowles, then the U.S. ambassador to India, telling him "Your San Francisco speech...is by all means the best policy statement on Asia that has been forthcoming from any source." Urging Stevenson to "spend at least 2 weeks here," he wrote, "Mrs. Roosevelt was here about 4 weeks and she felt her trip was a great success. It certainly was highly constructive from our standpoint."

Thus in January of 1953 Stevenson signed a contract with *LOOK* magazine for a series of articles in which he would share his experiences and reflections on a five-month journey through twenty-six countries in Asia. The magazine's 17 million readers would receive a comprehensive overview of the international complexities they would face over the foreseeable several decades. He planned to visit not just heads of state and diplomats but also trade union workers, educators, writers, and business people in their factories and offices, their pubs and sushi parlors so that he might discover what was truly on their minds and hearts. *LOOK*'s foreign editor William Attwood would accompany him to serve as editor, along with Stevenson's old friend William McCormick Blair Jr., former law partner and assistant when he was governor who served him in the same capacity during the 1952 campaign; Barry Bingham, publisher of the Louisville *Courier Journal*; and Walter Johnson, University of Chicago professor who was active in the previous year's campaign.[1] At the end of most days the group would discuss together what they had seen and heard and Stevenson's articles, subsequently edited by Attwood, would occasionally reflect those discussions. For Stevenson the journey would prove of enormous importance, an intensive self-education that not only found its way into numerous magazine and journal articles, and an important book, *Call to Greatness*[2], but also endowed his subsequent observations and foreign policy suggestions with an authority they probably would not otherwise have achieved. Though the trip began March 10, the first of his *LOOK* pieces appeared on June 2, the last on September 22.

Wherever he went he was greeted by huge crowds of people, clear evidence that across Asia the recent U.S. election had been closely followed. Typical was his reception in the capital of South Korea: "Thousands upon thousands of school children lined the dusty road into Pusan," wrote Walter Johnson,[3] "and there were 'Welcome Stevenson' banners sprinkled throughout the crowd." Everywhere he went Mrs. Roosevelt seemed to have preceded him: "The inquiries about you are constant in this region," he wrote her on April 18 from Singapore.

Two indelible impressions were left with the peoples he saw on his arduous journey: How closely and without prejudgment he listened to everyone he met, and consequently how informed were the views he expressed about the hopes and fears of the ordinary as well as the powerful members of the vastly diverse societies of the region. They remarked, too, on how irrepressible and guileless was the humor that marked nearly his every encounter, whether with the powerful or the lowly. "It's been a fabulous journey and I'm as tired as I was during the campaign," he wrote some Springfield neighbors on his return. "But we carried all of Asia!" When the mayor of Travancore-Cochin in South India welcomed him on behalf of the common people of the town, Stevenson mirthfully responded, "We of the Democratic Party also speak for the common people back home, and I have great pleasure in making all you good people of Travandrum honorary members of the Democratic Party."

A reporter who was there wrote, "At this the crowd roared with enthusiasm and laughter." Walter Johnson reported that "The local Communist party leader was overheard saying, 'Dash it all! First we have [Ambassador Chester] Bowles to contend with; then Mrs. Roosevelt had to come here—now we have Stevenson. And they're all so dashed human and attractive that it undoes months of propaganda on our part.' "[4]

A frequent complaint of governmental representatives throughout Asia concerned the pressure they felt to declare their allegiance to the United States in its cold war with the Soviet Union. Stevenson's ability to hear the nuances in such discussions was illustrated in an exchange he had with the secretary general of the Indian Ministry of External Affairs, Ragavan Pillai. When he began to discuss India's foreign policy, Stevenson said,

> I argued a long while with the prime minister that neutralism was "the wrong word to describe your foreign policy. You feel that you do not want to be caught in the East-West power conflict. [India is] not neutral, you are uncommitted."
>
> The minister replied, "You are absolutely right. We want time to tackle our own economic problems. But if the conflict comes, there is no doubt that we are anti-Soviet. ..."
>
> Stevenson replied, "I understand your feeling on this matter and perhaps the United States has been too quick to shout at others on this issue."[5]

According to Walter Johnson, Krishnalal Shridharani wrote, "Stevenson did an unusual thing for an American. He became one of the very few Americans to interpret India's foreign policy as India would like it to be interpreted."[6] In its issue of June 15, 1953, the *New Republic* magazine noted in a side-bar that Oliver Pirie, author of a piece titled "Sir, You Are in Solid Democratic Territory!" "represents five journalists who followed Stevenson in his Indian travels and whose collective efforts and separate reports are combined in this article." The article concluded, Stevenson "stood as a splendid example of an intelligent, responsible American leadership...a leader greatly respected and admired.... Throughout India he added to the stature of the United States."

A similarly nuanced understanding characterized Stevenson's description of Indonesia's situation:

> Defiantly independent, proud of their revolution, these men are touchy about being pushed around or appearing to be anyone's satellite; and they are determined to stay out of the world-wide contest between communism and democracy. But there is little anti-Americanism. They ask questions about America with eager, friendly curiosity. And they talk about their problems with disarming candor and transparent anxiety to find genuine friends and to draw closer to the America which was also born in a revolution against colonialism. ...

It seems that our best policy in Indonesia is one of benevolent detach-
ment. After all, it wasn't so long ago that we Americans were mighty sensitive
and suspicious of foreign influence and 'foreign entanglements.'[7]

In Burma that country's foreign minister, U Kyaw Nyein, hosted a reception for Stevenson and his party. Stevenson and Bill Blair had spent most
of the day in Mandalay while other members of their group had remained
in the capital. Arriving late at the reception, Stevenson joined a group of
Burmese officials who were discussing with the Yugoslav ambassador "a
news report that Senator McCarthy had just 'forced' the U.S. Information
Agency to investigate the writings of Mrs. Franklin D. Roosevelt and Adlai
E. Stevenson 'for any Communist leanings.'" "How do you Americans think
you can ever be a world leader if you act this way?" one person inquired.
Stevenson expressed his contempt for McCarthy but cautioned that the
senator should not be confused with the whole country. The acting foreign
minister remarked, "I look on Senator McCarthy as conducting a Spanish
Inquisition." He added, however, that he expected "American foreign policy to remain 'moderate' because of the influence of the Democrats in the
United States Senate."[8]

Even fifty years after they were written, his observations on Israel and her
relations with her neighbors have a tragic cogency:

> Israel's many friends in America should remember that good relations between
> Jews and Arabs are the only alternative to endless contributions of money
> to a permanently beleaguered fortress surrounded by embittered neighbors.
> Perhaps it is too much to expect that solutions will be worked out—as they
> should have been long ago—by the Arabs and Jews sitting down together.
> But they might welcome reasonable solutions imposed by outsiders willing to
> be damned by both sides. If this sounds like tough talk, I recall the pleading
> words of a sad-eyed old Mohammedan *caid*: "Two sick men need a doctor."
> He said it in Nazareth.[9]

In Yugoslavia toward the end of his trip, Stevenson had lengthy interviews with three of the nation's four vice presidents. Milovan Djilas, whom
President Tito later jailed twice for what he regarded as Djilas's subversive
books,[10] was widely regarded in the West as Communism's most perceptive critic. Edward Kardelj was Yugoslavia's chief financial minister. Koca
Popovic served as secretary of state for foreign affairs.

Then came a day and a half on Brioni, Tito's private island off the Adriatic
coast.

"It was the first meeting between Tito and an American statesman of Mr.
Stevenson's stature," wrote a Yugoslav journalist, "the first meeting between

two men who represent the best in their respective nations. And that is not insignificant."

At the conclusion of his visit, Stevenson told Yugoslav officials and reporters at the airport, "I leave you admiring all that you have done and all that you are now doing. I am proud that my country is contributing to the strength and vitality of Yugoslavia."

D.J. Jerkovic, a Yugoslav reporter, wrote,

No one answered him; there was no need.... He undoubtedly understood that here confidence in American democracy equaled the hopes which the entire world places in the United States.[11]

* * *

In the spring of 1953 Mrs. Roosevelt had accepted an invitation from Columbia University to join a group of U.S. citizens on a five-week good-will tour of Japan. On arrival she had given a press conference, commenting to her companions that she "had always heard that the Japanese were avid photographers, but I never expected to see so many news photographers as greeted us in Tokyo. I was told that Adlai Stevenson gazed in wonder at them during his trip to Japan and exclaimed: 'This is a photographic dictatorship!' "[12]

An objective of her tour was to discover the extent to which democratic institutions and practices were beginning to take root in what appeared to the victors this formerly feudal society. Wrote Mrs. Roosevelt,

The fact that the U.S. had rather arbitrarily insisted on giving the Japanese a democratic constitution, telling them that now they were going to be a democratic country, did not automatically change the old customs or turn feudalism into democracy. There were various articles in the new Japanese constitution that had been taken almost verbatim from Western documents, and some of these meant nothing to the Japanese or merely confused them because of the great differences between their social and economic background and [that of the United States.]...American methods were not entirely suited to the facts of life in Japan: the place of women in the industrial system, the necessity for children to contribute to the family income, the ability of the economy to support such public service.[13]

Mrs. Roosevelt tells readers of her *Autobiography* that when her goodwill tour ended, she and her companions proceeded home "the long way," stopping en route in Turkey, Greece, and Yugoslavia. Several months earlier she and Stevenson had arranged to meet on June 29 in Athens. Landing that morning in Athens in time to dictate her *My Day* column and the first draft of an article on her visit with the emperor and empress of Japan, she penned a letter to her daughter, Anna, that included these lines: "Maureen [Corr] is tired but Adlai Stevenson is coming in for tea & I think her curiosity will keep her awake to meet him." Then later, "Adlai Stevenson has been & gone, a most interesting man, with vision and common sense."[14.]

While at the United Nations she had made the acquaintance of the Yugoslav delegate. Though that delegation, frequently acting as cat's paw for the Soviets, had proven difficult, she had nonetheless been intrigued by Marshal Tito's temerity in defying Stalin and withdrawing his nation from the Comintern; she wanted to interview the president in person.

> His jaw juts out [she reported] and he speaks in the manner of a man who gives orders and expects them to be obeyed. But he has a sense of humor, he was pleasant to me, and he conveyed the impression of speaking frankly and honestly.... He is intelligent enough to recognize that he can have power in the long run only if the people give it to him voluntarily. As a result, I believe, he is concerned with providing a government that benefits the people, or at least enough of the people to maintain him in power. I concluded that he had a concept of self-government by the people quite different from ours, because there it comes from the top rather than from the bottom. But it did not seem impossible for our type of political philosophy to live and cooperate with the system that appeared to be developing in Yugoslavia.

A puzzling complication grew out of Mrs. Roosevelt's visit to Yugoslavia. Prior to her arrival there, President Tito had apparently exacted a promise from her: he would grant her an audience provided she would see to it that a full report of their interview appeared in a major U.S. publication. This she (or, more likely, her agent) had arranged with the same magazine, *LOOK*, with whom Stevenson had signed his contract. A letter she wrote her son, John, from Athens on June 30 described her perplexity:

> We arrived in Athens a little ahead of time. Adlai Stevenson came for tea at five and an hour with me. Why *LOOK* magazine is having him write an article about Yugoslavia as well as me, I don't know. They have already paid me 1500 dollars so I think they will probably take my article though heaven knows when they will publish it.

By year's end no action had resolved the dilemma; indeed, as late as March 1954 her article had still not appeared. She wrote Editorial Director Daniel Mich, reminding him of the understanding she had with the Yugoslav president: "Also I feel if you are not going to print my article (though the misunderstanding came about through another agreement which was made with Mr. Stevenson in your office), that I am obligated to return the money advanced to me." Mr. Mich replied, "as embarrassed as possible by what happened," urging Mrs. Roosevelt to keep the money as the fault was clearly the magazine's.[15] There is no evidence that Mrs. Roosevelt ever revealed the mix-up to Stevenson, though she did discuss it briefly with William Attwood. In any event, it seems to have left no scars on either principal.

* * *

London was Stevenson's final stop on what had proved for him and his companions a thoroughly exhausting journey. England had always been kind to him. The deliberations eight years before of the Preparatory Commission during the birth pangs of the United Nations were among the happiest moments of his public career. His current journey ended, then, among some of his warmest admirers—and at a time, it so happened, when the British edition of his "Major Campaign Speeches" had just been published. Even before their plane had landed at Heathrow, his editor from *LOOK* magazine, William Attwood, noted in his diary that evening, Stevenson "started talking about the possibility of making a swing around Africa next winter. Talk about chronic stamina.... It was a great trip. Never again."

The BBC aired a special program on "Speeches of Adlai Stevenson," during which the commentator described them as "the only really interesting and responsible political speeches the world has seen since the end of the war."[16] A press conference the following day, however, and a panel discussion with British editors that night qualified somewhat the media's enthusiasm. The *New Statesman and Nation* suggested that Stevenson "should never have become the darling of American progressives" and further that "although he would have made a better Republican President than General Eisenhower, he was selected as a Democrat." Malcolm Muggeridge, editor of *Punch* magazine, nonetheless couldn't contain himself toward the end of the interview. He confessed that he "couldn't resist" asking Stevenson "whether it is your present intention to accept a Presidential nomination in the next Presidential election...in 1956." Stevenson shot back, "I am obliged to say to you that if I could answer your question, which I can't, I wouldn't."

The September 22 issue of *LOOK* ran his final report on "The World I Saw." In capsule form it foreshadowed many of the assumptions underlying proposals he would make over the next several years, especially those relative to Asia and the Middle East.

> There is widespread feeling that we are impetuous, inflexible, and dedicated to the extermination of Communism; and that we have confused a military policy with a foreign policy. ...

The phenomenon of McCarthyism...and of fear and repression in mighty America were subjects that came up in every press conference from Tokyo to London. (One of Western Europe's most responsible and respected leaders told me that McCarthyism had done America more harm in eight months than Soviet propaganda had done in eight years.)...Faith in American leadership [this, an obvious reference to President Eisenhower and his administration] is shaken as confidence declines in America's self-confidence.

Coaxing that Communist colossus to accept the terms for full membership in the family of nations to which democratically inclined nations subscribe, he thought, would require extended and delicate negotiations, but "a broad basis for [such] negotiation" was already present, "China wants peace and trade above all."

[Japan is] now striving to graft a peaceful, democratic system onto autocratic, expansionist roots. (Someone told me that 80 different Japanese words have been used to attempt to convey the idea of "democracy.") Because of her large industrial plant and skilled, hard-working population, Japan can be a mighty dike against the tide of Asian Communism.

The Middle East Stevenson regarded as a region where

strong men and personal governments are the rule, but genuine democracy and representative institutions are the avowed goals....Communism is less a problem than economic and political maturity....The Jews and Arabs can find at least a *modus vivendi*....We can help, and in doing so we don't have to play favorites. Being proud of our part in creating the Jewish home state doesn't mean disregard or less concern for the Arabs.

Suggesting a dimension of foreign policy too often overlooked, he wrote,

One thinks of the possibilities of creating a pool of capital from the excess resources of the oil-rich states for development projects among their needier brethren.

Finally, on a general note, he demonstrated a practical, hard-headed knowledge acquired from years of experience as a negotiator when he wrote,

I doubt very much if peace and security will ever come out of one grand world-wide peace conference.[17] We will have to make progress bit by bit, item by item, place by place. We can define and agree with our allies and friends on common aims, minimal conditions and methods, and negotiate partial solutions in the framework of such common policy. The process may be slow and frustrating, but the stakes are epic in their transition from the world we know to a world we don't know.

Ugly illusions about the United States are all too prevalent, but there is also a touching, moving admiration.... And our illusions about the rest of the world are just as serious: that we have a monopoly of energy, know-how, culture and morality; that other people live and think as we do—or should. But if an illiterate Burmese peasant has an excuse not to understand America better, we Americans, with all the means of communication at our disposal, have none. So I am convinced that we must know more about our world to live up to the leadership that has been thrust upon us by circumstances.

* * *

Mrs. Roosevelt had arrived back in New York in July and, after checking on current developments at the office of the AAUN, proceeded to her beloved Val-Kill in Hyde Park. There was the annual picnic for the boys of Wiltwyck School and their families to prepare for, in addition to the customary list of visitors who kept beating a path to her door. Her "long journey home" had left her feeling troubled. Just as Adlai Stevenson's had been a disturbing journey for him, so was hers, and for similar reasons. Everywhere she and Maureen Corr had gone she was asked probing questions, particularly about Senator Joseph McCarthy's zealous crusade to root out of public life persons he considered Communists or "pinkos." His campaign had resulted in the dismissal of overseas as well as home-based persons in the State Department and U.S. Information Agency's employ. Many of them were men and women of long service with the government who had won the trust of the populations among whom they worked. An example was the case of Theodore Kaghan, public affairs officer in the Berlin office of the United States Information Agency who, after Senator McCarthy had attacked him, was sacked despite testimonial letters from Berlin's Mayor Reuter and ex-chancellor Figl of Austria, both of whom attested to Kaghan's strong anti-Communist convictions. More than that, books had been removed from U.S.I.A. libraries and in one or two instances provided the fuel for public book burnings.

Senator McCarthy had sent two staff "investigators," Roy M. Cohn and G. David Schine, to Europe to seek out consular officials of questionable loyalty and to remove "subversive" books from U.S.I.A. libraries. Europeans were chagrined. Mrs. Roosevelt was incensed:

> The first question you are asked in Europe [she wrote in a *LOOK* magazine article][18] is "What about Senator McCarthy?" and the second question is, "Is it customary in your country to go over 200 books in a few hours and remove

them from a library?" These questions are based on the trip taken by Mr. Cohn and Mr. Schine. Also you are asked in Europe if people are investigated in the U.S. as rapidly as these two young gentlemen did their investigations. When you reply by saying that what Senator McCarthy has done is not very important in the minds of most of the American people but that some people think he is doing a patriotic duty, the Europeans say, "Ah, but you did not watch a Hitler or a Stalin come to power." That is difficult to answer and that is why I said that this trip which these young men took so hurriedly and for purposes which Mr. McCarthy dictated, did harm to our prestige in Europe.

On her trip Mrs. Roosevelt had alluded to the "great damage" she thought the senator had done to American prestige abroad; now that she was home she became even more alarmed at the extent to which his campaign seemed to have cowed even members of Congress into total inaction if not submission. At an Americans for Democratic Action dinner in April 1950, she had said,

> The day I'm afraid to sit down with people I do not know because five years from now someone will say five of those people were Communists and there- fore you are a Communist—that will be a very bad day.
>
> I want to be able to sit down with anyone who may have a new idea and not be afraid of contamination by association. In a democracy you must be able to meet with people and argue your point of view—people whom you have not screened beforehand. That must be part of the freedom of people in the United States.[19]

Within hours of arriving home she sensed that that freedom was in seri- ous jeopardy. On September 8, she received a note from Adlai Stevenson, responding to one from her. Thanking her for a clipping she'd sent him from England, he went on to say,

> I had a busy time, as you will understand. Now I find myself relaxing so utterly that I can't summon the wits or energy to do much of anything. Some time you must tell me how to avoid total collapse after total effort—for years and years!

That same day the *Washington Post* carried a lengthy article noting that Mrs. Roosevelt, "disturbed by what she called a 'reactionary trend' in the coun- try," had come to Washington to announce formation of a new, nonpartisan organization, the National Issues Committee. "Our friends throughout the world are beginning to lose confidence in America," she said. Asked what she meant, the paper summarized: "The same forces which have blunted the edge of America's world leadership," according to Mrs. Roosevelt, "are largely responsible for the talk about a 'controlled recession,' for all but destroying the Federal housing program, for abandoning the Hell's Canyon project, and for lost ground in the fields of health and education." Insisting that the conflict is not between Republicans and Democrats, she said, "In every case both Republicans and Democrats will be found on each side. Instead, I feel sure that the whole trend I have outlined results chiefly from a lack of reliable, straightforward information available to the people. We are going to fill this gap to the best of our ability through the National Issues Committee." "A miasma of confusion and uncertainty which has overtaken us in recent years" she said, has helped feed the "disturbing trend" and "in this atmosphere the know-nothing and the demagogue have their opportunity and make the most of it, although they speak only for a tiny minority. The task we have set ourselves, therefore, is to redefine the great issues which confront this nation, to restate them in simple and popular terms as objectively as possible, and to see to it that the people get the facts upon which the making of sound judgment depends."

It was an ambitious goal, a lofty goal, one that demonstrated an absolute faith in the fundamentally rational nature of people: Give them the facts, straight and unvarnished, and there would be no question that a majority, at least, would choose the right path. It was a faith wholeheartedly shared by her friend Adlai Stevenson.

Curiously, Mrs. Roosevelt's initiative was mirrored by one that was brewing at the same moment in the minds of a number of the Democratic Party's leadership, Adlai Stevenson among them. A major party gathering was scheduled for September 13 and 14 in Chicago, ostensibly to hear Stevenson's report on his Asian trip. More to the point, the meeting would sound the tocsin for the party's campaign to win control of Congress in the 1954 midterm elections and the White House in 1956. Stevenson's speech would be the highlight, and nationwide radio and television broadcasts were scheduled. President Truman attended and wired Stevenson the following day that it had been "a great one," this despite his inability earlier in the week to persuade Stevenson to take the reins of party leadership. Not even his desperate *cri de coeur*—"Adlai, if a knuckle-head like me can be President and not do too badly, think what a really smart guy like you could do in the job"[20]—had persuaded Stevenson that he was the party's ablest spokesman.

Over the previous summer a number of intellectuals who had been drawn to Stevenson's side by his presidential campaign—John Kenneth Galbraith, Arthur Schlesinger, Jr., Chester Bowles, George Ball, Thomas Finletter, and others—had independently been pondering Stevenson's statement following his defeat that he wanted to make the Democratic National Committee "something really useful" during the years his party would be out of office. Several of these men had provided drafts for various Stevenson stump speeches during the campaign, but the scope of their thinking had now begun to broaden to embrace something resembling the institute or "think tank" of a later era. John Bartlow Martin recounts a conversation initiated with Stevenson by Galbraith on September 23, when the Harvard professor of economics said he had discussed with Averell Harriman "a problem that has been bothering me a long time, " namely, "How can we do the most to keep the Democratic Party intellectually alert and positive during these years in the wilderness?"[21] Galbraith envisioned a group of "accomplished students" of national and international problems producing position papers on the full gamut of issues from international trade to farm policy to civil rights. Ideas from such papers might be adopted by members of Congress, result in legislation, or end up in speeches by the party's presidential candidate; the point was to demonstrate the intellectual vitality and policy imagination of the Democratic Party.

Given the strong resemblance between Mrs. Roosevelt's "National Issues Committee"[22] and what would shortly become "the Finletter Group," it is hard to explain the apparent lack of coordination between Stevenson and Mrs. Roosevelt over the late summer and early fall on a matter of such magnitude, particularly when the Democratic Party's future could be so greatly affected by the mechanism its leaders chose for implementing so bold an initiative. Their correspondence had lapsed during July and August and when he arrived home Stevenson could hardly wait to retreat to his farm in Libertyville, to spend time there sorting his impressions and consolidating the insights he felt he'd won over the previous five months. Even as late as September 8, as we have seen, he still felt emotionally and physically drained of his storied "chronic stamina," while Eleanor's seemed evergreen.

In any case, Stevenson's response to Galbraith's initiative was to suggest that they meet at Chester Bowles' Connecticut home on October 3 and 4 where the three, joined by George Kennan, created what became known as "the Finletter Group." So named for its chair, Tom Finletter, President Roosevelt's former air force secretary, it grew to include a wide circle of experts[23] on a vast number of policy matters: social security, agricultural subsidies, wire tapping, monetary policy, disarmament, national power policy, foreign policy alternatives, among others. Martin credits that "think tank" with creating the intellectual foundations for both John F. Kennedy's "New Frontier" movement and Lyndon B. Johnson's "Great Society." Mrs. Roosevelt's "National Issues Committee" seems to have faded away within a few months.

The frayed connection between the two principals of our story during the late summer and early fall of 1953 may be partially explained by a note Joseph Lash confided to his diary on October 28. There he reported on a dinner party hosted that evening by Mrs. Roosevelt at her Val-Kill cottage

with the [Samuel] Rosenmans, [David] Levys, Harry Hooker and myself.... Talk turned to mediocre quality of leadership today. Mrs. R asked who of today's leaders could stand up to and deal with people of caliber of F.D.R., Churchill and Stalin. Mrs. R thought Tito. Stevenson might after he developed more self-confidence. Sam demurred about latter. He had great reservations about Stevenson's lack of political instinct. Said he had run into Cardinal Spellman who asked him to get Stevenson to speak at Al Smith dinner this year... that Stevenson had turned them down year before. When Sam saw Stevenson latter said he had two invites—one from Al Smith dinner, other from Woodrow Wilson Foundation—wasn't sure which he would accept. Sam said: "You have to make up your mind whether you want to be a statesman or a politician."[24]

This last is one of the most perceptive insights about Stevenson's sensibility offered by any of his contemporaries.

In a letter to Martha Gellhorn a week later, Mrs. Roosevelt revealed a further uneasiness about her favorite presidential candidate. He had not yet seen how to strike a balance between giving the impression "that we are a divided country on most issues but he must disagree enough with the administration to have some points of difference in the campaign. I don't think he is in full swing as the leader of the party and I hope he gets there soon."[25]

Her misgivings, however, didn't cloud her desire to engage with Stevenson before audiences of policymakers where his brilliance and moral stature could shine, hence a letter she wrote him in November urging him to attend Columbia University's Fourth Bicentennial Conference in June 1954. She expected it to be "very worthwhile and one which you will find interesting." Stevenson replied a few days later to say he had accepted Columbia's invitation "and am beginning to quake with anxiety already. I wish I had mastered the speech preparation problem like you have—and a lot of other things besides!"

On January 14 she wrote to thank him for the picture of himself "which you so kindly inscribed for me. I am delighted to have it and want to thank you warmly for your kindness."

*   *   *

Despite his protestations about physical and emotional exhaustion, Stevenson had been deliberating how he would deploy his (temporarily exhausted) "chronic stamina" in the twelve months prior to the midterm elections. Reflecting some years later on his role as titular party leader, he wrote,

In our country this role is a very ambiguous one. The titular head has no clear and defined authority within his party. He has no party office, no staff, no funds, nor is there any system of consultation whereby he may be advised of party policy and through which he may help to shape that policy. There are no devices such as the British have developed through which he can communicate directly and responsibly with the leaders of the party in power. Yet he is generally deemed the leading spokesman of his party. And he has—or so it seemed to me—an obligation to help wipe out the inevitable deficit accumulated by his party during a losing campaign, and also to do what he can to revive, reorganize and rebuild the party.[26]

There was his job description for the coming year. The only cure for what he saw as a dangerously inept and inattentive administration was to recapture a Democratic majority in Congress. If he could reach a significant portion of the public between February and November, he might be able to accomplish that goal. He would spend his fabled energies on the political campaign trail, setting out his party's positions on major domestic and foreign policy issues and contrasting them, sometimes directly, sometimes by inference, with those of President Eisenhower. With such exertion he might also be able to retire his party's debt that, at the end of the presidential race, stood at some $800,000. It would be a grueling year, one that would rule out the possibility of more than an occasional fleeting visit with Mrs. Roosevelt.

One of his early speeches that spring had demonstrably fateful consequences. In Miami on March 5, against the counsel of several advisors (they included Richard Russell, Hubert Humphrey, and Lyndon Johnson), Stevenson directly confronted the junior senator from Wisconsin, Joseph R. McCarthy, whose campaign to rid the government—and American society itself—of persons he regarded as "subversives," Stevenson thought, had become a dangerously corrosive force domestically and internationally. (At the time of the speech, according to the government's figures, 2,200 government employees had been dismissed or had resigned under Eisenhower's security program—a figure that grew to 9,600 by the end of the following year.)

Stevenson minced no words in his indictment of the program and his description of the true costs of McCarthy's reckless crusade. But more than the senator's crude methods were the target of the speech: Stevenson was aiming with equal force at the president himself for what he regarded as Eisenhower's political calculation that McCarthy's campaign was scoring points for the Republicans while showing up the Democrats' "coddling of domestic enemies."

> It is wicked and it is subversive [he began] for public officials to try deliberately to replace reason with passion; to substitute hatred for honest difference...When one party says that the other is the party of traitors who have deliberately conspired to betray America, to fill our government with Communists and spies, to send our young men to unnecessary death in

Korea, they violate not only the limits of partisanship, they offend not only the credulity of the people, but they stain the vision of America and of democracy for us and for the world we seek to lead.

That such things are said under the official sponsorship of the Republican party in celebration of the birthday of Abraham Lincoln adds desecration to defamation. This is the first time that politicians, Republicans at that, have sought to split the Union—in Lincoln's honor.

This system of ours is wholly dependent upon a mutual confidence in the loyalty, the patriotism, the integrity of purpose of both parties.... When demagoguery and deceit become a national political movement, we Americans are in trouble; not just Democrats, but all of us.

Our State Department has been abused and demoralized. The American voice abroad has been enfeebled. Our educational system has been attacked; our press threatened; our servants of God impugned; a former President maligned; the executive departments invaded; our foreign policy confused; the President himself patronized; and the integrity, loyalty, and the morale of the United States Army assailed.

The logic of all this is—not only the intimidation and silencing of all independent institutions and opinion in our society, but the capture of one of our great instruments of political action—the Republican party. The end result, in short, is a malign and fatal totalitarianism.

And why, you ask, do the demagogues triumph so often?

The answer is inescapable: because a group of political plungers has persuaded the President that McCarthyism is the best Republican formula for political success.

The only thing we know for sure is the government's reluctant admission that out of more than two million federal employees only one alleged active Communist has been found.... We await ... the administration's apologies to the many innocent, loyal people who have been injured by this unscrupulous, un-American numbers racket.[27]

It was a challenge the administration could not ignore. President Eisenhower appointed his vice president, Richard Nixon, to deliver the Republican response to Stevenson's indictment. It was a carefully framed statement[28] designed to exculpate the Republican Party as well as its top leadership— "Men who in the past have done effective work exposing Communists in this country have, by reckless talk and questionable methods, made themselves the issue rather than the cause they believe in so deeply."—but it signaled Republican willingness to allow the Army to begin hearings on McCarthy's libelous attacks on the integrity of several of its decorated officers. The hearings began on April 22.

An appointment to deliver the annual Godkin Lectures at Harvard in mid-March had been causing Stevenson considerable anxiety since his return from Asia. He decided to use the occasion to paint a (small-d) democrat's vision of the world as it might be, incorporating considerable material from his recent Asian trip as well as what he thought he had learned over a lifetime about America's relationship with the rest of the world. The three addresses were published by Harper Brothers under the title *Call to Greatness* and became the best-selling of all his books.

Following the Cambridge lectures, he decided to allow himself a few days rest with his sister Buffie Ives and her husband in North Carolina. There he suffered a kidney attack that required his return to Chicago. He wrote Mrs. Roosevelt a letter to be read at an ADA meeting later that week where he'd been scheduled to speak: "Instead +I'm talking with Chicago doctors, which should provide even better opportunity for missionary work. The trouble is they are doing most of the talking!"

The following week Mrs. Roosevelt wrote him (on April 12, the anniversary of her husband's death): "I hear you are to be operated on Monday. I only hope it will cure your troubles and that you will not be too uncomfortable so that your recovery will be rapid. You must not be ill for too long. We need you too much in the action fray."

She kept in close touch all through Stevenson's convalescence, which lasted for six weeks, writing him in a motherly tone: "I am distressed that you have suffered so much and I can fully understand your distaste for even the thought of campaigning at the moment. I hope your recovery will be rapid and that with increased strength things will look better." At the top of the page she had crossed out the typed "Dear Mr. Stevenson" salutation, replacing it with "Dear Adlai." It was a gesture of affection her recipient was moved by.

He replied,

Thank you so much for your sweet letter. When I read in the newspaper of your travels I am the more mortified that I fell by the wayside. I have recovered rapidly and soundly but I shall never catch up with you. Affectionately and devotedly,

ER's barnstorming for her candidate must rank as one of the most frenzied in twentieth-century politics, but Stevenson's recovery was apparently as complete as he reported. John Bartlow Martin provides a glimpse[29] of the pace Stevenson was able to maintain between April and November despite his hospitalization and extended convalescence. This was "a day in the life" when he was in New York:

9:30— Jack Fischer and Cass Canfield [of Harper Brothers, publishers]
10:30— Harold Ober [literary agent]
12:00— Mr. D'Alessandro [artist]

12:15— Lou Cowan [television producer]
12:30— Chester Bowles
 2:15— Roger Stevens [Democratic money man]
 2:30— Miss Hirsch [*Colliers*]
 2:45— Frank Karelsen [lawyer, educationist, ADA board member]
 3:00— Mr. Stewart (Arizona)
 3:15— Jim Farley
 3:25— Lloyd Garrison
 4:15— Wayne Morse [Democratic Senator from Oregon]
Evening— dinner and show; Leonard Lyons [gossip columnist]

The McCarthy hearings, which had begun on April 22, were temporarily halted at the height of the fall campaign. On December 2, the House of Representatives voted to censure McCarthy for conduct unbecoming a member of the Congress. His influence gradually waned from then on, but the damage he had wrought to the country and to thousands of its citizens was profound and the pall of fear and suspicion he created would last for several more years. Indicative of the nation's final assessment of the man was its adoption of the term "McCarthyism" to mean *unprincipled character assassination under the guise of rescuing the nation from evildoers.*

As for the results of Stevenson's intensive campaign on the hustings, Election Day 1954 gave the Democrats control of both houses of Congress—by a margin of one in the Senate, while nineteen new members in the House increased the party's majority to twenty-nine. Stevenson received plaudits from many political operatives for his part in achieving that outcome. By January 1955 he had traveled to most of the forty-eight states, given more than eighty speeches, and succeeded in wiping the party's debt off the books.

CHAPTER 3

RACE AS AN ISSUE

ON MAY 17, 1954, the U.S. Supreme Court handed down its unanimous decision in the case of *Brown vs. Board of Education* (of Topeka, Kansas). The opinion declared unconstitutional the "separate but equal" doctrine that had provided legal cover since 1886 for the desperate circumstances under which schools for black children had operated (without such justification) since the Republic's founding. The decision was the culmination of several decades of careful work by a cadre of dedicated members of the legal profession led by attorneys from the Legal Defense Fund of the National Association for the Advancement of Colored People (NAACP). Thurgood Marshall, later elevated by President Lyndon B. Johnson to the Supreme Court, headed the agency's team. Its effort was supported by academics and dozens of grassroots civic groups, fraternal organizations, churches, and labor unions who considered discrimination on the basis of race a denial of the equal rights guaranteed by the Constitution.

President Eisenhower reacted to the Court's action as he had chosen to do toward Senator McCarthy's "crusade": He would remain "above the battle" to maintain a neutral stance toward civil rights issues as long as possible—that is, until matters came to a head and neutrality was no longer a defensible position. (Biographer Marquis Childs recalled that "in 1948 the general had laughed when liberal Democrats started wooing him. He was, he told a reporter, a strong believer in states' rights: '...if he had to name any single individual whose outlook he agreed with it would probably be Senator Harry F. Byrd of Virginia.'")[1]

The consequences of the president's decision were incalculable. Supreme Court Associate Justice William O. Douglas thought them disastrous. Had the president used his "bully pulpit" to secure public compliance with the Supreme Court's order, he could have struck a blow for freedom. Sadly, the associate justice wrote, the president's "ominous silence" emboldened the racist forces throughout the country to resist the desegregation cause.[2]

The differing reactions of Stevenson and Mrs. Roosevelt are instructive for this study. Beyond whatever impression their public statements may have created in the minds of the electorate, the way in which each responded to the event itself would complicate their future collaboration. Mrs. Roosevelt's response came from a woman who had long been intentionally engaged with the African American leaders of her country. It was an engagement that resulted from a deliberately chosen, rigorous self-education about the actual conditions of the poorest members of the nation. In August 1933, at the urging of her close friend Lorena Hickok, she had traveled to West Virginia's Monongalia County, encountering there the marginal existence of white and black citizens of "the land of the free"[3] whose deprivations were legion even before the Great Depression had engulfed them. She was shocked and shamed by what she saw and, in true Eleanor Roosevelt fashion, had determined to do something about it. One outcome was "Arthurdale," the first of a series of fifty-two such projects constructed under the Subsistence Homestead Division of the National Recovery Act of 1933. The program envisioned the construction of livable homes to replace the miserable shacks that were the only shelter for millions of families, white or black, through-out much of the "Deep South." The homes would be constructed of locally available materials, have windows in every room, and—most importantly—indoor plumbing; 165 homes were eventually built on the 1,200 acres owned by Richard Arthur in Reedsville, West Virginia.

ER had imagined Arthurdale as the flagship demonstration model for the rest of the Subsistence Homestead project. As such it would include black as well as white households. But resistance to such integration from the whites effectively blocked her dream. Disappointed but undaunted, on January 26, 1934 she convened a White House council of war, inviting the deputy director of the program, Clarence Pickett (who was also executive director of the American Friends Service Committee), and six of the country's most prominent Negro leaders.[4] From their discussion that lasted past midnight " 'ER' promised to make every effort to ensure black participation in all federal work and relief programs," furthermore assuring the leaders that "her door was always open, her heart with them."[5] By 1945, she had decided she needed to educate herself more fully about how African Americans experienced their lives in American society and had accepted an invitation to serve on the Board of Directors of the NAACP. Elected co-chair in 1950, in 1951 she was named vice president of the organization. An emotional commitment to full equality of all African American citizens was a vital part of who Eleanor Roosevelt was.

The Supreme Court's opinion in *Brown v. Board of Education,* therefore, represented for her a significant and welcome forward step in this nation's arduous—and clearly reluctant, even grudging—journey toward the full human rights every human being deserved and for which she had labored so long both nationally and internationally. But she recognized that for many Americans the road ahead would be difficult. Three days after its issuance she featured the decision in her *My Day* column, greeting it in her characteristically succinct way of expanding her readers' horizon while seeming only to explain her response to the event. Between the lines any alert reader could see that she expected the decision to be met with stiff resistance, perhaps especially in the Southern states. She had no hesitation, however, in publicly identifying herself with the justices' unequivocal stand that segregation on the basis of race is de facto discrimination and, therefore, unconstitutional: "Segregation in itself means inequality, and the mere fact that you cannot move freely anywhere in your country and be as acceptable everywhere as your neighbor creates an inequality."

It was ten days, however, before the titular head of the Democratic Party found his voice on the subject; even then it was far from the clear one with which Stevenson usually spoke. Desegregation was a national problem requiring nationwide compliance, but all Americans should realize the particularly painful changes the decision would require of not just Southern schools but Southern social norms as well. The rest of the country should extend the hand of fellowship, patience, and understanding to the South in sharing that burden. As Stevenson biographer John Bartlow Martin has pointed out, this statement was hardly an unambiguously liberal response. Stevenson's enthusiasm was lukewarm and his sympathy was directed primarily toward the South.

Martin thought the speech "a curious statement from a man widely considered a liberal. True, it was prophetic in proclaiming the problem a national, not exclusively a Southern one. But it contained no praise of the decision itself, nor any statement that it was a justified one."[6]

These two quite divergent views of the Court's opinion might be at least partially explained by the apparently different lenses through which in the spring of 1954 our two protagonists were viewing the world. We have just reviewed the convictions that guided Mrs. Roosevelt's behavior and public utterance. Those that shaped Stevenson's were somewhat more complex. Only recently returned from Asia, he saw tensions in the nation's life against the backdrop of the cold war with the Soviet Union. That "war" was heating up in the mid-1950s with actual fighting on the Korean Peninsula and in Viet Nam. In his recent tour Stevenson had been impressed by how, wherever he went, he had been asked about Senator McCarthy and his "anti-Communist" campaign. Were Americans losing faith in their own country and its institutions? they asked. Why else was the senator allowed to continue his demagogic "crusade" unchallenged? Stevenson had also noted that the Soviets seemed peculiarly alert to every suggestion of weakness in

American society and ready to exploit the smallest opening they thought they saw in its otherwise impenetrable armor. Propaganda initiatives of the U.S.S.R. amongst Asian peoples constantly pointed to the discriminatory practices in the United States of the white majority against people of color, thereby implying that the Asians' "revolution of rising expectations" would be met with similarly repressive measures from the United States.[7] Partially conditioning Stevenson's response to the Court's decision was doubtless a fear that, unless desegregating America's schools could be accomplished by general agreement among all affected parties without rancor and without fuss, the U.S.S.R. could score a substantial propaganda victory in the court of world opinion. That concern had prompted him to say at Los Angeles on March 28, referring directly to the issue of racial discrimination, "The fate of the world depends today on unity among Americans."

More important still, however, was his recognition that the Supreme Court decision, which Southern Democrats quickly condemned, threatened the potential break-up of the Democratic Party. That concern would shape much of his thinking and speaking about domestic policy matters, especially civil rights, throughout the next two years.

Stevenson had demonstrated his strong commitment to minority rights throughout his career in public life. Before World War II he had served as first chairman of the Chicago Bar Association's Civil Rights Committee (1939). As aide to Secretary of the Navy Frank Knox in World War II, he had advocated the commissioning of Negro officers. As governor of Illinois he had desegregated state parks and insisted on the integration of schools in the southern part of the state; he had urged passage of a state Fair Employment Practices bill (though he had been unable to change the two votes that defeated it); he had used the National Guard to put down race riots in Cicero.[8] In 1952, following a thorough study of candidates running in both parties for the presidency and the vice presidency, the Board of Directors of the NAACP had passed a resolution saying that Stevenson's position on civil rights was "the most forthright" of any of the candidates of either party.[9] He certainly had nothing to apologize for so far as his record on civil rights was concerned. But the next two years would severely test his conviction—at the time, shared by Mrs. Roosevelt—that the way forward in civil rights should be blazed by education and persuasion rather than by forceful action, whether by the courts, by federal troops, or by a combination of both.

Did either—or perhaps both—of them underestimate the depth and the bitterness of the struggle that was on the horizon? Such a struggle had been hinted at by a Swedish sociologist a decade before. In 1944, Gunnar Myrdal's 2,000-page study, *An American Dilemma: The Negro Problem in America*,[10] had attracted widespread attention and debate, not only in the academy and the press but throughout American society; no leader worthy of the name had failed to become acquainted with the study.

In it Professor Myrdal had asserted,

> The treatment of the Negro is America's greatest and most conspicuous scandal. For the colored peoples all over the world this scandal is salt in their wounds. If America in actual practice could show the world a progressive trend by which the Negro became finally integrated into modern democracy, all mankind would be given faith again. And America would have a spiritual power many times stronger than all her financial and military resources—the power of the trust and support of all good people on earth.[11]

A gathering tide of determination had begun to build during World War II throughout American society. Many whites—ER and Stevenson among them—were uncomfortable about the sloganeering that tried to justify the purposes for which the United States and its allies were fighting abroad while at home overt discrimination, both personal and institutional, gave the lie to our protestations. The war over, resistance to the blatant racism of American society was increasing, particularly among African Americans. Pressure came from African American soldiers who, having fought for their country in the only "good" war in memory, were unwilling to submit any longer to separate and unequal status in their home communities. They exposed discriminatory practices of banks that were "red-lining" certain neighborhoods as off limits to blacks seeking loans for better housing, and of realtors whose national association's "ethical" code contained a prohibition against selling to blacks a house in a previously all-white neighborhood.[12] They began disobeying laws that validated discrimination in public accommodations— hotels, restaurants, theaters, buses, and trains. Pressure was exerted against educational institutions: By 1952, African American graduate students were being accepted in nine southern and border states: Oklahoma, Texas, Tennessee, Arkansas, Missouri, Kentucky, North Carolina, Virginia, and Delaware. Between 50 and 70 percent of ex-G.I.s returning home to Deep South states, however, found no places in Negro colleges—those state legislatures had provided funds only for enlarging white schools.[13]

Over much of 1953 Stevenson had had considerable exposure to the thinking of those African American leaders who were at the forefront of what became the civil rights struggle of the next decade. He had had several exchanges with the NAACP's Roy Wilkins and Walter White, secretary and executive director respectively. White had written him a sternly critical letter[14] following Stevenson's address at the Jefferson-Jackson Day Dinner in February, condemning his favorable mention of Senators Sam Rayburn and Lyndon B. Johnson as "great Americans." Was Stevenson not aware that "Senator Johnson has voted without exception against every civil rights measure which has come before the Senate? The record of Mr. Rayburn has been no better." Had Stevenson forgotten Walter White's concern? Had he forgotten the warning that Roy Wilkins had given him in September 1952, when the NAACP secretary had said that "Southerners [had] demonstrated by past actions that they...never came forward with any proposal that really changed the old order," and advised him to "examine most closely any so-called 'compromise' offer brought forward by the Southerners"?[15]

The advice of the two men was not entirely lost on Stevenson, but another, as he thought, more substantive concern was weighing on his mind: He realized, more than most at the time, that *Brown* presaged a significant struggle in the North as well as the South, but most bitterly in the South, one that would be spearheaded by Southern members of his own party, and that the chances of the struggle's splitting that party asunder were great indeed. The only hope, as he saw it and would reiterate time and again over the next two years would be to avoid the hardening of ideological positions from which no retreat was possible. Throughout the campaign that concern dominated much of his thought and determined the way in which he responded to queries on the subject from the media as well as from others. As events would show, he would be swimming against a powerful tide right up to Election Night, two years hence.

He would never, however, allow the demands of politics to preempt the delights of friendship, and on September 28 he composed a charming letter regretting having to miss Mrs. Roosevelt's seventieth birthday celebration in October. It concluded,

> Personally I am not sure we should celebrate your birthday or that we should be reminded that time passes for you as for the rest of us. There are some people for whom time seems to stand still and who can bridge all the genera-tions of their interval on earth, but they are very rare. You are one, and for me you will always be the same age, and no age.

* * *

The fact that the first reactions he and his mentor, Mrs. Roosevelt, expe-rienced toward the *Brown* decision differed quite so strongly suggests that they were relatively out of touch with each other during this time, as indeed they were. Stevenson was also doubtless somewhat preoccupied with his son Adlai III's pending marriage to Nancy Anderson of Louisville, Kentucky. The Roosevelt-Stevenson correspondence over the next year was sporadic at best, though there are numerous notes by each regretting their inability to arrange a meeting. Perhaps they were putting one off until each could see and articulate to their own satisfaction the way forward for the Democratic

Party and for the country. More likely, however, was the fact that in 1955 she seemed forever "on the go" on behalf of the AAUN—to Tennessee, Arkansas, Louisiana, Texas, and Colorado in the winter; France, Italy, and Israel in March; and an extended trip to Asia for the international federation of United Nations associations (Tokyo, Hong Kong, Djakarta, Manila, Bali, and Bangkok), while he was in Africa during April and May. On his return Stevenson was preoccupied with forming the team that would conduct his presidential bid in the 1956 campaign. (His only regret about the Africa trip, he reported, was that he'd been unable to include a visit with Albert Schweitzer, "whom many call 'the greatest living man.'" "I wanted to confirm the epitaph he has written in case he is eaten by cannibals: 'He was good to the last.'")[16] It would soon be recognized by both himself and Mrs. Roosevelt that an hour or two together that each had regarded as a profitable, always enjoyable luxury could prove of critical consequence for Stevenson's future career. But somehow life kept frustrating their best-laid plans for such a meeting.

At the end of its 1954–55 term, the Supreme Court issued proposals for implementing its decision in the *Brown* case taken the year before. The seven-paragraph unanimous decision came to be known as *Brown II*. It reiterated the court's statement in *Brown I* that branded racial discrimination in public education unconstitutional and noted that federal district courts would be responsible for supervising locally devised plans to end such practices. Acknowledging that in some jurisdictions community attitudes and mores might make the transition difficult, the opinion warned that "the vitality of these constitutional principles cannot be allowed to yield simply because of disagreement with them."

For Stevenson and Mrs. Roosevelt, however, both the political landscape and their interpersonal one were roiled when they learned that the NAACP was considering framing an amendment to an education bill that would require the federal government to withhold funding from any school that, despite the court's opinion, continued to maintain segregated classes. Mrs. Roosevelt favored such a move; it had actually been the official position adopted by the NAACP Board of Directors as early as 1950.[17] Stevenson, however, differed with the NAACP leadership on this point and told Senator Humphrey that he saw it as a product of "Negro stubbornness...and perhaps even reaction." [18]

He explained why in a speech to the National Education Association on July 6, 1955. There he shared his fear that public opinion was hardening into two polarized camps while the only hope of resolving the dilemmas posed by racial discrimination would lie in an enlightened public opinion. He had hoped, he said, "that what is good for all will not be lost to all by any linking together of the school aid and desegregation issues [this, a clear reference to the amendment being considered by the NAACP] which would delay realization of our hopes and expectations on either or both of these vital fronts. In the long run segregation and discrimination...will yield quickly to the general advance of education."[19]

Subsequent events would not permit such an outcome; the tide of resistance to the Supreme Court's order was running more strongly than he—or Mrs. Roosevelt—fully realized. Nor could it have escaped the notice of either of them that their divergence on the issues raised by *Brown* could spell trouble unless an early meeting could be arranged.

Just here the question obtrudes itself: Was she beginning to question "her" candidate's dedication to the principles that were now so native to her bone; in other words, was Stevenson's response to the issues raised by *Brown* and by the NAACP's contemplated amendment beginning to lead her to the view, later expressed by John Bartlow Martin, that Stevenson "did have a deep private commitment to civil liberties but a much shallower one to civil rights."?[20] That question would loom ever larger in coming months. It would also be a major force in bringing them into much closer collaboration than had been practicable since their friendship began.

CHAPTER 4

A SECOND RUN FOR
THE PRESIDENCY

PRESIDENT EISENHOWER'S STATE OF THE UNION ADDRESS TO CONGRESS, as reported in *Time* magazine's January 17, 1955 issue, sought to reassure the public that all was well, the government in capable hands: "In tone and content," said *Time*, Ike's speech "reflected the condition of the nation— watchfully peaceable, prosperous and united." That was clearly the national mood the administration in Washington was trying to encourage. The reality, however, was quite otherwise: Indeed, the entire decade of the fifties was shadowed by a vague but pervasive unease, a persistent atmosphere of foreboding that formed the backdrop for the nation's public life. A caustic Gore Vidal described the populace as "other-directed, hydrogen-haunted,— [the first hydrogen bomb test would be staged in March]—artificially traumatized, and doggedly-togethered." There were data to support his view. Earlier attempts to secure international control of the atomic "genie" having failed, both sides in the cold war periodically threatened to invoke its use. In mid-February the Technological Capabilities Panel, appointed by the president a year earlier, submitted its report, *Meeting the Threat of Surprise Attack*. The panel urged that "without military and civil defense, America's vulnerability *invited* surprise attack. The only way forward was to acquire defensive capabilities of every type."[1] The specter of "McCarthyism" still haunted public discourse. Though in December 1954 Joseph McCarthy was finally censured by the U.S. House of Representatives, the toxic poisons his "witch-hunts" had unleashed took several more years to subside. At first largely unrecognized as such, the fifties were a period that witnessed the first rumblings of the nation's third great convulsion since its birth—the Revolution itself and the Civil War being the other two. Prescriptions for sedatives tripled between 1955 and 1957,[2] and throughout the decade, as Sharon Ghamari-Tabrizi writes, "paranoia wiggled and curled in the sporadic surges of enthusiasm for civil defense, from the intricate plans to billet urban evacuees in rural villages that were drawn up during the Korean War, to the boomlet in fallout shelter construction during the Berlin Crisis of 1961."[3]

By April, international tension was approaching the boiling point in Asia. A million men of deposed Chinese president Chiang Kai-shek's army, fleeing before the Communist forces of Mao Tse-tung, retreated to the island of Formosa (Taiwan). Chiang then began fortifying the coastal islands of Quemoy and Matsu, a move that was widely interpreted as a prelude to an invasion of the Chinese mainland. Secretary of State John Foster Dulles was perfecting a new form of diplomacy that he would soon define in an article for *LIFE* magazine[4] as "the ability to get to the verge without getting into war. Of course, we were brought to the verge of war. The ability to get to the verge without getting into war is the necessary art. If you cannot master it, you inevitably get into war. If you try and run away from it, if you are scared to go to the brink, you are lost. . . . We walked to the brink and we looked it in the face. We took strong action."

Sabers were rattling in the U.S. Congress too, Senate Republican leader William F. Knowland and the chairman of the Republican Policy Committee, Senator Styles Bridges of New Hampshire, calling for U.S. intervention should the Chinese Communists try to reassert their sovereignty over Taiwan. There was even mention of the possible use of "tactical" nuclear bombs against China if such should be deemed necessary.

Stevenson decided to confront what he considered the possibility of a war on the Asian mainland. In a nationally televised address—his first in four months—he outlined a strategy for stepping back from the abyss. The United States together with as many nations as would join should propose that collective action in defense of Formosa would be their response should the Chinese Communists employ force in the Formosa Strait. Such a move, Stevenson thought, would add "moral solidarity to military strength" and assure that "Quemoy and Matsu would have little further importance to the Nationalists, let alone to us."[5]

It was a practical proposal of an experienced statesman for extricating his nation from a tangle that could well have lighted the fuse of World War III. Secretary of State Dulles met it with a condescending and dismissive comment: "Mr. Stevenson," he said, "has in fact echoed the administration's program in relation to Formosa." If such was the case, the administration's "program" had not previously been made clear to either the media or the general public. Adlai Stevenson, however, had precisely described the anxieties and the hopes of his fellow citizens while simultaneously proffering a strategy whereby the president without losing face could back away from the pressures coming from the Chinese and from members of his own party.

That was just what the president did at a summit conference in Geneva in July, whereupon the Asian crisis subsided.

Stevenson shared with Agnes Meyer his own assessment of the Geneva meeting: Had Eisenhower not chosen to reverse "most of what [his administration] had said and done for two and a half years," he thought the meeting would have stalemated. In the event, it proved "only one thing: people want peace. I think we are learning to live in an age of perpetual peril, albeit slowly, with convulsions of pessimism and optimism."[6]

In his tribute to Stevenson at the United Nations on July 19, 1965, Archibald MacLeish said of the man whose life and work were so closely intertwined with those of Eleanor Roosevelt from 1946 until her death in 1962: "He had no taste for power, no desire for it.... The two disastrous and superb campaigns which he conducted were proof that his reluctance at the start was not the reluctance of political calculation but of passionate belief."[7] It was a generous, large-hearted eulogy and, like most such rhetorical feats, more flattering than true—accurate, perhaps, as to Stevenson's temperamental stance in 1952, but hardly so for his 1956 run. He himself would say in his acceptance speech on August 17, 1956: "Four years ago I did not seek the honor you bestowed upon me. This time it was not entirely unsolicited."[8] This last comment drew "laughter and applause," his hearers fully aware that he had had to fight a gargantuan battle to eliminate powerful rivals for his party's endorsement.

In 1952 he had conducted the campaign following his own instincts rather than those of his advisors. Not surprisingly, they thought it had cost him the election. So this time he had decided to follow their advice, at least on most occasions. He recognized that four years earlier he had several times spoken "off the cuff," only to find that he had set unnecessary traps from which it was painful to extricate himself. He had insisted on giving speeches on topics that his advisors thought were too complex or too controversial to be helpful to his cause and they had usually been proven right. Following his own drummer had deprived him of the prize; now he would march to theirs. The prospect prompted a moment of reflection he shared with Agnes Meyer:

> Having long denounced, inwardly and certainly, the presumption, arrogance and insensitivity of anyone who would seek a Presidential nomination, here I am doing just that! So I feel in a way that all the exertions of the past 3 months is [sic] but inexorable retribution and that I am doomed to pay and pay for my apostasy.[9]

If this was more than just another example of Stevenson's flirtatious delight in wordsmithing, his letter may reflect a genuine ambivalence about the decision he had made—possibly for the reason Archibald MacLeish described—and would carry into the campaign that was about to begin. His relationship with Mrs. Roosevelt was certainly made no easier thereby. She, the penultimate politician, had lived her entire adult life at the pinnacle of political power and acquired one of the keenest strategic political minds of her generation.[10] She would play a crucial role in guiding both Stevenson and the Democratic Party at several dangerous crossroads over the next several months. That, even then, she would find herself on opposite sides from Stevenson on several issues certainly complicated their relationship to a degree, but neither would allow such differences visibly to dampen their affection and respect for each other.

In her *Autobiography* Mrs. Roosevelt reports she decided to get back into politics in the 1956 campaign. A major reason was that "during my own world travels I had been greatly interested in the impression [Stevenson] had made on foreign statesmen. Again and again they told me that [he] was the kind of man who listened, who wanted to learn all the facts." She then recalls a visit "the Gov" paid her following his African journey when he asked her whether there weren't others who she felt "could do better" than himself as Democratic Party leader. She answered in the negative, saying she knew no one as experienced and farsighted as he. She then writes, "Though I urged Governor Stevenson to run, I did not expect to take an important part in the campaign."[11] That expectation would not be fulfilled.

According to a March 16 Gallup poll only 16 percent of the electorate was finding anything whatever to complain about the Eisenhower administration. The president seemed content on the whole to keep a low profile and to give his cabinet officers and their underlings a relatively free hand to run the country according to their lights. Congress seemed edgier than the rest of the populace. Earlier in the year the Senate voted 84–0 to continue investigations of "Communist activities" of government employees; it also extended Selective Service for another two years. Now it was summer, and the country was enjoying "unprecedented" prosperity. Domestically the citizenry seemed to be in a somewhat befuddled state, uncertain about the future while generally accepting of the status quo. The Deep Southern states were an exception, where White Citizen Councils, emboldened by the president's silence on the *Brown* decision, were digging in their heels to resist desegregation of schools and other public facilities. As Harry Ashmore observed, "The ostentatious neutrality of the executive branch encouraged denigration of the [Supreme] Court, which now began to come under direct fire from right wing organizations that identified minority rights with Communist conspiracy."[12]

The president could point to a civil rights bill his administration had introduced in the Congress in April, but neither he nor congressional members had pressed for its passage. A discouraged correspondent wrote the *New York Times* that

> the Eighty-fourth Congress adhered to its eighty-year-old tradition when it adjourned without enacting a single civil rights measure. One cannot respect an administration which, with four years to present a legislative program on civil rights, waits till April of the fourth year, knowing that no bill introduced at that late date has any chance of overcoming…Congressional procedural barriers.[13]

In late August, Emmett Till, a fourteen-year-old African American boy from Chicago on a visit to Mississippi relatives, was alleged to have either whistled or told a pretty white storekeeper woman, "on a dare from some local boys, 'Bye, baby.'"[14] He was kidnapped in the middle of the night, brutally beaten, his body barbwired to a hundred-pound cotton gin fan and thrown into the Tallahatchie River. Though the television cameras recorded the trial, only those who packed the courtroom were actual witnesses of "Jim Crow justice" at work. An unfazed all-white jury, determined to uphold "the Southern Way of Life," after only an hour's deliberation acquitted the two white men who were identified by eyewitnesses as the perpetrators.[15] (A year later they would boast to a *LOOK* magazine reporter that they had "taken care of" Till.) The news made headlines across the world. Ten thousand people rioted in the streets of New York's Harlem. President Eisenhower resisted pleas for a statement condemning the murder and disallowed a federal investigation. Stevenson too said nothing about the affair until four months later when James Wechsler, *New York Post* editor, wondered aloud about his silence. "No one can approve of the Till case," Stevenson snapped in December, "and anyone can say so over and over again." He supposed he could "just shout," but that "helps things very little."[16] His irritation was palpable. He was voicing white public opinion at large: America's Caucasian majority was deaf to the rising chorus of the nation's African Americans who were now determined to put an end once and for all to 200 years of racial discrimination and injustice.

Stevenson was eager for the presidential contest to begin. Polls were unreliable: Didn't his party's midterm election triumphs the year before demonstrate a pervasive uneasiness in the electorate? The political winds were surely blowing in his direction. Learning in July that President Truman would be attending a Shriners parade in Chicago, he arranged a quiet meeting in the hope that he might receive the president's blessing. Truman came away without making any such promise, only urging Stevenson to announce his candidacy soon. By now Truman had concluded that the party's "titular head" lacked the fire in his belly that is essential for anyone seeking political office, most especially the presidency. On August 5–6, a Stevenson strategy session at the Libertyville farm revealed that even some of his top advisers were doubtful that Ike could be beaten.

Nonetheless, he began forming the team that would conduct his second campaign for the presidency. For the next twelve months the statesman would contend with the politician in Stevenson's psyche. Seeking, among others, to add a sophisticated newsman to his staff who could help him "reflect thoughtfully over the news and the image [he should] present" as the campaign developed, he turned to Harry Ashmore, editor of the *Arkansas Gazette*. Ashmore had been a member of "The Elks," Stevenson's speechwriter corps in the 1952 campaign, and would be able to help the candidate with his "Southern strategy."[17]

From August 9 to 12 the National Governors Conference was held in Chicago. During that week twenty-two of the twenty-seven Democratic governors made appointments to see him in order to urge him to run again. He took this as a favorable sign, though questions were raised later as to what portion of these sentiments could be interpreted as "endorsements." His three sons also expressed their support.

Then on September 24 came a bolt of lightning that would dramatically change both the form and tone of the forthcoming campaign: On a golfing vacation in Denver, Colorado, while visiting his wife Mamie's relatives, President Eisenhower played twenty-seven holes in an afternoon. That night he was stricken by a heart attack and at 2 A.M. was rushed to Fitzsimons Army Hospital. Suddenly all previous political calculations and strategies had to be reexamined. Republicans had to assess the likely consequences of Richard Nixon inheriting the Oval Office and what that could mean for Republican congressional campaigns. On September 26, the *New York Times* featured several articles under the banner "Three Republicans in Spotlight Due to President's Illness." Among Democrats the possibility of a wholly new contest seemed suddenly to loom. Both Tennessee senator Estes Kefauver and New York governor Averell Harriman moved aggressively toward winning their party's nod for the prize that many pols as well as members of the public felt Stevenson had proved in 1952 he couldn't win. (Harriman had earlier said he was "for Stevenson" but now told the press that that didn't mean he would back "The Gov's" candidacy a second time.) President Truman remained silent until October 10, when he was quoted as saying "It would be improper of him to dictate the choice" of the Democrats' candidate. His decision appeared to be based on his expectation that if, as now seemed likely, a close contest within his own party should emerge, he would be called upon to arbitrate.

On October 18, sixteen governors of Southern states—fourteen of them Democrats—met at Point Clear, Alabama, for their annual conference. A major topic of discussion at the meeting, according to press reports, was "a move to form a powerful centrist coalition within the Democratic Party to strengthen the Southern position next year in the selection of a Presidential nominee and the writing of a party platform."[18] Expressions of surprise that none of them had apparently been contacted in advance about the proposal but instead had learned of it only from reports in the press brought an admission from Lyndon B. Johnson, Democratic majority leader in the Senate, that he had broached the idea as a trial balloon the day before through the device of a press release. When contacted, he told the *San Antonio Express* that he was "not trying to line up a coalition against an automatic nomination of Mr. Stevenson." Calling himself "not a conservative but a moderate," he said, "the moderates would try to have influence in writing the platform."[19] (The "Southern position" by now had been made clear through the White Citizens Councils and the growing resistance to desegregation of the schools. Its signature tactic endorsed by governors and some Southern senators was touted as "interposition.") At first cool to the idea of a "coalition" (doubtless because they hadn't been consulted), the governors seemed on reflection to be attracted by the notion of wielding coordinated influence in the convention both on the choice of presidential candidate and on the language of the platform.

Mrs. Roosevelt, however, was convinced that once again Stevenson was her party's strongest candidate. Her October 19 *My Day* column stressed that international affairs increasingly impinged on national decision-making. The candidates for both parties should be "men who have had experience in dealing with people from many other nations and who know conditions in many other parts of the world." She called Stevenson's "executive experience as governor of Illinois an added asset."

Stevenson's hopes that he could avoid the grueling pace of the 1952 campaign by skipping primary contests were torpedoed by the shifts in the political situation that followed Eisenhower's heart attack. If he meant to win, his advisers told him, he would have to enter primaries in at least a half dozen states. "Then I'm not running," he spluttered. "I have no interest in this.... I'm not going to those supermarkets."[20] But in the end he relented, writing Mrs. Roosevelt on November 7 that he planned on making a "statement" on the 14th. He assumed she would know its intent.

The day she received his letter Eleanor Roosevelt sought out Barry Bingham, campaign manager for New York's Stevenson-for-President Committee. In a memo to Jane Dick, Bingham reported on "a long talk with Mrs. Roosevelt"[21] in which she expressed herself "ready to do anything we wanted her to do." She urged the Stevenson-for-President Committee to engage in "as much activity as possible with women and young people," underscoring the suggestion with a list of "four able women" she thought could coordinate activity in New England, the Middle West, the South, and the Far West, and stressing the ease of organizing on college campuses.

As Stevenson had anticipated there was little surprise on November 15 when he announced his intention to run. On the 19th he gave the keynote speech at the National Committee dinner in Chicago.[22] Conceived by his team as the party's opening salvo in the 1956 campaign, it was a disaster; he had labored over every paragraph so long that it had entirely lost the punch of his speeches in the 1952 campaign. The result fell flat as a collapsed soufflé and the campaign was off to a dismal start.

Earlier in the month there were signals coming to Stevenson headquarters that all was not promising for an eventual victory. On November 14, a second cousin of Averell Harriman, a long-time member of the Democratic National Committee (DNC) for the District of Columbia and former ambassador to Norway (1933–40), had written Stevenson to inform him that due to family pressure she was resigning from the DNC: her family thought she should be "neutral" in the forthcoming contest. Two days later came a letter from Stevenson's distant cousin Richard Russell, prominent Georgia senator, predicting that he would be elected president provided the party adopted a "reasonable platform." It was a shot across the bow, not only of the candidate but also of the party leadership, to warn against language committing Democrats to what Russell and, by implication, "most Southerners" would consider an unacceptable stand on civil rights.

Stevenson was painfully aware of most of these pressures and counterpressures as he was preparing his speech for the National Committee. He began forthrightly enough, noting that an unwonted preponderance of the appointments to high executive positions in the current administration had been awarded to people from big business. A Democratic administration would "return the public interest to the center of public policy, and restore the sense that government is the concern not of a single dominant economic interest but of all the American people."

Then came a carefully crafted paragraph alluding, albeit indirectly, to the question of civil rights—or so it was interpreted:

> I agree that moderation is the spirit of the times. But we best take care lest we confuse moderation with mediocrity, or settle for half answers to hard problems.... Moderation, yes! Stagnation, no!

Stevenson was pleading for a spirit of give and take, for a recognition of the futility of rigid ideological stances toward infinitely complex economic and social problems, civil rights beings one of the most pressing as well as most intransigent. But to ambitious politicians the word "moderation" was a red flag. His old friend Averell Harriman, now competing for the party's nod at next year's convention, saw an opening. Following Stevenson to the podium, he threw down the gauntlet, thundering, "There is no such word as 'moderation' in the Democratic Party vocabulary." Similar reaction would soon come from other party leaders and the press would echo the taunt throughout the campaign.

The "new" candidate scheduled a press conference the day after announcing his intention to run for a second time. As expected, topics ranged from major foreign policy questions to who would constitute his leadership team for the campaign to whether or not he had made any "deals" that might assure his nomination at the forthcoming party convention. Through it all shone the old Stevenson verve and love of bantering repartee. A reporter asked how he would finance his pre-convention campaign. "With money" was the quick reply. "Will you have a finance committee to raise the funds?" another wanted to know. "I have an individual," Stevenson replied. "I don't know that it is a committee and at the moment I'm not prepared to tell you about it. I will later. I hope he is busy." A *Dallas News* reporter, fully aware that in 1952 Governor Allan Shivers led Texas Democrats to switch to Eisenhower and that an even more drastic split was looming for the upcoming party convention, queried: "Will you comment on Governor Shivers' qualifications to sit in the next national convention?" Stevenson's riposte: "No sir, I won't, because I don't know what they are."

Even though President Eisenhower's medical condition had served to open the floodgates to a clutch of potential alternative Republican candidates for the presidency, the general himself was apparently of two minds about running: Mamie was known to favor retiring to their Gettysburg farm. Party managers decided to let confusion about the president's plans envelop the Democrats and frustrate their arriving at a sharp focus for their campaign. Meanwhile a vacuum would serve the Grand Old Party well until Ike made up his mind. He would not announce his intentions until February 29.

Unremarked, at first, by the media, a seemingly minor incident was occurring in the capitol of the Old Confederacy, Montgomery, Alabama, one that heralded the imminent approach of a tectonic shift in the relations between the nation's black and white citizens. A humble, dignified biracial woman of forty-two named Rosa Parks, who hemmed and ironed garments in the city's upscale Montgomery Fair department store, had simply refused the order of a racist bus driver to give up her seat to a white man. It was the holiday season, December 1, 1955, and the end of a long hard day. As she later explained, "When I declined to give up my seat, it was not that day, or bus, in particular. I just wanted to be free like everybody else. I did not want to be continually humiliated over something I had no control over: the color of my skin."[23] Her simple act led to the Montgomery Bus Boycott which the city's 17,500 blacks (who normally provided 90 percent of the bus company's patrons) maintained for over a year, walking instead of riding to work to protest the racially discriminatory laws of the State of Alabama. A *New York Times* reporter was alerted to the emergence of a twenty-five-year-old African American minister named Martin Luther King, Jr., newly called to Montgomery's Dexter Avenue Baptist Church, who had been asked to head the boycott's "Montgomery Improvement Association." The media were calling King an example of "the New Negro," educated, articulate, self-assured. The *Times* reporter recorded the comment of a Negro mail carrier: "It's not a New Negro—it's the new times. Only we know it, and the white folks here haven't caught on to it yet."[24] He was describing the plight of white folks nationwide, very few of whom as of December 1955 had "caught on." Eleanor Roosevelt and Adlai Stevenson would wrestle with the consequences of that blindness throughout the campaign of 1956.

As the holiday season approached, Stevenson began planning "for a few delicious days," as he wrote Agnes Meyer, "in the country with my children" at the Libertyville farm. Fate, however, intervened to frustrate his plans. On December 21, his youngest son, John Fell, was driving home to Illinois with three Harvard classmates, friends since childhood. Near Goshen, Indiana, a truck that was trying to pass another truck plowed head-on into the car John Fell was driving. Two of the boys were killed, the third suffered minor injuries. John Fell's kneecap was shattered, he lost many teeth and was badly bruised and cut. A considerable part of Stevenson's holiday season was spent at John Fell's bedside. Throughout his son's convalescence, both Mrs. Meyer and Mrs. Roosevelt maintained daily telephone contact with Stevenson.

On December 27, Mrs. Roosevelt sent him a handwritten note asking if he could arrange a meeting "to talk farming" with her sons Elliott and Franklin, Jr., one a rancher, the other a New York farmer. He replied a few days later saying,

> I have visited Frank's splendid farm, and indeed he presented me with a splendid Suffolk ram more than a year ago in, I suppose, an heroic effort to improve the sheep population of Illinois! Well, the ram has increased it but I can't guarantee that he has improved it.

Replying to her query about his older son's recovery, he wrote, "John Fell is mending rapidly in body, but the spirit will be slower, I fear." In a letter that he wrote her ten days later, it seems clear that he'd taken time to reflect more deeply on the spiritual price his son's accident was likely to exact.

> I shipped John Fell back to Harvard yesterday—with a cast, a crutch and some fine new teeth. I think he is in good shape with no remorse or self-reproach, but, I have no doubt, a profound and everlasting wound which he will bear in silence, as we all do.

To have been the agent, however innocently, of another's death leaves, in any but the most callous, a damaged heart. Adlai Stevenson had known that truth since he was twelve years old.*

Arthur Schlesinger, Jr., writing in 1960 about the respective attitudes toward power of Stevenson and John F. Kennedy, surely was thinking of this event's possible influence on Stevenson's public behavior:

> The thought of power induces in Stevenson doubt, reluctance, even guilt. He is obsessively concerned with the awesome responsibilities of the presidential office.... Lauren Bacall once argued persuasively to me that he had a political death wish. I have never believed that Stevenson is essentially indecisive... [or that] he would balk for a moment at executive necessities.... Yet the exercise of power does present a problem for him.[25]

---

*At a 1912 Christmas party Buffie hosted for neighborhood friends, one of them, home from military school, asked if there was a gun in the house. An old .22 rifle was retrieved from the attic for the young man who snappily demonstrated the manual of arms for the group. Adlai, who had been watching from upstairs, raised the gun to his own shoulder and pulled the trigger. At that moment, one of Buffie's friends came into the line of fire. The Stevenson parents, returning from next door, entered the house as the young girl, receiving a bullet to her head, dropped to the floor dead. "I did it," cried Adlai, disappearing to his mother's bedroom.

A week later, Helen Stevenson took Adlai to Chicago, then to South Carolina, telling her journal, "Adlai needs to forget and we will make a wall of silence never to speak of [the accident] again." The family kept that vow for forty years until it came to light in 1952 when a *TIME* magazine reporter, researching Adlai's early years, discovered the tragedy.

CHAPTER 5

CIVIL RIGHTS AGAIN

HAVING ACCEPTED THE NECESSITY OF ENTERING PRIMARY CONTESTS in as many as six states, Stevenson flew to Minneapolis on January 17 to file as a presidential candidate in the Minnesota November primary. The Stevenson team had chosen Minnesota, Illinois, Pennsylvania, Florida, and California to expose "Middle America" and the two coasts to the candidate's agenda for the nation. Estes Kefauver, who had been stumping in Minnesota and other states during the previous year, wired Stevenson the next day that he too would seek the Democratic Party's nomination. Stevenson's managers thought "the Gov's" candidacy would be safe in Minnesota inasmuch as its senior senator Hubert Humphrey as well as Governor Orville Freeman had already pledged their support. He would, therefore, start his campaigning in California in February.

Key adviser Arthur Schlesinger, Jr. had recently spent time trying to assess his candidate's strength in that key state. He wrote Stevenson about his "image" there: that the 1952 candidate had campaigned with negligible concern for the political consequences of positions he espoused, but now four years later his nearly every speech bore the marks of his advisors' political calculation. Schlesinger cited two examples of what he meant: the candidate's stand on offshore drilling for natural gas, and civil rights. On the former issue he said Stevenson "sounded like Eisenhower" (states should control their offshore rights), while on civil rights Californians thought Kefauver was taking a more forthright position than Stevenson.[1]

Stevenson expressed his frustration at this state of affairs in two letters,[2] the first to Alicia Patterson, the second to Agnes Meyer, both written on February 8. He was speaking to six or eight rallies a day, he told Alicia, trying despite "a constantly hostile press" not to obscure his image. He was bothered by "a party element more focused on the racial issue, Israel, etc. than on winning elections." That element, he thought, "puts temperate behavior in the posture of reaction very quickly." To Agnes Meyer he complained of the "slapstick politics" and extempore speaking that were his daily diet that assured a confused image and "misquotations as numerous as the accuracies." Most of the pressures were "either for irresponsibility or banality."

A few days earlier he had given one of his politically most important speeches before the California Democratic Council's annual convention. He had so belabored it before delivery that it was a total failure; the press dubbed it "the Fresno Fiasco." It was full of lofty generalities—"A nation which...settles for...'security' is a nation sick and in mortal danger, for security as an end and aim is a sick man's vain delusion....Nations are secure when they are alive and moving toward the ends they dream of....The future demands of us no departure from principle, no restrictive new political doctrine. It simply demands that we continue with good heart to adapt to an age of change." The pressures of campaigning were beginning to sap his energy reserves.

Estes Kefauver was quoted as promising African American leaders that, if elected, he would order all federal funding denied to schools that defied the desegregation order of the Supreme Court. His remark was an allusion to Congressman Adam Clayton "Powell's amendment" which the NAACP's Board of Directors was strongly supporting. Mrs. Roosevelt was vice president of the NAACP Board of Directors and had initially opposed its position from a tactical point of view. Now, however, as she would say on several subsequent occasions, she too was committed to the board's position.

Stevenson was weary "after as rugged an ordeal as I can recall," and impatient with the political calculation and hedging involved with seemingly every sentence he uttered. Furthermore he felt let down by Harry Ashmore, the Southern liberal editor whom he had been relying on for guidance on civil rights issues. Referring to the Powell Amendment, he complained: "I have no thoughtful advice on this sort of thing in spite of the fact that Harry Ashmore has been traveling with me continuously."[3]

He was also already violating his earlier resolve to listen more closely to his advisers about campaign strategy. Thus at a February 7 meeting in Los Angeles with a largely African American and Mexican American audience he reiterated his opposition to the Powell Amendment and said he opposed using federal troops to enforce the Supreme Court's *Brown* decision. (His Chicago office, according to NAACP secretary Roy Wilkins, "had hoped to have him avoid any further discussion of the [civil rights] matter until he could make a speech in Detroit, March 15, when he would go into the civil rights issue exhaustively.")[4] It was a brief speech in order to allow for a longer question and answer period, and there he seemed to trip over his own feet as he expanded on the reasons for his opposition; to some it sounded as though he was trying to convince himself of the position he was taking. Federal force, he said, was the precipitating cause of the Civil War. "Troops or bayonets" would not secure compliance with the Court's ruling. To persuade Southerners to abandon the segregated way of life they had practiced since the nation's founding, "we will have to proceed gradually," he said. "You do not upset the habits and traditions that are older than the Republic overnight." Pressed yet further, he lost his cool: "I'm not running for this office for the honor of it, my friend," he blurted, "[and I will] do everything I can to bring about [national] unity even if I have to ask some of you to come about it gradually." He had used the anathema "g" word. A veteran *New York Times* reporter pounced on the term and declared Stevenson had, in essence, wounded himself unnecessarily. Other papers took up the cry, prompting him to issue a "clarifying" statement in Portland a few days later. It contained a single sentence that, far from helping his cause, complicated it further. "We will not...reduce race prejudice," he said, "by denying to areas afflicted with it the means of improving the educational standards of all their people."

AFL-CIO chief George Meaney, who had played a major role in getting Stevenson the presidential nomination in 1952, now lashed out in condemnation of the candidate's stand:

> For Mr. Stevenson to say that he would not withhold Federal money from a state violating a specific decision of the highest court in the land is nonsense to me. My God, if he were to give funds to such states, he would be acting in complete disregard of what the Supreme Court says the Constitution requires.[5]

It was cold comfort for the Stevenson camp that Meaney made it clear that his "criticism was confined to the segregation issue" and would not decide on whether to back any candidate till after both Republicans and Democrats had held their conventions.

Having read next morning about the gaffe, NAACP secretary Roy Wilkins fired off an angry three-page letter[6] in which he sought to educate the candidate on his use of language that to African American ears sounded at best patronizing and at worst incendiary:

> "Gradual" to vast numbers of white Southerners means never at all. So when you tell a Negro audience, early in 1956, that they must be patient and abide by a "gradual" approach to the solution of their problems you are scraping a raw nerve.... Uppermost in the minds of every person in that audience were the Emmett Till killing, the bloody suppression of the Negro vote and other atrocities in Mississippi; the cowardly economic pressure campaign and the vicious racial propaganda of the White Citizens Councils; the open defiance of the U.S. Supreme Court by certain state legislatures and state officials; the organized drive to intimidate citizens, to deny freedom of assembly and

speech, to curb the right of petition; and the scene on the campus of the University of Alabama where a mob of 1000 young men threw missiles at a lone Negro woman student.... [Autherine Lucy, the University of Alabama Law School's first African American applicant.]

By inference your Los Angeles speech supported the currently fashionable contention in some quarters that the Negro citizen, in his request for implementation of the Supreme Court opinion in the public school segregation cases, is "going too fast." The question is: is the federal law supreme, or is it not?

Responding to a request from Mrs. Roosevelt, John Morsell, Roy Wilkins' assistant, sent her a copy of his boss's letter. (Though biding her time until comment from her would carry maximum weight, she was following closely her candidate's every public utterance.) She made a note in the margin opposite the second paragraph quoted above: "This is a condescending letter." She would shortly take Wilkins to task for writing it.

New York State's senior senator Herbert H. Lehman, one of that body's most highly respected members, reacted, he wrote Stevenson, with a similar "sense of disquietude over the stand you have taken, or at least, over the way you have expressed your attitude, as reported in the newspapers." "I do not know," he wrote,

whether you appreciate what the word "gradualism" and the word "education" mean to Negroes and to White [sic] people who are deeply concerned with the civil rights issue. To advocates of civil rights, these are words of frustration and denial.

It is difficult to speak of the enlightening effects of "education" in a situation such as we have...chiefly [in] some parts of the South, where all the active education is in the direction of prejudice and discrimination. [Adlai underlined the word "active" and wrote "No!" in the margin opposite this sentence.] People who go to segregated schools...are conditioned not only to the separation of the races, but to the existence of distinctions on the basis of race. The most powerful and effective forces at work in these areas are those bent on maintaining the status quo....Integration in the Armed Services, abolition of discrimination in interstate travel, and all the rest of progress that has been recorded, resulted from administrative, legislative or judicial fiat, and not from "education."

The denial of voting rights,...the question of physical violence and security and...the denial of the protection of the Bill of Rights and of the Fifteenth Amendment...must be confronted in one way or another....[Stevenson underlined "confronted."]

Summing up, the senator urged that "To set a distant target date merely postpones for that length of time coming to grips with the problem."[7]

Though they were on a first-name basis, we have seen no evidence of a Stevenson reply to Senator Lehman.

Returning to her New York apartment after a speaking tour in the Southeast (Florida, Georgia and South Carolina), on February 11 Mrs. Roosevelt wrote Stevenson that she had just visited with presidential adviser Bernard Baruch who was "very anxious" to talk with Stevenson in March or April about some financial issues. He would help Stevenson handle them adroitly and could "show you how Secretary [of the Treasury (George) Humphrey] can be put in a hole." The old gentleman was "very alert and much better than I have seen him in a long time."

Three days later she sought to extricate Stevenson from what she saw as the media's distortion of his proven civil rights record. In Chicago, speaking on behalf of the New York State Stevenson-for-President Committee, she said she found the "confusion and misunderstanding" about Stevenson's civil rights position "difficult to understand." Cataloguing his achievements in this field as governor of Illinois, she asserted that "no one of the candidates has a clearer [civil rights] record." She found her candidate's opposition to the use of force—"troops and bayonets will not bring about a change"—"entirely correct" and placed herself squarely at his side on this issue. Like Stevenson, she was worried about the rising tide of impatience among blacks that was mirrored by the growing intransigence of racist whites as represented by their Citizens Councils. If this trend continued the likely result would be a polarization from which no resolution could emerge. She was trying to interject a note of calm reason into the situation.

Turning to her divergence from Stevenson over the Powell Amendment, she clarified the subtle legislative issue that initiative had created: She favored amending the Federal Aid to Education bill (though she didn't mention it here), by including the Powell Amendment, but if inclusion of an amendment threatened defeat for the entire bill, she would favor passage of the bill without the amendment.

She had avoided mention of her candidate's outright rejection of the Powell Amendment while simultaneously explaining the reasons for her strategic approach to the matter. She had also expressed her willingness, if the amendment would cause defeat of the bill itself, to drop her support for the amendment. Despite their differing positions in the matter, her statement concluded with an expression of her absolute confidence in Stevenson's assessment of the situation: "I know that Mr. Stevenson sees this question in its broadest context. I know that he believes we must be a nation with equality and justice for all our citizens and I trust in his integrity and in his judgment as to the best methods to be employed."[8]

It was a magnanimous gesture as well as a crucially helpful one. Stevenson promptly sent an ecstatic telegram from Seattle:

HAVE JUST RECEIVED HERE A COPY OF YOUR WONDERFUL STATEMENT SUPPORTING MY STAND ON CIVIL RIGHTS. THIS OF COURSE WILL BE HELPFUL IN THE CAMPAIGN, BUT IT IS MOST VALUABLE TO ME PERSONALLY AS EVIDENCE OF YOUR UNDERSTANDING.

The nation's press, however, with a mindset divided, as usual, between its constitutional role to educate the populace and the commercial value of controversy, was playing up the fall-out from Stevenson's use of the term "gradually" in his Los Angeles appearances. New York papers carried a slurring comment from NAACP secretary Roy Wilkins, taking the governor to task for suggesting that Negroes should moderate their pressure for change. Mrs. Roosevelt wrote Mr. Wilkins a stern letter, saying

> I have had before me the exact conversation in Los Angeles between Mr. Stevenson and the Negro group, and it does not coincide with the statement you made in this morning's papers. I did not like your statement which I read in the New York papers before I left.
>
> I have had a long talk with Mr. Stevenson and in addition I have looked up his record very carefully and found it excellent as governor and previously. I have come to the conclusion that his stand on civil rights is the correct one in every way. I regret that the NAACP which has done such remarkable work should come out with a statement from you which I think shows lack of consideration and very hasty speaking. We will need great wisdom and patience in the next few months, not hotheaded bursting into print.
>
> I know it is difficult for NAACP not to take extreme positions but these positions will not help to achieve the results we want achieved. We certainly must press forward but we must do it wisely and in the proper way.[9]

Civil rights, it was now clear, would be a major issue, even a dominant one, for the rest of the campaign, one that President Eisenhower would happily ignore almost entirely while he and his campaign managers would relish watching Stevenson and his advisers tie themselves in knots trying to explain their position. Meanwhile, Southern members of Congress, who held a majority of the most powerful committee chairmanships, would stand at the ready to exercise their veto power over any initiative they regarded as a threat to the Southern Way of Life, or, if deemed necessary, to bolt from the Democratic Party itself.

Mrs. Roosevelt's February 18 *My Day* column, written in San Francisco where she and Stevenson were both attending a combined Democratic Advisory

Committee and National Committee meeting, spelled out the context that had thrust the civil rights issue to the foreground of national attention.

> Governor Harriman...agrees with [New York] Senator [Herbert] Lehman that the President and the Republican Administration have not faced up to their responsibility as regards integration in this country. They also agree that the Democratic Party, because of its Southern membership, has not come out strongly and honestly in its stand, and they are determined that there shall be a clear-cut decision as to where the Democratic Party does stand.
>
> They acknowledge the fact that this may bring a political explosion, since this is the question which deeply divides the Democratic Party. The South...has held, because of seniority, many of the most important and influential party positions in the Congress. The Congressional leaders in both the Senate and the House are opposed to anything which will mean a clear-cut stand on civil rights legislation....For the liberals in the North to force on the whole party a stand which is impossible for the South to accept is going to be a very serious step, and I hope that wisdom and patience will be used in the discussions which are to go on in the next few days.

A clearer statement of the dilemma her party was facing would have been hard to imagine, and her sensitive reader could feel how deeply she was grieving that any misstep would bring down the party she loved. For the next eight months she would spend a considerable portion of her energies to help her Democratic compatriots extricate themselves from the situation their opposing convictions had driven them to. The task would demand every shred of persuasiveness, every scintilla of sensitivity she possessed.

For the moment, though, she and Stevenson seemed to be "on the same page" on civil rights. Time would test the accuracy of that perception more than once during the remainder of the campaign. But from the San Francisco meetings until Election Day our two principals would be brought much closer together than their long-distance "mutual admiration society" had heretofore managed to accomplish. Following the National Committee meetings she returned to New York and immediately sought a meeting with Ralph Bunche, under-secretary-general at the United Nations, whose judgment on interracial matters she considered without equal. Among those she considered "responsible" African American leaders, he was usually the first to come to mind. She was preparing for the contest ahead.

Back at her apartment on East 65th Street, she found a letter waiting from Pauli Murray, an African American woman attorney she had befriended when Pauli had tried, without success, to enter the University of North Carolina's law school in 1938. Having earned her law degree from the University of California Law School, Ms. Murray was practicing civil rights law in New York City. She was one of the founders of the Congress of

Racial Equality (CORE) in 1942, the organization that introduced to the civil rights struggle Mahatma Gandhi's teaching of nonviolent resistance (*ahimsa*). She was also a poet and a prolific writer on behalf of civil rights issues. Thurgood Marshall called her book *States' Laws on Race and Color* "the Bible for civil rights lawyers." She and Mrs. Roosevelt exchanged views on civil rights matters periodically and in February 1956 she was trying to decide how genuine was Adlai Stevenson's loyalty to the values she herself held. Mrs. Roosevelt responded to her query on February 22, summarizing her view of the strategic legislative landscape as well as her assessment of Stevenson's convictions and her own.[10]

She had consulted Ralph Bunche, perhaps her most trusted source of intelligence on African American issues, and concluded that she and Stevenson shared his views of the situation. She lamented Roy Wilkins' "hot-headed statement" as well as the manner in which the media had reported Stevenson's Los Angeles appearance. She acknowledged the candidate's unfortunate use of the word "gradual" but argued that his understanding of the word was wholly opposite that of African Americans. "The only thing on which Stevenson and I differ with some of the Negro leaders is in the support of the Powell amendment. His feeling is that aid should not be withheld from the states that need education most in order to improve." She thought it risky for "Negro" leaders to be "tearing down Stevenson who is after all the only real hope they have."

There was another letter in the same mail with Pauli Murray's, this one from "Poppy" (Mrs. Walter F.) White, wife of the NAACP's executive director. She, too, was finding Mr. Stevenson's position on civil rights hard to understand. Mrs. Roosevelt tried to help:

> I am really not puzzled about Mr. Stevenson's attitude. I am puzzled at the way he was reported and the reaction of the colored people. Mr. Stevenson's basic attitude is excellent and his record is excellent. I feel that at some point he must show his real indignation about some of the things that are happening in the Southern states but if the Negroes forget his record and forget the courageous statements he made in the South during his last campaign and attack him now, he will be accused, when he does say what he feels on civil rights, of doing so in order to gain the Negro vote, and that is something I think he will find extremely difficult to take because he is a man of great integrity and says what he believes is right regardless of its effects on his personal fortunes [*sic*]. This is a very difficult situation at present and one which requires a great deal of calm leadership.[11]

Her letter did not satisfy "Poppy" White, who responded next day:

> At times like these when so many seem to be turning their backs on civil rights, I think that colored people and others who are concerned, need a

great deal of reassurance—just as a friend in trouble needs some expression of sympathy and regard. Certainly this has not been forthcoming from Mr. Stevenson.

I do agree that civil rights should not become a political football. Don't you think that the only way to take it out of the arena is for the Liberal Democrat to express views at least as strong as those of the Republican party? Such a strategy would make the Dixiecrats politically homeless—to use Walter's phrase.[12]

"Poppy" White had described the logical course of action for the Democratic Party to take. But to render the Southern wing of their party "homeless" would have required its unequivocal endorsement of the *Brown* decision and all that it implied. Mrs. Roosevelt, Adlai Stevenson, and the entire Democratic leadership were convinced that such a direct confrontation with institutional racism's discriminatory practices would be a politically suicidal act: It would result in the massive departure of the Southern contingent of the party and the rout of the Democratic cause at the polls in November. Whether the party could ever recover from such a blow seemed, at best, a dubious prospect. So verbal avoidance and prevarication would have the upper hand for the remainder of the campaign. Such was the rationale Mrs. Roosevelt, Adlai Stevenson, and the entire Democratic Party apparatus were using—indeed, they felt they were *forced* to use it in the 1956 presidential contest. Theirs was a calculated *political* strategy in which principle played a very minor part, indeed.

All the actors in the drama of 1956, Republican and Democrat alike, were, in Garry Wills' phrase, "trammeled in a net" in which either party's return to power depended on collusion with a system that was corrupt and inhuman at its core. To play the "game of politics" at all required the Faustian bargain of ignoring that reality. Mrs. Roosevelt had tacitly admitted as much in her letter to Pauli Murray when she described Stevenson as "the only hope the Negroes have."

* * *

Stevenson, meanwhile, was chafing under the difficulty he was having making the case for moderation in individual and state responses to the Supreme Court's mandate in *Brown II*. Were there no reasonable voices among the Negroes of America, no "responsible Negro leaders who would express preference for integration by persuasion rather than force? Certainly there must be many," he mused, "if they can be induced to say anything in view of the clamor of the NAACP."[13]

He decided a high-level council of advisers needed to develop definitive position statements on a variety of civil rights questions that he could use in coming speeches. Such a group convened for a two-day meeting in New York in mid-February. They included Arthur Schlesinger, Jr., Harvard history professor; Lloyd Garrison and Thomas Finletter, both attorneys; and Stuart Gerry Brown, political science professor at Syracuse University's Maxwell School of Politics. (The absence of Harry Ashmore was noteworthy.) Their efforts contributed to an important speech in Hartford, Connecticut, on February 25. Abandoning the high-flown generalities that had characterized many of his recent efforts, the speech brought the issue of civil rights into the living rooms of ordinary people in unmistakably clear and forthright language:

> "Equal rights for all, special privileges for none"...means equal rights for all regardless of race and color. America is nothing unless it stands for equal treatment for all citizens under the law. And freedom is unfinished business until all citizens may vote and go to school and work without encountering in their daily lives barriers which we reject in our law, our conscience and our religion.

This last sentence emphasized Stevenson's conviction that the Supreme Court's directives had more than legal force; they were an expression of what all law-abiding American citizens knew in their heart of hearts to be right and just. He followed these statements with a brief and pointed history lesson on the subject of "interposition." Andrew Jackson had been the first U.S. president to encounter such a challenge to federal authority, Stevenson said, and had dealt with it forthrightly:

> "I consider," Jackson wrote, "the power to annul a law of the United States, assumed by one State, incompatible with the existence of the Union, contradicted expressly by the letter of the Constitution, unauthorized by its spirit, inconsistent with every principle on which it was founded, and destructive of the great object for which it was formed." That [said Stevenson] was essential Democratic doctrine—and American doctrine—120 years ago. It is essential Democratic—and American—doctrine today.

No Southern leader, no media representative could fail to understand the message Stevenson was sending: All resistance to the Supreme Court rulings in *Brown I* and *II* was on its face illegal.

A week later he flew to the twin cities of Minnesota, then campaigned for five days crisscrossing the state on icy roads while temperatures hovered slightly above or below zero, and delivered as many as eight speeches a day. He seemed exhilarated by the experience. That same week Mrs. Roosevelt was campaigning for him in the northern part of the state, though they did not manage a meeting. Jane Dick was traveling with her. On her return to

New York on February 12, Mrs. Dick wrote Stevenson's sister, Buffie: "I spent two days with Mrs. Roosevelt on the Iron Range and believe me, it was an experience! What a woman, and what a job she does for Adlai!"[14] Despite the declared support for Stevenson, however, of Governor Orville Freeman, Senator Humphrey, and the State Democratic Party organization, Kefauver's poll numbers were climbing in response to his stance as the underdog and his claim that Stevenson was a tool of "party bosses." Stevenson, relying on Freeman's and Humphrey's assessment, wrote Mrs. Roosevelt he was not worried about the outcome; it had been "a most successful and encouraging journey."

> I had ecstatic reports about your conquest of [Minneapolis] and of the Iron Range. The exclamations that stick in my mind about you…are "adored" and "terrific." Jane Dick says you are the best campaigner she has seen and that the speeches you made on my behalf were the most successful she has heard. Need I say that I am grateful beyond words.

As things turned out, Governor Freeman and Senator Humphrey had miscalculated: On Election Day Kefauver overwhelmed his opponent, winning twenty-six of the state's thirty delegates to the party convention. State law allowed members of one party to vote for candidates of the other party and the Republican organization had encouraged such "cross-over" voting in order to defeat Stevenson. Democrats thought the ploy had figured heavily in Stevenson's defeat. (The only counties solidly in the Stevenson camp were the two in the Iron Range where Mrs. Roosevelt had campaigned.) Henceforth he would have to wage an even more vigorous fight in every primary contest he entered.

CHAPTER 6

STRAINS IN THE ALLIANCE

SENATOR KEFAUVER'S OVERWHELMING WIN IN MINNESOTA was a bitter pill for Stevenson supporters. Coming on the heels of a similar rout in the New Hampshire primary—though he had decided not to campaign there—the defeat made the Stevenson team decide to revamp their campaign strategy. Arthur Schlesinger wrote that in his speeches Stevenson should "become more concrete, programmatic, down-to-earth and less rhetorical...[and] positive," while Harry Ashmore was convinced that "the Guv's" insistence on having a script, even for every whistle-stop appearance, was at the root of his not getting across to his hearers. To the former Stevenson wrote, "I confess I am perplexed about the complaint that I have not been positive and concrete enough on issues. I am sometimes put to it to think of one I haven't taken a position on in speeches, articles, etc," then, putting his finger squarely on the main difficulty, "Perhaps the explanation is that my language has been too complicated."

Ashmore, admitting his "failure to produce the endless flow of deathless prose he thought he needed," tried to wean Stevenson from his scriptural dependence. "The real trouble," he later reported, "was that the primaries required a candidate to run as though he were standing for county sheriff; the voters wanted to look their candidate in the eye and press the flesh...what he said didn't matter half as much as the fact that he was present and available in their home town....The irony was that he was really very good at it, sustained, I think, by his own amusement at the very absurdity of much of what he was required to do," whereupon Ashmore gives us an example of the extent to which campaigning can try the patience of even the most patient human being:

> Once when we were hop-scotching from town to town down the spine of Florida, he asked me how he had done at the last supermarket stop. "Well,

Governor," I replied, "when a little girl in a starched white dress suddenly steps out of a crowd and hands you a stuffed alligator, what you say is, 'I've always wanted one of these to go on the mantelpiece at Libertyville.' What you don't say is what you did say, 'For Christ's sake, what's this?' "

He concludes:

> He was delighted, and repeated the conversation in his remarks at every stop for the rest of that day, in the process no doubt losing votes to Estes Kefauver, who was born knowing what to do with a stuffed alligator.[1]

It was clear that Senator Kefauver was becoming a thorn in Stevenson's side. Contending with a president who was revered by an adoring public was hard enough; on top of that, Kefauver's candidacy was requiring the governor to fight a two-front war, the second against a member of his own party. Had the coonskin-capped Tennessean not been so aggressively dedicated to campaigning, Stevenson would not have exhausted himself barnstorming as he did, and 1956 would have been, emotionally as well as physically, a far less debilitating year. Nonetheless, as he wrote Marietta and Ronald Tree, "I am not as downhearted as perhaps I should be.... I shall take my armor off the kitchen door and rouse my sleeping charger and take after him."[2] For the next seven months "he ran, as he said, 'like a singed cat.'"[3]

On March 28 he returned to California to try to heal some of the wounds that his performance there the preceding month—along with the Minnesota defeat—had dealt his own cause. The first part of his speech, defensive in tone, was an extended attack on his challenger's tactics. The fact that he had secured endorsements from Minnesota's governor, senior senator, and many other leaders of the state's party organization amply proved, Kefauver claimed, that Stevenson was the tool of "party bosses" who were trying to dictate the party's choice. "And now I am advised that Senator Kefauver personally sought the support of these very same people...and a score of others. Here in California, as in New Hampshire and Minnesota, the endorsement of the leaders of our party evidently becomes reprehensible only when the Senator doesn't get it."[4] His actions would only help the Republicans. Turning to his assessment of the campaign thus far, he confessed the strain was beginning to annoy him: "When I read in the papers...that I am spending too much time discussing the issues and not enough time shaking hands, and that I'm more concerned about issues than about people—well, frankly, it makes me disgusted, and then it makes me just plain mad."[5]

But the major purpose of the speech was to assure Californians about what he had meant when he spoke of the necessity of proceeding "gradually" on the civil rights front. He had had in mind the very real possibility that public rejection of the spirit of compromise and accommodation could well split the nation into warring camps, with the inevitable result that blood would flow in the streets of many an American city and town. Though he would never have drawn the analogy, it seems likely that Adlai Stevenson was feeling that his duty, like that of another native son of Illinois not quite a hundred years before, was to save the union at all costs. This was the larger issue before which the plaints of the Roy Wilkinses, the Lyndon Johnsons, the Herbert Lehmans, the Richard Russells, and all the rest of the contenders for one or the other "side" in the so-called Civil Rights Debate paled to near insignificance.

His remarks about the Supreme Court's decisions in *Brown I* and *II* were the most substantive as well as the most forceful of any he had previously uttered:

> I want [America] to be a place where men and women and children of every race, creed and color share alike the opportunities that this great country has to offer. I feel that the Supreme Court has decreed what our reason told us was inevitable and our conscience told us was right. I feel equally strongly that whether you agree with that decision or not, it is the law and should be obeyed. The job that has to be done now is to find even in the conflicting counsel of those who disagree so violently the best course by which the Court's decision can be carried out. The longer we drift the greater the danger—the danger from those who would violate the spirit of the Court decision by either lawless resistance or by undue provocation.

He concluded this part of his speech with a single sentence that harked back to the plea he had made when the *Brown* decisions first came down, convinced as he was that presidential leadership was indispensable whenever public opinion on a question of such national importance was divided: "I have suggested that the President should promptly bring together white and Negro leaders to search out the way to meet this problem as a united people."

He had made this latter plea on several previous occasions, but without success. President Eisenhower maintained his "above-the-battle" posture and would continue to do so until, three and a half years after the opinions were issued, the confrontation at Little Rock's Central High School would compel him to call in federal troops to restore order. By then, the possibility of the kind of meeting Stevenson had in mind had disappeared and the power of rational persuasion had been trampled by the momentum of events.

* * *

Reading his speech, Eleanor Roosevelt sensed that campaigning was taking too great a toll on his spirit. On April 2 she wrote that he was "often in

[her] thoughts and commiserated with what she felt was "the hardest part of [his] struggle." But once the primaries and the convention were behind him, the campaign would seem "very easy in comparison!"[6] He replied that he wasn't "as discouraged as [he] had a right to be." It wasn't "in [his] nature." He would go about "whatever the people may deem my responsibility. That I shall continue to do—my way" (an echo of Frank Sinatra's theme song unmistakable there). And a week later,

> The road is long and weary, as you know so well, and I am by no means sure that I am traversing it wisely or effectively, but at least I am traversing it! Your confidence and encouragement are perhaps as meaningful to me as anything.[7]

She too was keeping up her furious pace on the campaign trail. They seemed almost to be competing with each other to see who could chalk up the greatest mileage flown and number of speeches given. California attorney general (later governor) Edmund G. Brown, chairman of the California Stevenson campaign committee, wired Mrs. Roosevelt urging her to give two speeches in the state: one at a luncheon in San Francisco and a second in Los Angeles. She replied that she could manage a luncheon in either city plus a dinner in the other: "I will take a midnight plane on Sunday, May 27th to wherever you want me to go and I must return on a midnight plane on May 28th as I cannot give any more time."[8]

Agnes Meyer had apparently learned from her California friends that the state's Democratic organization was in disarray and needed help. Only Mrs. Roosevelt, she thought, could provide the needed stimulus to Stevenson's cause. Evidently unaware that Mrs. Roosevelt had already responded affirmatively to Pat Brown's request, she wrote the candidate that she thought she had persuaded the First Lady to make the effort. Stevenson alluded to Mrs. Meyer's letter in a note to Mrs. Roosevelt, thanking her for her decision, "but I must insist that you do not undertake this unless it is not too inconvenient or too much of a strain. I am afraid Mrs. Meyer's energies would exhaust me but I must not let her exhaust you!"[9]

Nearly a fortnight had passed since Stevenson's Los Angeles speech that Mrs. Roosevelt had been stewing about. Both for his sake as well as to give herself time to clarify her feelings about her protégé's grasp of his purpose, she had delayed but finally decided to write him at length about several matters that were disturbing her. The result was a three-page missive on April 11, to that date the most substantive communication of their relationship. He had left the day before for six days of barnstorming in Florida, followed by two in North Carolina and Pennsylvania, then another five in Washington D.C. They would see each other briefly on April 25 when he spoke at a $100-per-plate fund-raiser in New York City, though whether her letter had by then finally caught up with him is unknown, his pace that spring being as frenzied as ever that year. If they had an opportunity for meeting on the 26th is likewise unknown, but he was far from ever ignoring any observation of hers. The next time he wrote her (May 1) he would make no mention of receiving it.

Her letter read,

Dear Adlai,

I am really worried about one or two things that I think I should say at the present time. It seems to me that it is unwise to be attacking Mr. Kefauver as much as you have been doing. The things that need to be attacked are the issues that need to be made clear to the man in the street in the simplest possible terms. The people need to feel that you have done all the agonizing over how to meet situations, that you are sure of what you would do if you were starting it today. In a primary campaign I think these issues can be stated in a somewhat exaggerated way as far as one's certainty of how one intends to begin. It is obvious that no solution is certain and that you may have to change your approach but the people have turned to Eisenhower because they feel, simply because he said very little, that he knew the answers. Kefauver has so far said nothing worth listening to but he has said it in a way that makes the people feel he also is someone who has the answers. That is not quite honest but it is reassuring and many people need reassurance particularly when they don't want to have to think things out for themselves.

I also feel strongly that Mr. Finnegan [national campaign manager] should be mapping out his strategy and getting things set up for the convention so that he knows exactly whom he is counting upon to make each move. [He] should have his finger on every single state with a man and a woman in each state dealing not only with the regular Democrats but with the volunteers, so that he pools the two together and they operate to complement each other.

You should be giving yourself to thinking out the speeches and the trips and where your strategic points are. You should have someone with you— someone who...would act for you as Sherman Adams acts for the President, who would have the power and do the job. Otherwise you are not free. Everyone around you is devoted but I have a feeling that just because of their devotion they are not gauging well the public sentiment and giving you the reports. A Sherman Adams would see that he was getting the proper kind of reports from Mr. Finnegan and the same would be so of any other people working in the field. I get a feeling of a bad set-up on public relations, of an inferior public relations organizational job being done, and of your being pressed without the proper balance of information or the time to think of the things you ought to be thinking about.

The problems of today are serious enough. Nobody knows the answers but the people must feel that the man who is their candidate knows where he is going to begin, that he is not so tortured by his own search that he can't give them reassurance and security.

I think it is important to get this kind of organization started immediately. This is not meant to be a discouraging letter but an encouraging one. If I did not think you could win, it would not be worth doing a good job.

With every good wish, and looking forward to seeing you on the 25th, and please forgive me if I have been too blunt.[10]

Remarkable for its author's political as well as her psychological sophistication, this letter signals a new stage in the relationship between the Democratic Party's principal players in what Theodore H. White has called "the last election in which the old patrician élite of American life would be in control."[11] Given the anxiety that prompted its writing, might we conclude that the letter betrays Eleanor Roosevelt's doubts about "her" candidate's grasp of his proper mission? Or, alternatively, can we read between the lines of this so-carefully-composed letter an unspoken intuition that her own powers might themselves be starting to wane ever so slightly? The former possibility seems far closer to the mark than the latter. Her speeches and her extraordinary stamina on the year's grueling campaign trail conveyed the distinct impression that she was in no doubt whatsoever about Stevenson's abilities. If doubt existed, she kept it to herself. Furthermore, her pivotal role in party councils concerning the party platform as well as in the coming Democratic National Convention would prove beyond question that her political skills throughout this year were at their peak.

Stevenson, however, had returned from California utterly exhausted—alarmingly so. Arthur Schlesinger thought he looked "exceptionally tired," while Marietta Tree was "horrified at his condition, so horrified that I almost lost faith in him. He was so exhausted he was making no sense."[12] Porter McKeever comments on the absence of the very sort of gyroscopic person Mrs. Roosevelt had identified as missing among his advisers: "In the absence of the calm, firm hand of Carl McGowan, from the 1952 campaign, a veritable cacophony of advice from uncertain 'pros' and more certain nonpros engulfed him."[13] His breakneck schedule, designed to contrast his robust vigor with Eisenhower's fragility, took no account of the physical cost it exacted, and "the lack of direction suggested by the 'singed cat' figure of speech was evident as he traveled to Florida, Pennsylvania, Washington..., New York, back to Florida, Chicago for eleven hours, Oregon where he made as many as sixteen different whistle-stop speeches a day, California for more extended and even more hectic barnstorming, making more than fifty speeches in a single week, back to Oregon, then on to Florida and back to California, all in less than six weeks."[14] And it was *only April*; the crucial battles of the campaign were still before him.

On April 21 in Washington D.C. he delivered one of the most important addresses of his career to the American Society of Newspaper Editors. In it he attacked what he considered the foreign policy failures of the Republican administration and proposed some bold Democratic Party alternatives. Uppermost in his mind was reduction of the international jitters that were poisoning the global atmosphere, an inevitable consequence, Stevenson thought, of the "brinkmanship" policies of Eisenhower's secretary of state, John Foster Dulles. Centerpiece of his talk was a proposal that the United States should unilaterally declare an end to all U.S. testing of the hydrogen bomb.

> I would call on other nations, the Soviet Union, to follow our lead, and if they don't and persist in further tests we will know about it and can reconsider our policy. I deeply believe that if we are to make progress toward the effective reduction and control of armaments, it will probably come a step at a time. And this is a step which, it seems to me, we might now take, a step which would reflect our determination never to plunge the world into a nuclear holocaust, a step which would reaffirm our purpose to act with humility and a decent concern for world opinion.

Though never far from his consciousness since August 1945, the development and control of atomic energy had periodically risen to the top of Stevenson's priority concerns. He had followed closely the debates in the United Nations that early on was considered the logical locus of control for such devastating power. He had monitored the fate of the Baruch Plan and similar initiatives at the hands of both the Soviet Union and the United States that foreclosed the ceding of atomic energy concerns to the United Nations. Stevenson also consulted from time to time not only with diplomats but also with scientists working in the field of atomic energy and its control. Particularly since February he had been actively researching this issue, requesting opinions from a broadly representative sampling of the scientific community and received significant support for the proposal. Indeed, just nine days before this speech Commissioner Thomas Murray of the Atomic Energy Commission had suggested precisely such an initiative to the Senate Foreign Relations subcommittee. Predictably, the president dismissed the proposal out of hand as naive and dangerous (though Eisenhower a few months after being reelected would himself write Admiral Lewis Strauss, chairman of the Atomic Energy Commission, about "my hope that the need for atomic tests would gradually lift and possibly soon disappear").[15] Predictably, too, the public seemed willing in a dangerous world to trust in such matters a military father figure over a well-meaning but relatively unknown layman.

Although it put forward a militarily defensible position, Stevenson's address was without question a politically self-destructive initiative. His staff had advised against it. That he chose to make it anyway was an example of what Stuart Gerry Brown called Stevenson's "conscience in politics." (This, after all, was the man who, years earlier, on being advised against raising an issue because it would lose him votes, had retorted that there were more important things than getting elected: "But I don't have to win.") Five months later, in an address to the American Legion, he proposed a similarly penetrating but, for his candidacy, devastating step involving the military: Scrap the draft and adopt a policy of a career military establishment. Both these major proposals would be implemented by future administrations— one Democratic (Kennedy-Johnson) and one Republican (Nixon). A Limited Nuclear Test Ban treaty was signed in Moscow in August 1963 and five years later Richard Nixon ended the military draft by signing into law "the policy Adlai had advocated."[16]

CHAPTER 7

CROSSCURRENTS ON RACE

As the '56 primary campaigns approached their midpoint, most voters seemed to agree that the Republican campaign mantra, "Peace, Progress, and Prosperity," described the only concerns that mattered. The media, however, perennially on the hunt for controversy, smelled blood in the issue of civil rights. Thus, while delighting in covering Stevenson's appearances—he was quick, witty, urbane, and taught his hearers a very great deal about a great many issues throughout the campaign—reporters seemed also to sense ambivalence in his civil rights position statements. The consequence was that press conferences frequently featured somewhat heated exchanges between the candidate and his interrogators. Were his critics mistaking the candidate's statesmanship for cowardice, his desire to achieve understanding among contending interests without violence, for weakness? As the campaign's intensity grew, his "utterances" on the subject also became bolder, a fact that not only confused and angered portions of the electorate but also occasionally complicated his friendship with Mrs. Roosevelt.

For her, the winds of doubt and fear, of suspicion and prejudice, that swirled around civil rights questions this year called for all the resourcefulness she could muster. There were many levels on which she had to operate effectively and persuasively: first, with her hundreds of concerned friends and then with civic organizational leaders and special interest groups such as the unions and women's groups—among these, especially with the officers and Board of Directors of the NAACP; and the framers of the Democratic Party Platform, as well as other national, state, and local party politicians; and with the public at large, via her hundreds of speeches on the campaign trail and her syndicated newspaper column *My Day*. With each constituency she employed her unparalleled capacity for empathy when required and toughness when appropriate—all in the service of persuading her listeners that Adlai Stevenson possessed the qualities of leadership and vision the nation and the world required in a president of the United States.

Both principals were disturbed by the rigidity of partisans on both sides of the civil rights ideological spectrum, and in April Mrs. Roosevelt found herself sharing Stevenson's impatience with the NAACP's executive director, Roy Wilkins. He had delivered what she felt an unnecessarily incendiary address in Chicago in which he seemed to threaten the Democrats with a mass walkout from the party unless its leadership became more militant in their advocacy of civil rights measures. He had given a similar talk in New York a few days earlier.

> Southern governors, state legislatures, senators and congressmen continue to slander and strangle Negro citizens in their states, economically, politically and socially. Up here we cannot vote for or against these men...but we can have something to say about the party that made [James O.] Eastland chairman of a committee [the Senate Judiciary Committee] which can choke us whether we live in Mississippi or Illinois or Montana. Up here we can strike a blow in defense of our brothers in the South, if necessary by swapping the known devil for the suspected witch. It could be that the witch [i.e., the Republican Party], if freed of the political necessity of teaming up with the devil [i.e., the Southern Democrats], just might do better by us.[1]

"One of Wilkins' bosses," as she could be described by virtue of her office as vice president of his board, dispatched a stern rebuke that not only took him aback but also caused consternation throughout the agency. She thought he had been "most unwise" in his recent public statements, as a consequence of which he was "losing the people who have done the most for you." She pointed out that a Republican victory would mean four more years of inaction on the racial justice front while a Democratic administration would clearly mean greater justice for people of color. Then, speaking of Wilkins' major error of judgment, she reproached him for using his office as NAACP secretary to advise "how citizens shall actually vote. I think it is the duty of the Association... to urge both parties to change their ways where necessary, to praise both parties when they do well, to criticize when they do badly and to do the same with individuals in those parties. To do what you did in Chicago and what you did by inference in New York...is going to tear the Association apart and reduce much of your support."

Then came a bombshell:

> I am unable to come to many meetings or spend the time to be a Board member and so I am herewith tendering my resignation[2]

Her letter sent a shudder through the NAACP leadership. Communiqués were exchanged, meetings held. Her resignation would deal a deadly blow to the social justice agenda she had fought for her whole lifetime and to the movement as a whole. The NAACP itself would be irremediably wounded. Would she please reconsider? The miscreant promised to mend his ways and Eleanor Roosevelt finally relented; she would allow her name to remain on the NAACP letterhead, but it was clear that this episode had dampened her enthusiasm for the agency. (Wilkins' retreat proved a mere temporary tactic: in a very few months he would persuade the NAACP to endorse Harriman's candidacy rather than Stevenson's.)

She and Adlai did see each other at the Waldorf Astoria dinner on the 25th. Eighteen-hundred Democrats turned out for the $100-per-plate "Tribute to Stevenson" affair. His advisors, with a view to playing their candidate's strongest card in a state where Harriman was taking a far more forthright stand than Stevenson on civil rights, had urged him to speak forcefully on some aspect of foreign policy. Stevenson ignored their counsel. The next day's *New York Times* ran a page-one story under a (distinctly unflattering) picture of Stevenson, Mrs. Roosevelt, and New York's senior senator Herbert H. Lehman. The headline read, "Stevenson Says President Shirks Duty on Integration." "Mr. Stevenson apparently chose his topic," wrote Leo Egan, "with a view to meeting the complaint that his position on the racial desegregation issue was unduly 'moderate.'"

The article continued, quoting Stevenson:

The Presidency is, above all, a place of moral leadership. Yet in these months of crucial importance no leadership has been provided. The immense prestige and influence of the office has been withheld from those who honestly seek to carry out the law in gathering storm and against rising resistance..

Mr. Egan omitted Stevenson's clearest explanation of Eisenhower's default:

The office [of the presidency] is the one office... apart from the courts, where the man who fills it represents all the people. Those in the Congress bear particular responsibilities to the citizens of the states they represent... Not so of the Presidency. And where the nation is divided, there is special demand on him to unite and lead the people toward the common goal.

The article went on to mention briefly the other major civil rights issue Stevenson had underscored, the Fifteenth Amendment's guarantee of the right to vote. Fully aware that here he was touching another raw Southern nerve, he made an unequivocal statement:

Wherever any American citizens have been denied by intimidation and violence the right to vote, then the right to vote of all American citizens is imperiled.... These laws should be enforced. And if they are inadequate, they should be strengthened. And I believe that all responsible citizens, south and north, would go along with a determination to assure the right to vote under the law.

To intransigent Southern whites, the franchise represented the outer breast-works that must be defended before the walls of the keep were exposed and full equality of citizenship could be won. (It would take another nine years before Stevenson's conviction would be addressed legislatively—in the Voting Rights Act of 1965.)

President Eisenhower's true sentiments about the *Brown* decisions doubt-less explained his silence about the Court that had promulgated them. A clue was given in a reported private conversation the president had had with Emmet John Hughes, one of his speech writers, following *Brown I*:

> I am convinced [he told Hughes] that the Supreme Court decision set *back* progress in the South *at least fifteen years.* . . . It's all very well to talk about school integration—you may be also talking about social *disintegration* and the fellow who tells me that you can do these things by *force* is just plain nuts.[3]

The president and Stevenson were in agreement, however, on the use of force question, while Eleanor at this juncture was wondering whether federal troops might be required to quell the rising tide of violence Stevenson had alluded to in his speech. She certainly would have disputed Eisenhower's assessment of the social cost of desegregation efforts thus far—as we have seen, she had enthusiastically welcomed the decisions when they were issued and was under no illusion that the struggle for justice would be without pain.

Their brief rendezvous over, Stevenson was off to Florida to continue his "endless ordeal," then to Oregon and California, while Mrs. Roosevelt flew south to firm up support for him in the nation's capital. A few days later she received a letter from Nancy Davis, chair of the D.C. rally, reporting that "Senator Kefauver told the press that your appearance turned the tide in Adlai's favor!"[4] Stevenson concurred, writing Mrs. Roosevelt, "I eagerly join even Kefauver in attributing the happy result to you."

The district's voters had endorsed his bid. Eleanor discounted her role: "Please don't bother to write," she wrote, "I really can do very little. Wait till it is over and we can sit down quietly and rejoice!"

* * *

A few days later she received from NAACP executive secretary Roy Wilkins an urgent confidential memorandum addressed to all Board of Directors members. He was enclosing "a draft of a suggested order to be issued in the

State of Texas vs. NAACP, et al.... Involved in this order... is the whole question of the future operation of the NAACP in the Southern states."[5]

Texas state authorities had designed a case against the organization that was intended not only to close every NAACP office and program throughout the South but also to foreclose even the possibility of the agency's challenging the State's initiative through normally available legal channels. Within months, legal actions similar to those of the State of Texas were adopted by the state legislatures of seven Southern states. Alabama, for example, fined the NAACP $100,000 for refusing to surrender its membership list, while Louisiana, without waiting for the federal court to act, issued a permanent injunction barring the agency from operating anywhere in the state. Southern legislators were declaring war on the NAACP and using legal maneuvers that would severely strain the agency's staff and drain its legal and financial resources throughout the next decade.[6]

Campaigning in Florida, Stevenson was feeling the stress in his bones. Midway in the flurry of whistle-stops he found time to scribble a note to Agnes Meyer. He complained of the awful ordeal of incessant appearances day after day, "all of which tire me nervously and emotionally. I don't speak easily off the cuff (Ashmore thought he was 'awfully good' at just such 'utterance') and I have never succeeded in getting a sort of set patter that I can use over and over again that satisfies me.... Sometimes I have had to speak as many as fifteen times a day, and every day is an interminable agony; but curiously enough I seem to find unexpected sources of strength, and... I have no major complaint as the endless days wear on."

He wrote another friend, "Do write me and send along any humorous bits that occur to you. I get drier, duller and emptier!" He appended a postscript: "A woman in the crowd said to me the other day, "Governor, you're better looking than your pictures—thank heavens!"[7]

As previously planned, he and Mrs. Roosevelt met again briefly at Los Angeles on May 28. They had arranged to land at the airport close to the same time, but she arrived early and by the time his plane landed she had gone to her motel. They appeared together later at a press conference (J.B. Martin thought the result was only "fair"), then she dashed off to a meeting in an African American district while Stevenson kept an appointment at a television station.

When the primary results were tallied in Florida, Stevenson had won by a slim 12,000 votes. In California, however, he swamped Kefauver with a vote of 1,129,964 to 680,722. Eleanor Roosevelt sent him a note: "Congratulations on primary results. Go away now for at least three weeks rest!" He replied with a long letter whose tone conveyed the impression that he was now seriously considering her as perhaps his chief campaign counselor. He was sure that the one day she had given to campaigning for him in California was "of more value than anything else that happened." (He had in mind especially his carrying the state's African American districts from four and one half to ten to one "in spite of NAACP opposition.") There followed some conjectures about Republican strategy attempting to portray Harriman as "the only authentic successor to the New Deal-Fair Deal," and Stevenson as "a pale imitation of Eisenhower."

Eleanor Roosevelt replied with another long letter. She thought his analysis of the Republican strategy "spot on" and welcomed his California win. "The people there seem to have come to their senses." The Republicans, of course, would try to cause a split in Democratic Party ranks, *and I don't know that there is any way one can hold it together and live up to one's convictions"* .(italics added). She thought the only resolution of black and white suspicions and hatred lay in calling the leaders on both sides together to try to work first steps out.[8]

Thus far in her letter she has stated precisely the views her candidate has himself been putting forward nearly every time he speaks on civil rights, whether in the North or the South. Regrettably, the president doesn't share their conviction that a "summit" of leaders from the nation's black and white communities is "the only possible solution" to the growing polarization between those groups.

But now she tells Adlai of an important new development: Paul Butler, Democratic national chairman, has asked her to come to Washington to help the Platform Committee frame its civil rights plank. It will have to be one that "will not mean the South will walk out of the Convention." She wasn't looking forward to the ordeal; it reminded her of the "endless hours" she spent at the United Nations debating about words and their meaning, "and I think that is what we shall have to do in this case."

Rather than invite Stevenson's suggestions on the subject, she had some preliminary thoughts about her assignment that may serve as prescriptions for his future conduct of the campaign as well as for the platform itself:

> It is essential for the Democratic party to keep the colored vote in line, so you can't take away the feeling that you want to live up to the Supreme Court decision and go forward, and that this can't be done in one fell swoop. Desegregation of schools in the South must follow a number of steps. Even in the North we have to desegregate housing before we can desegregate schools.
>
> Take a good rest now and get ready for the fight in the campaign which I know you will really enjoy.[9]

---

*Mrs. Roosevelt here speaks to Stevenson's as well as her own experience of conflict between moral principles and the demands of power politics. As Harry Ashmore noted, "Here the high road of conscience coincided with the low road of practical politics, for if that bridge could not be maintained there was no chance that a Democrat could be elected President" (*Hearts and Minds*, 198).

She closes by inviting him to come stay with her at Val-Kill "if you come East at any time and want complete rest."

Then comes a disturbing sentence: she plans to go to Europe on August 17, returning on September 9. The Democratic National Convention dates were August 13 to 17; surely she wasn't intending to absent herself from it altogether? It is difficult to read between the lines: Perhaps she was feeling that Stevenson had the nomination "in the bag." (She had said she was "impressed in New York state by the under-cover support you have and I feel sure that once released from Averell the great majority of the vote will come happily to you.") Perhaps she felt that after all he had proven himself incapable of winning the "common man's" confidence and hence stood little chance of winning the election? Or was she herself simply exhausted—she had every right to be—by her own campaigning on Stevenson's behalf and felt she had earned a rest? It is even possible that in the pre-Convention chaos the campaign staff had failed to communicate their hope that she would play one more life-saving role in party deliberations before the campaign itself began. In the event, though she would come for only two days, she would prove herself once again in those brief hours one of the nation's most astute political operatives.

Stevenson was delighted to receive her letter. To him it signaled a rapprochement between their views of relations between North and South as well as between the races; he had feared there was greater divergence between them than now appeared. He was right in his assessment. Eleanor Roosevelt had been moving away from the hardening ideological stance of her NAACP and ADA friends out of her conviction that their views, if endorsed by the party, would unquestionably result in a repeat of the 1948 convention's Southern walk-out. (A diary note Joe Lash made at the time seems to justify Stevenson's feeling: "[ER] said she was going down to Washington...to a key meeting...on a civil rights plank. The only Negro leader she really trusted was Ralph Bunche. She was disappointed in Channing Tobias because he accepted all of Roy Wilkins' positions.")[10] Stevenson responded to Mrs. Roosevelt's letter in an almost lyrical tone:

> Somehow this sort of understanding talk about the race problem coming from the voice most respected among Negroes—leaders and rank and file— has got to be given greater currency. I agree with you so emphatically that it excites me to read even these few sentences.... I would gladly withdraw from this political contest if it would serve in any manner to save the party from breaking up and enthroning the white extremists in the South or losing the Northern cities and thus the election. Either alternative is sad, but the former the saddest and most injurious to the Negro and his advancement toward full participation, not to mention the effect on our already diminished stature abroad where great decisions of the future are being made.

He ended with a suggestion that she write "an article for a popular magazine like *LOOK* or *COLLIERS*," presumably setting out in detail the argument she had sketched in her letter. A postscript read, "If I come East I most certainly will avail [myself of] your refuge in the country."

She demurred about a magazine article. She had two priorities: "I do better talking to the Negro leaders. I am doing this at every opportunity, and I told Mr. Butler I will go down for a meeting and try to work on getting an agreed plank for the platform. Though I confess I think it very difficult!"[11] Meanwhile she shared a letter from her friend Lord Elibank, an English MP whom she considered a reliable informant on Britain's political weather:

> I wish most ardently, [he told her], that, so far as your work for Mr. Stevenson is concerned, it may lead to a great victory for him in November. And that, I can assure you, is the wish of many—probably most—thinking persons over here, because, apart from having the advantage of Mr. Stevenson's great and foresighted knowledge of international affairs at the White House, we should also see the last of . . . "the brink of war" man, Mr. John Foster Dulles.[12]

A fortnight later, responding to her offer to give him as much time as her other commitments might allow, Stevenson replies that, if he is nominated, he wants her to "speak just as much as is humanly possible—and in your case this means superhumanly!" Apologizing, somewhat lamely, for being quite so demanding, he nonetheless asks her to "keep every possible date open" because "I should like to have you available all the time." A hand-written note he apparently decided to omit is crossed out at the end of the original draft of this letter: "I am coming to New York on or about August 1 and I hope to have a chance to run up to Hyde Park for at least a brief visit about the convention." There were many such hoped-for meetings that never materialized.

THE 1956 DEMOCRATIC NATIONAL CONVENTION

WHEN ELEANOR ROOSEVELT ACCEPTED THE INVITATION of Democratic national chairman Paul Butler to join a working group to frame a proposed plank on civil rights for the party platform, she knew what a delicate role she was being asked to take on. The media for weeks prior to the convention were speculating darkly over the possibility of a North-South split on the issue of civil rights that, by 1956, had begun nibbling at the nation's conscience. She, therefore, went to Washington D.C. keeping in mind not only the concerns she had mentioned in her June 13 letter to Stevenson but also three others: (1) Southern delegates' unconditional acceptance of the civil rights plank must be secured; (2) The plank must keep the Northern liberals from defecting to Harriman whose positions, especially his support of the Powell amendment and his willingness to use federal troops to enforce the Supreme Court decisions, made him sound—to inflexible liberals and to a majority of African Americans—the most attractive candidate; (3) The plank must persuade African Americans, as well as liberals from both North and South, that Stevenson's "moderation" was the only political stance on civil rights issues that could hold the party—and the country—together. It would be an exercise in an arena she knew well, one in which she could call on the finely honed skills she had developed during her work on the Universal Declaration of Human Rights.

Back at her New York apartment, she shared with Trude and Joe Lash her thoughts about the session. Hers had been a political high-wire act and she was clearly feeling she had met Paul Butler's expectations:

> It isn't going to be possible to meet what the colored leaders have drafted but the 2 Southerners seemed reasonable and I was surprised that they agreed to what seems to me a pretty good wording in both the plank on education and

[the one] on civil rights. It won't be strong enough for Harriman but I think it actually says all that needs to be said & would allow for any action one could take & still I think it won't divide the party.[1]

There was to be a fund-raising dinner in New York on August 1. In anticipation, ER sent off a hurried note to Adlai in response to a query from him as to her plans following that event. "I will be at the dinner on August 1st," she wrote, "but in Hyde Park from that night on and glad if you could spend even one twenty-four hours."

At the dinner she noticed how drained of energy he seemed. George Ball laid it to the stress of the primaries that he thought "destroyed [Stevenson's] élan and his resilience. No longer was he a confident, ebullient candidate; the querulous note was heard far too often as he looked toward the impending campaign as an ordeal rather than an opportunity." Jane Dick had written him earlier: "I don't think you have any idea how tired you are. I do know. I have been deeply concerned....In my considered judgment, this *one factor* of wearing you out, until you are just an animated shell of the *real* Adlai—has been *the major mistake* of the campaign."[2] Returning to her apartment after the dinner, ER sent Adlai a telegram: "If by chance you want to get out of New York August second and can come to H.P. for 24 hours I will promise you as much quiet as possible. It would be a great joy for me." Next morning she wrote David Gurewitsch, her doctor friend and intimate: "I also saw Ralph Bunche and Roy Wilkins and both said they accept the wording we worked out for the Civil Rights plank, now let's see how much gets thro' the platform committee."[3] (Bunche and Wilkins could be said to represent the North and South poles of African American public opinion of the time.)

As a (not entirely selfless) contribution to the fund-raising dinner for Stevenson, Estes Kefauver chose August 1 to announce his withdrawal from the race, requesting his followers to throw their support to Stevenson. His move prompted speculation that Harriman, considering this development a blow to his own cause, might follow suit. His team, however, announced that a Harriman dinner scheduled for August 2 would be held as planned. That evening the New York governor included in his remarks an attack on Stevenson, highlighting his opponent's position on civil rights:

> There are those who advise us to take it easy, those who talk about moderation as the spirit of our time. For my part, as Governor of New York and as a Democrat, I reject these counsels. They are the counsels of defeat.... With a fighting campaign and a fighting candidate, we can and will win in November.

A *New York Times* story next morning quoted the ever-alert Mrs. Roosevelt describing Stevenson "as devoted as Harriman to [the] principles of [the]

New and Fair Deals." Furthermore, "she saw no difference in the positions of Mr. Stevenson and Mr. Harriman on the civil rights issue." She had known Averell Harriman, she said, since he was a small boy. She had entertained him and his family at her Val-Kill cottage on more than one occasion. Now she was supporting a man for the presidency whose outlook and experience she felt superior to Harriman's. It was not a comfortable position to be in, but such was the world of politics.

At breakfast next morning she read of another old friend's defection from her cause: Samuel L. Rosenman, a former justice on the New York Supreme Court, described by the *Times* as "one of President Roosevelt's speech writers, confidants, strategy consultants and articulators of New Deal philosophy," had just declared his support for Harriman (whom he was also serving as legal counsel). The article took pains to note the judge's insistence that "he wanted it emphatically understood that he did not wish to engage in any dispute with Mrs. Roosevelt, with whom he has had a long friendship.[4] Then he said that he had read all of Mr. Stevenson's published views and declared: 'I see no trace of [that New Deal spirit] in Stevenson's speeches. I see it in Harriman's. The New Deal and Fair Deal are synonymous, and they are the antithesis of moderation,' [he said. Then, asked to give 'a definition of New Deal-ism,' the justice said it is] 'an insistence that the powers of government be used to help people who can't help themselves.'"

On July 20 Paul Butler sent Stevenson a copy of the plank that Eleanor had piloted through the drafting committee. Stevenson was uncertain about its wording and thought it could be stronger. On August 4 he sent a draft of his own to Butler, saying in his cover letter, "I hardly need tell you that I attach primary significance, as I know you do, to making this platform statement a constructive contribution to meeting the nation's No. 1 domestic problem.... It does seem to me that this draft does not state clearly and plainly enough what I have been saying in the primary campaign and what I feel strongly is right,"[5] whereupon he enclosed his own draft of such a plank. After three introductory paragraphs, it read,

> The Democratic Party stands firmly in support of the Supreme Court decisions regarding desegregation in the public schools and in other public facilities, including transportation, as we stand firmly in support of all Supreme Court decisions.
>
> Every American child, irrespective of race or national origin, economic status or place of residence, has full and equal right under the law to every educational opportunity to develop his potentialities.*

*This sentence was adopted *verbatim* by the Platform Committee to introduce the education plank (*Proceedings*, 307).

We favor legislation:

a. To protect all citizens in the exercise of their right to vote;
b. To secure the right to equal opportunity for employment;
c. To provide protection for the right to security of person;
d. To perfect and strengthen federal civil rights laws; and
e. To provide adequate administrative machinery for the protection of Civil Rights[6]

Given his severely exhausted condition, Stevenson may not have recognized how far removed these statements would sound to Southern ears from the carefully modulated positions he had been describing on the campaign trail, and how deeply they would offend much of the South. He decided to sound out Mrs. Roosevelt on her reactions to his draft and so traveled to Val-Kill the day after the Waldorf dinner ($75,000 raised). Regrettably, he felt under too much pressure to take advantage of the "restful twenty-four hours" she had envisaged. Nor, it seems, was he in a mood to concur with her judgment about a plank that would mollify the South.

That same day she wrote the Lashes: "Mr. S[tevenson] came here for a couple of hours to discuss Civil Rights and he wants much more specifically said in the platform which I would love to see done but I doubt if he can get by the Southerners."[7]

For her readers her *My Day* column next day bore a wistful tone. It is certainly one of the most revealing documents we have of her feelings for Stevenson. She had hoped the visit would provide a relaxed interval from the bruising pace of the campaign, but Stevenson had kept the focus of their meeting on the party platform, particularly its civil rights and education planks.

I had the privilege of a short visit from Adlai Stevenson last Thursday afternoon. One must talk of matters of state and of politics with him, for at the present Stevenson's whole life must be given to these questions. But he is the kind of man that you wish you might some time find sitting under a tree in a relaxed mood with nothing to do! There would be plenty to talk about and there would be many things I think that one could explore with pleasure.

Her imagination takes flight from there:

I always wonder, when I do not know people well or know only one side of their personalities, whether there would be things which could be mutually enjoyed. What would one read aloud? Would tastes in music or in pictures touch at any point? Would one like to travel and to sightsee in the same way? Would a view, or a child, or a bit of nature touch the same feelings in the other person and make companionship a pleasant adventure?

After all, getting to know people is an adventure, but often a new person will not interest you enough to make you want to go any further with the adventure. And then again, there will be someone with whom it would be fun to explore!

I feel regret because time is never long enough to really get started on a new adventure in friendship with someone as busy as this candidate for the Presidency.

Almost as though bent on lending credence to her plaint, Stevenson wrote Mrs. Roosevelt, enclosing a copy of his draft and telling her he was sharing only with Butler and herself his letter to Butler and his draft platform, but "want you to be fully advised as to what I have proposed" [Translation: "I want you to know, Dear Mentor, that I am marching to a different drummer, not yours"]. He then told her that he "made an unrehearsed, spontaneous remark to a casual interviewer a couple of days ago to the effect that I had a strong feeling 'that the platform should express unequivocal approval of the Court's decision, although it seems odd that you have to express your approval of the Constitution and its institutions,'" adding cryptically, "You will note that the enclosed draft speaks of 'support' rather than 'approval'" [Translation: "A party, like an individual, may support Supreme Court decisions as the law of the land. This need not imply we approve of them"]. Stevenson's pain at the calculation required to "hold" the African Americans *and* the Southerners' votes is palpable in this sentence. The net in which the politics of the mid-1950s was caught required such maneuverings, or so the principal actors in the drama thought. Calling ER's stance "opportunistic and unmilitant," Joseph Lash comments about this episode: "It was not the finest hour of either of these normally staunch supporters of civil rights."[8]

The 108 members of the Resolutions and Platform Committee assembled on August 6 for five days of solid work on the convention's major legislative agenda. They convened amidst what the *Times* called "somewhat hopeful omens" to begin "an urgent effort to write for the National Convention a civil rights platform bridging the North and South."[9]

Delegates appeared determined to put aside ideological differences and the squabbling that seemed an inevitable ingredient of every such gathering. Even Averell Harriman was reported to be in a "conciliatory" mood. As for the putative nominee himself, Stevenson was thought to have won the confidence of a considerable majority of the Southern delegates, while his popularity among Northern voters had been proven in the primaries. A week before Sam Rayburn's gavel would bring the convention to order, with 686½ votes needed to nominate, Stevenson was said to hold between 400 and 600 first-ballot votes, Kefauver 202. Harriman was far behind and Lyndon B. Johnson was bringing up the rear.

On August 7, Stevenson went on television to spell out his definitive stance on the subject of civil rights. According to press reports next day it "stirred Southern ire." "Stevenson Stand on Rights Perils First-Ballot Victory" and "Demand for an Integration Stand Brings Threat to Withdraw Support" were typical headlines. Georgia's Democratic state chairman was one of the first to declare that he "would not vote for Stevenson in this Convention." He called the candidate's newly revealed position "a stupid blunder which...may well deny to him and to the Democratic Party victory in the Presidential campaign." Kentucky governor A. B. ("Happy") Chandler said Stevenson had "knocked himself out of the race," though his view "was not accepted generally, even among Southern delegates." The *New York Times* reported that "a group of Southern Democrats met in the rooms of Gov. James P. Coleman of Mississippi. Reporters waiting outside in the corridor could hear angry comments concerning the stand outlined by Mr. Stevenson."[10] Calling the Illinoisan prior to this development "the best friend of the South among those actively contending for the nomination," the governor refused to predict how his delegation would be voting next week.

Times senior correspondent James ("Scotty") Reston's column commented next day:

> There was never any real justification for believing that a political party that split on civil rights during the Presidential elections of 1948 and 1952 would not divide openly in 1956 after all the emotion that followed the [Supreme Court's] desegregation order....It would have been a miracle if these two conflicting interests and philosophies had not produced an open row when the Northern and Southern factions met in Chicago.

Then, in an attempt to explain Stevenson's broader perspective, Reston wrote,

> Mr. Stevenson is not thinking only of discrimination against the Negro race in the South but also of discrimination in the North as well, not only of public school segregation in the South but also of housing segregation in the North. And actually he does not put the school segregation question first but fourth in his list of priorities. His view is that the platform should mention not only the public school issue but also equal voting opportunities for the Negroes, equal housing opportunities and employment rights, in that order. Integrated schools were fourth.

Party leaders moved quickly to dampen the controversy. Representative John W. McCormack, chair of the Platform and Resolutions Committee, named a drafting subcommittee, with himself as chair, charged with framing a civil rights plank acceptable to both North and South. Its makeup reportedly "greatly pleased the Southern wing of the party and was acceptable to the more liberal Northerners" as well as to Stevenson and his team. Noting that a "spirit of compromise is in the air," the *New York Times* editorial page described the issue before the committee: "The Southerners are simply trying to keep [the plank] as vague and meaningless as possible. The one thing they want least is an explicit declaration of approval of the Supreme Court's desegregation decision, which is the one thing many of the Northerners want most."

Let us pause briefly here to note the full import of these pressures for the friendship between Eleanor Roosevelt and Adlai Stevenson. The *Times* editorialist's last-quoted sentence (above) referred to church, fraternal, and civic groups in the North whose most outspoken leadership came from the unions, the NAACP, and Americans for Democratic Action. ER had been a member of the Board of Directors of the NAACP for more than a decade and, since 1951, its vice president. She had also been a founder in 1947, then honorary chairman, of the ADA whose mission was to articulate and work for a liberal, non-communist national and international agenda for the United States. Yet in the current controversy she was standing forthrightly *against* the positions espoused by both those organizations. She was guiding her actions by the hope that agreement could be achieved between North and South and a compromise forged around which the entire country could unite. Weeks before the Platform and Resolutions Committee convened, she had helped frame what she and her colleagues felt was precisely such a document. This was Eleanor Roosevelt the pragmatic politician speaking, the realist with an ear attuned to the sticking points and the tipping points at play in every important decision on the national or international stage—and she was one of the world's top players on that stage.

Stevenson sincerely believed, as he told Paul Butler, that he had just stated in unmistakably clear terms "what I have been saying in the primary campaign and what I strongly feel is right." His position, however, seemed on its face, at least to the media and to many Southerners as well as Northerners, to mark a departure from the more moderate one he had been putting forward during the primaries. There was speculation that he had moved leftward to undercut Harriman's support, or possibly to reassure Truman of his liberal credentials. Some such calculation may have played a role in the way he presented his views. Foremost, however, was his conviction that in the momentous decision the nation faced—in his letter to Butler he had called it "the nation's No. 1 domestic problem"—principle must take precedence over politics. To Mrs. Roosevelt's disappointment, that was the note on which he had left Val-Kill only a week earlier.

Thus did a woman whose whole life had drawn her closer to the plight of the forgotten and the abused decide, on the basis of "pragmatic realism," for a middle way—the only strategy she felt could win the prize—while the candidate, for whom such identification seemed emotionally beyond his reach, had declared his fealty to the highest principle yet enunciated in this political campaign. His was a stand that *almost guaranteed his rejection by the electorate* whose support he would be wooing in the final months of the campaign.

Two days later a compromise civil rights plank was adopted by the drafting committee. It contained no clause committing the party to implementing the Supreme Court's order and condemned any use of force. Another page-one story in the *Times* said, "it falls between the combined position of the labor unions, the Americans for Democratic Action and the National Association for the Advancement of Colored People on the one side and that of the Southerners at the other extreme." The story concluded with a note that, though she wouldn't arrive till the convention's opening day, "the authors of the plank...are understood to have the general support of Mrs. Franklin D. Roosevelt."[11]

Then President Harry Truman blew into town, a broad grin on his face wherever he appeared: he had a surprise to spring on conventioneers. When asked about who he was backing, he enjoyed putting the press off, coyly remarking that he would declare his preference the day before the lights went on in the Cow Palace. When the Sunday papers announced his preference for Harriman over Stevenson, few were surprised. Both Adlai and ER had hoped the president, as he had intimated he might, would not try to influence the outcome of the contest. According to Elliott Roosevelt, when she heard the news, ER commented, "Well, that's certainly no help to us, but we shall have to do the best we can."[12]

His move, said the media, "disrupts efforts to reach accord on civil rights."[13] Forces advocating a "hard civil rights" position seemed momentarily reenergized. But then Senator Lyndon B. Johnson emerged from the shadows to provide the Platform Committee and the convention itself "the bridge between North and South he has long been in the Senate." Johnson, said the *Times*, appeared to control "the largest uncommitted center of power in the convention," namely, Texas' fifty-six delegate votes "plus many standing offers of heavy support from elsewhere [in] the South."[14] He was exploiting the situation, he said, for two purposes: (1) in order "to force the adoption of a middle-road civil rights plank" and (2) "to bring about the greatest possible unity." (Biographers have written that for a time, both before and during the convention, LBJ really thought he had a chance, if civil rights split the convention wide open, that he might emerge as the party's compromise presidential candidate.)[15]

ER and Elliott flew to Chicago with Adlai, arriving Sunday afternoon, August 12, the day before the convention's official opening day. Elliott recalled the scene:

> His campaign manager, Jim Finnegan, had a car waiting for us at the airport. Mother and Adlai shared the back seat, while I eavesdropped from the jump seat in front of their knees. Even now, he wavered about seeking the nomination. She browbeat him for most of the ride into downtown Chicago. ["Mother," Elliott said, "treated Adlai like a bright child who had to be coached to win the college scholarship"]
>
> "There are many people who could wage this campaign just as well as myself. I don't know that I'd be the right candidate. I don't think I should carry on as the standard bearer—"
>
> "You are the only one who can possibly do it," Mother said flatly, "and you will do it."
>
> "But I'm not sure I want to."
>
> "Oh yes, you *do!*"[16]

The plan was to have her speak to a large press conference Finnegan had arranged at which she could deflate Truman's balloon. A crowded ballroom full of reporters and convention delegates would be awaiting her arrival as her limousine drove up to the Conrad Hilton Hotel door.

She was girded for battle. Monday's page-one headline read, "Truman Is Rebutted by Mrs. Roosevelt," the story opening, "Mrs. Franklin D. Roosevelt told Harry S. Truman today it was time to let the young folks run the country. She also let him know that she, too, had a voice in designating the heir to her late husband. Her choice, she made it clear, is still Adlai E. Stevenson."[17] The story continued:

> "We must have a candidate who is prepared to go forward," Mrs. Roosevelt told her news conference. "I'm old, of course," she said smilingly. "Mr. Truman is much younger." Queried about ages, Mrs. Roosevelt said she didn't know exactly how old Mr. Truman was. "I will be 72 in October," she said. Mr. Truman was 72 on May 8. Mr. Harriman will be 64 in November. Mr. Stevenson is 56.
>
> The country needs a President who is young and progressive enough to adapt old traditions to new situations, she added....
>
> Mr. Truman had said the day before that he had decided to endorse Mr. Harriman because crises in world affairs necessitated election to the Presidency of a man able to assume office immediately "without a period of costly trial and error." He also cited Mr. Harriman's wide experience in foreign affairs.
>
> Mrs. Roosevelt declared that Mr. Stevenson's record in foreign affairs is impressive. It is superior, she said, to Mr. Harriman's in Asia and Africa where, she remarked, the United States is most in need of friends.

Conceding that Mr. Harriman, whom she has known "ever since he was a boy," was well versed in Europe and Russia, Mrs. Roosevelt added that "what he said about Asia and Africa" did not demonstrate "an intimate knowledge."

The article concluded by noting that she was cheered by crowds as she left the hotel to go across the street to the Sheraton-Blackstone "where she had lunch with Mr. Truman." Arthur Schlesinger called hers "an adroit and ruthless performance."[18]

* * *

ER spent most of the next twenty-four hours with Adlai and John Fell visiting state delegations and putting the case for choosing Stevenson's experience, abilities, and vision over those of Harriman, Johnson, and any of the lesser folks who had thrown their hats in the ring. Then, on the opening night of the convention she addressed the delegates in a speech that not only sealed the case for Stevenson's nomination but also set the tone for the rest of the week's deliberations. Delivered, as was her custom, entirely without notes, it was a vivid demonstration of her intellectual power and political acumen, and it brought the delegates to their feet with a roar of approval. (Edward R. Murrow later called it "the greatest convention speech I ever heard.")

> It is a foolish thing to say that you pledge yourself to live up to the traditions of the New Deal and the Fair Deal—of course you are proud of those traditions, of course you are proud to have the advice of the elders in our party, but our party is young and vigorous. Our party may be the oldest democratic party, but our party must live as a young party, and it must have young leadership. It must have young people, and they must be allowed to lead. They must not lean on their tradition. They must be proud of it. They must take into account the advice of the elders, but they must have the courage to look ahead, to face new problems with new solutions.

She was underscoring the theme she had expressed at the previous day's press conference (and, we may surmise, at her luncheon with President Truman). Now she suggested a possible new frontier for Democratic Party initiative:

> You will remember that my husband said in one of his speeches that...we still had a third of our people who were ill-housed, ill-clothed and ill-fed. We have lessened that group in our country...but we still have a job to do. Twenty per cent today is the figure they give us.
> Could we have the vision of doing away in this great country with poverty? It would be a marvelous achievement, and I think it might be done if

you and I, each one of us as individuals, would really pledge ourselves and our party to think imaginatively of what can be done at home, what can make us not only the nation that has some of the richest people in the world but the nation where there are no people that have to live at a substandard level. That would be one of the very best arguments against Communism that we could possibly have.[19]

Her mission accomplished and confident the tide was now running strongly in Adlai's favor, she accepted her protégé's offer to accompany her to the airport. On the 17th she would be on a flight to Paris with two of her grandchildren.

There remained adoption of the party's platform and its choice of presidential and vice presidential nominees. The civil rights and education planks of the platform drew considerable comment. There was an unsuccessful attempt by Southerners to enter a minority report, and the liberal forces, led by Senators Herbert Lehman (NY) and Paul Douglas (IL), expressed their conviction that, if need be, Stevenson could win without the South. Chairman Sam Rayburn used his gavel to ram the majority report through to adoption.

In a novel departure from precedent, Stevenson asked conventioneers to name their choice for his vice presidential running mate. Massachusetts senator John F. Kennedy, who had delivered a rousing nominating speech for Adlai, looked for a while like the winner until Tennessee announced for Kefauver; the bandwagon veered in his direction and he was ultimately acclaimed the candidate.

Balloting for the top spot followed and Adlai won 905½ votes on the first ballot to Harriman's 210, Johnson's 80, and a scattering of ballots cast for favorite sons. Of the week's "major events" there then remained only Stevenson's acceptance speech the night before delegates departed for home. According to most observers the speech was a failure. Porter McKeever wrote, "The rhetoric was lofty but the content was diffuse, unfocussed, and disappointing."[20] John Bartlow Martin said, "He had won the nomination. But he had disappointed his own followers...and he had alienated Rayburn, Truman and others by throwing the convention open for Vice-President." Arthur Schlesinger noted, "One felt that the image of the New Stevenson, this grim, masterful figure had suddenly disappeared and in its place appeared the old Stevenson, the literary critic, the man obsessed with words and with portentous generalizations." It was an ominous note on which to launch a new presidential campaign.

CHAPTER 9

THE CAMPAIGN TRAIL AGAIN

THE CONVENTION OVER, Stevenson held a wide-ranging press conference at which he was queried about issues in domestic and foreign policy and his opinion on farm price supports, a volunteer versus drafted armed services, the Taft-Hartley labor law, civil rights, fiscal policy, and differences between his views and those of President Truman and President Eisenhower on several of these matters.

Peter Lisagor of the *Chicago Daily News* asked the candidate's position on the emerging problem of the Suez Canal (which Eleanor had sniffed in the wind a month before). In July, Britain and the United States, to mark their displeasure with Egypt's President Gamal Abdel Nasser, had withdrawn their previous offer of grants to finance construction of the Aswan Dam. Nasser, in response, had nationalized the canal's operating company and a new face-off with the Soviet Union was in the offing. "I had anticipated that someone might ask me about the Suez," Adlai replied and went on to add, "I have expressed particular misgivings about our policies in the Middle East, especially about Mr. Dulles' on-again off-again negotiations regarding the Aswan Dam. But this is an area of vital concern to the United States and to our Allies and I do not think that any comment or criticism by me at this critical moment would serve a constructive purpose....I do not want to add to the difficulties of the President and the Secretary of State in this delicate situation. I shall reserve any further comment on this until a later time."

He probably surprised most of his hearers when he commended the prompt and decisive action of the governors of Kentucky and Tennessee—their use "even in some cases of the National Guard"—to quell resistance to school integration that had occurred in both states. Though this statement seemed to contradict both his oft-repeated stand against the use of force to achieve compliance with the Supreme Court's desegregation order, as well as the Democratic Party's platform plank on the matter, nothing further was made of the discrepancy by the media.

Over the next few days he penned brief messages to a dozen or so persons who had either played crucial roles in the campaign to date or would do so in the course of its sprint to the November finish line. Then he and Kefauver left for a four-day, 5,000-mile whirlwind tour to strategize with party leaders in the Southwest, West, and South. While on that trip he wrote Dore Schary, "As for Jack Kennedy, I have a feeling that he was the real hero of the hour [Kennedy had narrated the film describing the history of the Democratic Party, and delivered a noteworthy nominating speech for Adlai], and that we shall hear a great deal more from this promising young man." Eleanor did not share his admiration for the Massachusetts senator.[1]

A letter* from a modestly educated but thoughtful Pennsylvania farmer confirmed that Stevenson's speeches were registering with blue- as well as white-collar audiences:[2]

Columbia, Penna.
August 28, 1956.

Mr. Adalia Stevenson;

Dear Sir:
Since listing and watching you speak on T.V. I have wanted to write to you. I am a farm labor and when you spoke about people like me it gave me encouragement. I am below average wage earner because I like farming. I feel by writting you maybe I can help you understand the needs of the many people like myself. Your [acceptance] speech struck time and time again at the real truth. We are in serious trouble when Mr. Truman was in office I earned the same as I do now an average of 160.00 per mo. Back then I could get along not to good but I was satisfied. Now its impossible for me to be able to make ends meet. ...

We small people have made this country what it is no man or woman can do his best when constantly beset by worry and uncertanty these big money men are being very foolish with there contempt and greed they are destroying this country. There actions have caused the small men to hate them where there is hate there is discontent and you know where that leads to sooner or later rebelion. ... What most of these money men don't realize is that most of these men have been thru a war many millions have fought dictators and if pressed they will fight them in this country. It may take a long time but some time they are going to realize that the only way to get along is to unite and strike together and hard.... Our lives are not our own any more.... Today it is more and more crime and Juvinile delinquency that what comes from harried and overworked parents. Its not the relaxing of parental care its the

*Misspellings in original

presser of the times causing the parents to neglect the children devoting all
there time to having to work to make a living.... No Sir Mr. Stevenson this is
not God's country anymore. You are our only hope Sir by fulfilling the terms
of your promises you made on your acceptance speech. You can give new life
to the average poor wage earner ...

I would be proud to help you in any way I can at anytime I am going to
vote for you and hope you get it. I have a lot of belief in you and hope you do
as you said you would.

> Sincerely yours,
> Thomas R. Parker
> R.D. 1
> Columbia, Penna.

The night before leaving the convention, Eleanor wrote to David Gurewitsch
to report that the Stevenson organization was devastated by Truman's
endorsement of Harriman. She thought it perhaps would work to Stevenson's
advantage, "He himself knows now that if he wins he is free and owes no
allegiance to Truman," and despite the fact that Truman was "using all his
influence and much Harriman money to defeat Stevenson," she thought the
situation far from hopeless.[3]

Back in New York, she wired Adlai her thanks "for the lovely orchids
and for all your many kindnesses" during her brief but remarkably effective
hours at the convention. He replied, saying he was "sure I failed utterly to
thank you properly for all you have done during these past many months,
and finally at the Convention itself. The latter came off better than I had
any right to expect." He closed, wishing her "a relaxing and diverting trip
with the young people. I can imagine the diversion, but not the relaxation"
and signed it "Devotedly, Adlai."

She wrote David again as her plane was over the Atlantic, telling him that
Stevenson was nominated and speculating that he and Kefauver should make
"a good team for the campaign," while she had reservations about how they
would work together once elected. She thought they had "a hard fight" ahead.
She also thought David "would like Stevenson's attitude on Truman."[4]

In Paris with her grandsons and David Gurewitsch's daughter, Grania, she
wrote Adlai from the Hotel Crillon that she was enjoying "a busy, but on the
whole pleasant time," adding, "I think the boys are enjoying it much more
since Grania Gurewitsch joined us." She had been thinking about the campaign ahead. The crucial issue in the campaign was to persuade the electorate
that a Republican defeat would not mean an end to the prosperity the country
was enjoying. She had talked with the Queen of the Netherlands about the
issue of New Guinea and Indonesia that "is tied up with our whole position
on the colonial question." She was worried about the Suez situation, another
of her characteristically premonitory concerns for future trouble: "The Soviets

have a knack for standing back and being enigmatic and letting us wonder what they will do while they shove somebody else to the fore, usually a weaker nation that would never dare stand up on its own." Two months later the Suez crisis flared, viewed by many as the opening scene of the final act in the history of colonialism.

She was still hoping for a *nonpolitical* visit with Stevenson, one of like-minded friends, but framed her invitation in terms she thought he would find irresistible. She planned on being in New York on September 9 "and Hyde Park from the 10th to the 12th. I think I saw you were going to be in New York about that time [and] if you let me know, I would love to have a chance to talk with you and hear something of your plans and campaign preparations."

She hoped campaign manager Finnegan would send her dates she could fill, "also any suggestions of what he would particularly like me to cover in speaking. Since the Republican convention I feel more certain than ever that you can win. They seem to me empty and void of imagination or content."[5]

*   *   *

Throughout the next eight weeks "The Guv" would sustain a merciless pace, his 72-year-old mentor running him a very close second. His schedule for September is illustrative: September 24: Oklahoma City; September 25: Shreveport and Miami; September 26: Jacksonville and Tampa—overnight in Kansas City; September 27: Kansas City and St. Louis; September 28: Indianapolis and Milwaukee; September 29: Minneapolis, returning to Washington D.C. that evening. Porter McKeever observed, "It would have been a man-killing pace for one starting out completely rested, which, of course, he wasn't."[6]

Eleanor meanwhile seemed to have decided to grant her candidate's springtime wish, that she would be available to "speak just as much as is humanly possible" (and he seemed to have forgotten his protective note of April 17 saying he didn't want Agnes Meyer exhausting her). Tamara Hareven reports that

> in October, Earl Banner of the *Boston Globe* joined her on her tour. After a *Globe* editor had seen her itinerary, as issued by the Democratic National Committee, he assigned Banner to prove that the announced schedule was an exaggeration. Only with great difficulty did Banner keep up with her for some days, until he was convinced that she was indeed carrying out the schedule. After the election her children told her that she had been working too hard. "They may have been right," she said, "but I noticed that I could often keep going longer than they, and I thought that it was never easy to know what one could do or not do at some time in the future. I was seventy-two in 1956 and sometimes I felt very old and sometimes I felt very young."[7]

Her first public foray on Adlai's behalf came on September 16 when she appeared on "Meet the Press." In a devastating performance,[8] she showed her mastery of the thrust-and-parry game such programs depend on to win in the court of public opinion. The first question came from May Craig of the Portland, Maine *Press-Herald*. She quoted former president Truman as saying at the convention that the nation could not afford "a period of trial and error in U.S. foreign policy, particularly in such a dangerous time." Didn't Mrs. Roosevelt feel that President Eisenhower would be better equipped to handle the crisis over the Suez Canal?

ER's response was clear and deft:

> No, Mrs. Craig, I don't. I feel Pres. Eisenhower gained his knowledge of foreign affairs as a general in the European theatre. He was a general carrying out the policies that were *made* by other people. When you're doing that you learn to be skillful in carrying out policies made by other people. I don't think that's the same as having to *think out* policies for yourself.
>
> My experience is that Mr. Stevenson has taken a great deal of trouble to inform himself on the background of Asia and Africa with which this question is closely tied. I don't think it would be a period of trial and error, I think it would be a transition to a man who has a policy which is perhaps more basically thought out than the policies which have been pursued in the last few years, which have met crises over and over again, but which never seem to have any connection with a thought-out world policy.

"Could you tell us how you feel about Mr. Nixon's running for the vice-presidency?" she was asked. Many of her Republican friends, "particularly young people," she replied, [say] "he has matured and grown in many ways."

> I happen to remember very clearly his campaign for the Senatorship. I have no respect for the way in which he accused Helen Gahagan Douglas of being a Communist because he knew that was how he would be elected, and I have no respect for the kind of character that takes advantage and does something they know is not true. He knew that she might be a liberal but he knew quite well, having known her and worked with her, that she was not a Communist. I have always felt that anyone who wanted an election so much that they would use those means did not have the character that I really admired in public life.

Then, asked whether she subscribed to the view, advanced by Stevenson, that "President Eisenhower himself wants prosperity only for big business and that he doesn't care about the little guy?" she responded:

> Oh no! The President is a good man and he would always want to do the right thing as he saw it, but he has a great admiration for the achievement of the successful business man because he has never been a successful business man and you always admire what you don't really understand.

Adlai wired his thanks and congratulations: "If you are neither statesman nor politician, then pray tell me what is it I am pretending to? This was the wisest, most gracious and convincing performance in my recollection. I thank you, I congratulate you and I bless you."[9] She replied, saying she didn't know how he could find the time "to watch such things as 'Meet the Press,' [he wasn't watching the *program*, he was watching *her*]" but that she was "surprised and delighted" by his telegram "more than I can say"

Campaign managers shared Agnes Meyer's conviction that she was "Adlai's greatest asset" and scheduled her accordingly. Joe Lash wrote in his diary that her "Meet the Press" performance had "scorched the Eisenhower-Nixon ticket." He thought she was "showing rare gusto these days…primarily because she has become so needed in Stevenson's campaign." But she was "frightened" at the way the campaign organizers had come to rely on her "to perform magic. 'If you go here,' they told her, 'still you have to be in Harlem with Adlai on the 4th, even though it means flying back from Michigan in the afternoon and out to Wisconsin the next morning.' The pressures were remorseless but she loved it all, and for a time it looked as if she might perform the miracle that the Stevenson workers were expecting of her."[10]

A few days later, Adlai sent a memo to Jim Finnegan, his national campaign manager, urging him to arrange joint appearances for himself and Mrs. Roosevelt: "October 4th at the Harlem rally," he thought, might be "one such occasion [Did this suggestion betray Stevenson's anxiety over facing a Harlem audience?] and possibly the major rally before the election." He thought her "Meet the Press" performance "masterful, especially the characterization of Ike as a man whose experience lay in carrying out policies, not in formulating them, and her reminder that Nixon had called Helen Gahagan Douglas a communist, even though he knew it was untrue."[11]

That same day Eleanor forwarded a "memorandum to Mr. Stevenson from Bernard M. Baruch via Eleanor Roosevelt." He advised that "just at present the South is so annoyed with Mr. Eisenhower that they are all for Mr. Stevenson. It would seem to be wiser not to go there and to let them pull against Mr. Eisenhower and not run the danger of antagonizing any of them." It was a memo written out of Mr. Baruch's friendship with Eleanor Roosevelt; he did not share her admiration of Stevenson and would vote for Eisenhower in November.

On September 20, Eleanor sent Adlai a note appropriate to her big-sisterly role: She had "some very remarkable cold tablets" that he need only request of her secretary, Maureen Corr, "and she will send them right on to you."[12]

Throughout the fall she issued periodic statements,[13] as the occasion demanded, explaining her reasons for supporting Stevenson's candidacy, the question of race always a prominent concern. One released in late August emphasized that, having educated himself about other parts of the world, he was no longer the reluctant candidate he had been in 1952, but ready to be "a full-time president," a role she felt Eisenhower had shown himself incapable of fulfilling. He simply did not know *how* to lead the nation. "The greatest educator of the people of the United States should be the president, [but] you have not been made to feel a part of the problem and I think that is essential for the president of the United States to do. Being a man of war does not necessarily mean you know how to fight the civilian battles."

Another, dated September 25, spoke to the racial issue. She was confident that Stevenson would "see that the law of the land is complied with" and be sensitive to "how the Negro people in the U.S. feel who have waited so long for their full rights as citizens, but that he would also be aware of "how the Southern White people feel whose way of life is being changed, otherwise we may find ourselves involved in violence and bloodshed." (To be sure, it was a statement about justice, but did it also reveal an ambivalence she and Stevenson both shared about its full realization?)

Though each of them was careening back and forth across the country in pursuit of victory and, therefore, found it well nigh impossible to arrange even the briefest meeting, there were few days on which each was not present in the other's thought and care. Thus at Yale University on October 5, taking up the theme she had made the central point of her speech at the convention in August, namely, the need for new Democratic Party leadership, Adlai invited his hearers to reflect with him on the example Eleanor Roosevelt had offered delegates of courage and self-denial: At the convention she had urged Democrats to "take into account the advice of the elders" but to also heed the voices of the party's younger members "who must have the courage to face new problems with new solutions."[14]

A week later Eleanor was campaigning in West Virginia and reflecting not only on the time she and Stevenson met in London in 1946 but also on their interchanges over the years since. We can surmise that she was engaging in a rigorous reappraisal of "her" candidate as the 1956 campaign was peaking. Somehow it seemed to be lacking both the focus and the momentum required for victory with elections just one brief month away:

> I remember after the 1952 elections Adlai Stevenson went on a trip around the world. I followed him in most places and particularly in Asia. Always I was told "We like your Mr. Stevenson—he listened to what we had to say." This taught me a lesson: We Americans have a reputation for doing all the talking. If you don't know much about the people and their background, doing all the talking and not finding out their ideas is not a wise thing to do....Adlai Stevenson took his trip to Africa because he had not seen this Continent which he realized was one area where our problems would lie in the next few years, and he felt obliged to learn about these people. A person must take the

trouble to learn what he needs to know if new problems are to be solved in new ways[15]

*   *   *

Stevenson's 1956 campaign differed from his previous run in many ways—in 1952 he was introducing himself and winning public confidence; now he was as familiar as an old shoe—(one with a hole in it became the symbol of his relentless pursuit on the campaign trail and won photographer William M. Gallagher a Pulitzer Prize.) No longer a fresh voice, he was determined to articulate the issues as clearly and comprehensively as he could, in the belief that such was the only true reason for having a political contest in the first place. Here he constantly met with resistance from members of his staff for whom the strictures of television, for the first time in the nation's history, were imposing new and relentless pressure on candidates. The "sound-bite" campaigns of the future loomed.

But he was also inordinately tired. Commentators observed that one day (or night) he would "come across" with all the effervescence and bounce as well as the articulateness of his old 1952 self and then, within hours, appear nervous, even irritable, at being where he was and doing what he was doing. Early in October, Mrs. Roosevelt received a letter from a worker in the New York campaign committee's headquarters commenting on this phenomenon:

> A number of people are distressed because his advisers have suggested that he talk on a more "common" level. They feel that he isn't being natural on that level and is ill-at-ease. I have great faith in the mass of people and believe that he can be his natural, articulate, intellectual, humorous self and not lose a vote. He seemed quite ill-at-ease in his T.V. appearance at Milwaukee last week. I think you might reassure him on this point if you agree with me.[16]

The writer was Pauli Murray,[17] an old friend, whose opinion Eleanor always found astute and in this case she did agree. A week later she wrote Adlai expressing her hope that he would "take a rest whenever you can. It troubles me that the grueling campaign you have [under-] taken must take so much out of you physically." Then she spoke, again with the affectionate tone of an older sister, assuring him that she was "not hearing any objection any more to your humor, so don't worry about that! Just let it come naturally. If you can speak to the mass of people as though you were talking to any one individual in your living room at Libertyville, you will reach their hearts and that is all that you have to bother about." Her reassurance was comforting. Next day he wired her, "The entire Stevenson entourage sends our affectionate greetings to our most effective and beloved supporter."

On the campaign trail

The tide, though, had for some time been flowing in President Eisenhower's direction, and events on the world stage were about to seal Stevenson's fate. Meanwhile, a letter from "Poppy" (Mrs. Walter) White dated October 16 must have come as a body blow to Eleanor Roosevelt. She doubtless saw that it prefigured a likely trend in November among African American voters:

> After a great deal of soul-searching, I have decided that in this election I have to be on the opposite side of the fence from you. This is the first time, and I want you to know that your stand has made the decision very difficult indeed. I am afraid it really is "Hobson's choice" this year.[18]

CHAPTER 10

AFTERMATH: TIME FOR REFLECTION

DURING THE CLOSING WEEKS OF THE 1956 CAMPAIGN Adlai Stevenson sought to win citizen support for the two major defense policy initiatives he had described in earlier speeches: replacement of the military draft by an all-volunteer army and a moratorium on testing of the hydrogen bomb. Members of his staff had warned him against the trap he was setting for himself, but Stevenson seemed bent on arguing his case before the court of public opinion. On both issues he had arrived at his conclusions only after exhaustive consultation with experts in these two fields—military experts in the former case, physicists, statesmen, and nuclear scientists in the latter. By the time he started pressing the testing proposal he had secured signatures of support from more than 270 scientists. Eleanor did her part in several *My Day* columns, calling the initiative "the one gesture we can make with the least risk" and one that "will bring other nations who do not want war to feel that we are making a genuine effort to move forward." [1] Two days later she accused the president and his advisers of adopting on this issue a "philosophy of standing still." [2]

When Stevenson first broached the initiatives, however, he had failed to present the full array of arguments that brought him to suggest such radical departures from current policy and practice. To do so now, so late in the campaign, made his move seem an act of desperation. It also appeared that he was entirely ignoring the political dimensions of his proposals. Newton Minow, law partner, FCC chairman, ambassador, and one of Adlai's close friends, said,

> There are those, and I confess I was among them, who believed, more in sorrow than anger, that the Gov did not have acute political instincts. In many of his campaign moves, including the ban on nuclear testing, he did make wrong

political decisions. In the narrow sense of politics, in the adding-machine verdict of vote gains and losses, our judgment was often superior to his.

But what we failed to comprehend immediately, and only began to understand later, was that his political instincts were generally keener than ours. He was very much aware of the political repercussions and drawbacks of many of the moves he made on the chessboard of electoral politics. The point is that he knew the political hazards and still rejected these short-term considerations.

He was marching to a distant drummer, ... to the beat, not of his personal victory but of mankind's.[3]

But, tactically speaking, that was beside the point: his move gave President Eisenhower and his advisers an opportunity to, first, distort his proposals and then to dismiss them as "irresponsible...a theatrical gesture." Emmet John Hughes, Eisenhower's speechwriter, opined that "from the standpoint of the White House, it would have been impossible to have wished for a greater political gift." Several members of the White House staff, he reported, "were concerned about many aspects of the administration's defense and foreign policies but they now immediately perceived the opportunity to divert attention from their vulnerabilities."[4] The largely Republican media dutifully purveyed the administration's line, and the damage Stevenson's advisers had foreseen dealt a devastating blow to his cause. In response, Mrs. Roosevelt lobbed a blockbuster bomb into the Republican camp in the form of a powerfully reasoned column about the Suez crisis: How was it possible, she asked,

> that we would find ourselves lined up with the Soviet Union and the dictator of Egypt against Great Britain and France and the only democratic country in the Near East, Israel! Where has our influence, which ought to help shape such decisions in the world, failed so that we find ourselves today in such a position?...Do we want to continue with the kind of leadership that has led to a war in which, if we are not with our old allies, we have to side with the Kremlin and the dictator of Egypt?[5]

But the convergence of the Middle East crisis[6] and the Soviets' forceful suppression of a Hungarian attempt to overthrow their Communist rulers—both in the headlines just days before Election Day—tipped the scales and persuaded the public that the country would be "safer" under a military president than it would under the former governor of Illinois.[7]

Over the months Stevenson had labored mightily to shape a campaign in which issues were thoroughly aired. Such airing as there was had come primarily from himself, save the few cases in which he had succeeded in drawing the Republican lion from his den, as he had done on both these latter

two topics. (Several years later Stevenson prophetically expressed his reluctant conclusion that in the age of television presidential campaigns would
be reduced to sound bites and personality contests.) But he had few regrets
about the way he had conducted his part of the contest.

Eleanor Roosevelt campaigned for her candidate right up to the final
day before the election, returning to Hyde Park in time to cast her vote—
"the last if not least important thing I could do in behalf of Governor
Stevenson."[8] But victory had eluded him once again. That 62 percent of
daily newspapers (1760) had backed Eisenhower and only 15 percent (189)
supported Stevenson's candidacy[9] appeared to justify the latter's charge that
ours was "a one-party press in a two-party country," but that was a contributing and not the decisive factor. The final tally gave Eisenhower a landslide
victory: 35,585,316 votes to the governor's 26,031,322 (which translated
in the Electoral College to a vote of 457 to 73). Forty-one of the forty-
eight states were in the president's column, Stevenson carrying only seven
Southern states, not a single Northern one. Significant numbers of African
American voters, especially in the North and West, declared their allegiance
to the Republicans. In both houses of Congress, however, Democrats had
won a majority, making this only the second time in American history since
1848 that the president was confronted with a majority in both houses under
control of the opposite party. The bitter irony of that fact alone must have
mortified Adlai Stevenson.

Nonetheless, his concession speech had the grace, gallantry, and magna-
nimity the nation had become accustomed to over the arduous months of a
campaign it would gladly have seen shortened by half:

> I say to you, my dear and loyal friends, there are things more precious than
> political victory; there is the right to political contest. And who knows better
> how vigorous and alive it is than you who bear the fresh, painful wounds of
> battle.... We are ready for the test that we know history has set for us.... What
> unites us is deeper than what divides us—love of freedom, love of justice, love
> of peace. ...
>
> Now I bid you good night, with a full heart and a fervent prayer that we
> will meet again in the liberals' everlasting battle against ignorance, poverty,
> misery and war.
>
> As for me, let there be no tears. I lost an election but won a grandchild!

Eleanor wrote him the day after the returns had been tabulated, touching on the
heart of the matter: He had conducted "a magnificent fight. No one could have
done more, but the love affair between President Eisenhower and the American
people is too acute at the present for any changes evidently to occur." She hoped
he would "take a real rest and holiday," and if he happened to be in the vicinity
she hoped he would "come and see your very devoted friend and admirer."

She had given her all for Adlai and subsequently told several friends she hoped "she would not again have a candidate she wanted so badly to win that she felt she had to campaign for him day and night."[10] The price they both had paid at the gaming table of "practical politics" had played a significant part, though probably not a decisive one, in the election's outcome. Joe Lash concluded that "because she had been so heavily committed to the success of the Stevenson candidacy, she had failed to do justice to the urgency of the civil rights issue."[11] That conclusion seems inescapable—for them both.

Her column on November 9 betrayed her disappointment, verging on bitterness, at the election's outcome. Praising Adlai's message to the president in which he had wished him "all success in the years that lie ahead," there was a barb in her line:

All of us will pray for the President's health in the next four years,

Her next comment was uncharacteristically acidic:

Though one may doubt the wisdom of the people, we believe that the will of the people must be accepted and that it is always best to trust that in time the wisdom of the majority of the people will be greater and more dependable and those who are in the minority must accept their defeat with grace.

She would now return to her work with the American Association for the United Nations, following every move in that body "with keen interest, for [it] seems to me the one hope of restricting the passions of the world." Then comes a comment—possibly traceable to a conversation with Joe Lash—on what she called the major unresolved issue that was exposed during the campaign just concluded: civil rights. Only the collaboration of congressional Republicans and liberal Democrats would provide adequate pressure on Southern Democrats to achieve "any advance in civil rights in this country." Adlai's thinking was already moving along this same path.

*   *   *

Whatever the source—a peculiar alignment of the planets or a sudden release of pent-up libidinal energy that had so long been channeled on behalf of a political prize—in the latter weeks of 1956 and the early ones of the following year, the emotional lives of both principals of this story began, separately, to claim a greater share of their attention. Since her discovery in 1918 of Franklin's infidelity that marked the end of their physical relationship, Eleanor had sought out a particular person in whom to confide, on whom to lavish her enormous capacity to love, and with whom to fulfill her need to feel needed. Nancy Cook and Marion Dickerman, Lorena Hickok and Earl Miller had each in their turn experienced the privilege and the weight of her affection. Joe Lash himself had played that role for a time, had been "the one to whom she confessed...a shoulder on which to lean, the 'other' who, by the alchemy of psychic relationships, becomes the person who excites and encourages growth and intimacy." But he had found that role "only partially satisfactory."[12] He and Trude were well on their way to matrimony when ER had chosen him as her confidant, so when David Gurewitsch entered the picture his appearance had provided them a welcome impetus for a shift of emotional gears.

David was a tall and strikingly handsome man with an aristocratic bearing. Having been born (in Zurich) of Russian parents and spent his first seven years in Vitebsk, his native language was Russian. He attended medical school at Freiburg and Berlin, but with the rise of Hitler he transferred to Basel University in his native Switzerland. There he received his medical degree in 1933. Following a stint in an Israeli kibbutz, he accepted a fellowship at New York's Mt. Sinai Hospital in 1936 and in 1938 joined the staff of Columbia-Presbyterian Hospital's Rehabilitation Institute. There he spent the next thirty-five years as attending physician in physical medicine and clinical professor of rehabilitation medicine, specializing in patients with severely debilitating diseases such as cerebral palsy, multiple sclerosis, and stroke.

By late 1956, as Lash expressed it, "David had [Eleanor's] heart in a way the rest of us did not. Her love poured forth but...it was love for a man who was inaccessible."[13] Eighteen years his senior, ER had been introduced to David by one of his patients, Lash's wife, Trude. In December 1947, she had asked Eleanor's help in securing a seat for him on a plane to Geneva. He had contracted tuberculosis and was promised a place at a sanitarium in Davos, Switzerland. Eleanor herself was flying to Geneva for a meeting of the United Nations Human Rights Commission and arranged that she and David had adjacent seats. As ER discovered, he was debating with himself about seeking a divorce from his wife. From that time on he had been the recipient of what can only be called her strongly erotic affection, frequently writing him late at night after finishing her answers to the day's mail, as in this paragraph written only days after their flight:

> Don't ever worry about being a nuisance. I've always liked you and been drawn to you since we first met and the trip just made me sure that we could be friends. I never want to burden my young friends and with all my outward assurance, I still have some of my old shyness and insecurity left when it comes to close relationships and that is probably what makes you feel shy. I've really taken you into my heart however, so there need never be a question of bother again. You can know that anything I can do will always be a pleasure for me and being with you is a joy....My love and thoughts are always with you. E.R.[14]

But now, nine years later, David had shaken Eleanor's confidence to its roots when, following a theatre evening together, he had suggested they look in on a reception being held at the Museum of Modern Art. There he introduced ER to Edna Perkel, with whom he clearly was smitten. By spring their romance was ripening and Eleanor wrote him an agonized letter revealing her struggle with the emotional consequences for herself:

> David darling.
> I am writing this because I may not have the courage to say it all. I love you so dearly that you can hurt me more than anyone else....I've always known I couldn't mean much to you but suddenly I had to face how little I meant to you....If you can feel it in your heart now & then to want me a little & to ask for my presence it would help my self-respect. Otherwise I do all the asking, a beggar wanting & asking too much & therefore feeling ashamed.
> Forgive me, for your mere presence, a look, the sound of your voice means so much to me, it is ironic. E.R.[15]

Through these overwrought paragraphs echo ER's childhood feelings of abandonment whose periodic recurrence she experienced lifelong.

*   *   *

Adlai, meanwhile, was feeling his way into the shape of his new life as an "unsuccessful politician" (his description of himself as he accepted an honorary Doctor of Civil Law degree from Oxford in May). The post-Election let-down prompted some introspective moments. He had begun to feel that his headlong pace of the previous decade and more was at the expense of his own emotional wellbeing. Agnes Meyer had been suggesting as much before she invited both him and Eleanor to join 200 other guests for her 70th birthday party in Washington. The next morning she engaged him in what must clearly have been a frank and searching exchange about the place of romantic love, if any, in his life. Having been seated the night before, as she described it, between "my most wicked and gifted offspring" (her daughter Elizabeth) and "the seductive Mrs. David Bruce,"[16] wife of the U.S. ambassador to Great Britain, he may have been readier to listen to her advice than he had on previous occasions. At any rate, he wrote Eleanor a few days later saying "I have had a very personal and most helpful talk with Agnes Meyer following her birthday party. She said some things that made me want very much to see you if you can spare an hour alone some time."[17] That meeting was held at the end of January. A few days later ER wrote Anna: "I had quite a talk with Adlai the other day & readjustments are hard for men but I think he's going back to law & trying to do largely international work which should be good." That same day Adlai gave Agnes Meyer a report of his hour with

ER: "Homeward bound after satisfactory visit to N.Y. Also good visit with Eleanor....P.S. Eleanor admonished me to do nothing impetuous romantically, & I guess there is no likelihood anyway. But she was a dear and so very, very wise and comforting." Eleanor wanted Agnes Meyer to hear her side of the story and wrote she had had "an hour with Adlai. He was bothered by "the loneliness of his personal life" and the care of running a farm and a house "when he is not there most of the time." She had told him it would be folly to marry "just for the sake of being married!" She thought him "rather helpless and lost." She and Agnes would "just have to keep in touch with him as much as we possibly can."[18]

Some time in late January, the columnist Drew Pearson apparently started (or was it repeated?) a rumor that Adlai and Mary Lasker might be romantically involved.[19] Stevenson was frequently seen in public with glamorous women and speculation was not unusual. It nonetheless prompted an inquiry from his sister, "Buffie" Ives: "I keep hearing about my engagement and I am sure I don't know what the message you had referred to but I suppose it was Drew Pearson's story about Mary Lasker. Relax! I will let you know if anything is cooking."[20] A similar query from his psychiatrist friend Karl Menninger, who sounded delighted, drew this reply: "The news about Mary Lasker to which you refer is flattering in the extreme but highly exaggerated."[21]

He was still floundering when May arrived, writing plaintively to Mrs. Meyer following a visit:

> I think you are right that I've been so busy most of my life with impersonal things, and still am, that I'm not a very fit candidate for marriage and probably never was....But its not easy to wholly dismiss the idea of marriage as you enjoin me because I would make a bad husband when my best chance of being a proper person & of fulfillment is by love & marriage. I don't even have an *idea* about...the "integration of passion and reason within my personality," as you put it....But, madam! I protest that "mother's boy has in self-defense never loved anyone but himself." He has, he does, love, really love many people and very especially a great tutor, benefactor and comrade on this exciting, fearful, beautiful journey we call life....And someday could we talk of *you* instead of *me!!*[22]

Mrs. Meyer replied that, "of course," he should marry. "Eleanor and I only wanted it postponed until you were rested....Fear not—you will find the mate you deserve."[23]

*   *   *

From the moment his divorce from Ellen was finalized in December 1949, Adlai Stevenson was never without a multitude of women clamoring for his attention. He had everything many women would delight in: a quick, effer-vescent wit, courtly manners, a contagious spirit of bonhomie that warmed up a room the moment he entered it, a broad acquaintance with most of the world and its leading statesmen, and despite its traumas, a fundamentally optimistic outlook about the most stubborn conundrums confronting his generation and its successors. Perhaps most important of all, he invariably gave the person with whom he was speaking his undivided attention. John Bartlow Martin, though, remarks on a curious aspect of his relations with the important women in his life: "He was tender to those unattainable, and coolest to those close."[24] To illustrate his point he selects the manner in which Adlai advised Alicia Patterson (Guggenheim), with whom he main-tained one of the closest and longest of his relationships, about her own divorce that she was contemplating in the latter months of 1951. She had written him to tell that she was planning to divorce her husband, Harry Guggenheim. Adlai, Martin tells us, "a year or two earlier had thought of marrying Alicia, now he seemed downright alarmed that she might make it possible." He had been divorced and now was finding peace and serenity; he wanted peace and serenity for her but "advised against divorce."[25]

Martin seems not to connect that advice with the fact that at the time Adlai was deeply involved with Dorothy Fosdick, that they were even con-templating the possibility of marriage. And while it is true that most of his female "inner circle" were, indeed, "unattainable,"—(Alicia herself, Marietta Tree, Jane Dick)—Dorothy Fosdick was unencumbered by a spouse. She was sending him papers on U.S.-China relations, U.S.-Soviet relations, and other subjects of statecraft she knew concerned him, as well as love let-ters "at least once a week and sometimes oftener." They were also meeting frequently, for a weekend, three or four days, or a single twenty-four-hour period—in Washington D.C. and Springfield, Illinois. They spent four days together with Adlai's three boys at Southern Pines, North Carolina, with the obvious hope that she would "hit it off" with Adlai's sons. She had clearly displaced Alicia in Adlai's affections at the time. Porter McKeever attri-butes the cooling of Dorothy's ardor over the next year to Buffie Ives' "overt antagonism."[26] His sister's interference in his personal life at several periods was an embarrassment and a source of irritation for Adlai.

Agnes Meyer, by contrast, played a critical, though by no means roman-tic role in Adlai Stevenson's life. Whereas both Alicia and Dorothy were genuine amours, Agnes Meyer's interest in Adlai was primarily intellectual, though she too professed she loved him deeply. Introduced to him by fellow journalist Irving Dilliard, editorial page editor of the *St. Louis Post-Dispatch*, at Columbia University's Fourth Bicentennial celebration, she testified that she and Adlai "were instantaneous friends."[27] "We didn't talk politics at first; it was a very personal relationship." It was one that, from the start, observed accepted boundaries, which made it relatively easy for him to "let his hair down" with her. For her, "It was a beautiful and incredible friendship. It was harder than a love affair." The dominant tone of their relationship almost from the beginning resembled that of beloved psychiatric consultant to equally beloved patient. His letters to her are the most probing and self-revealing, with the possible exception of those to Alicia Patterson, that Adlai wrote. By contrast, hers to him frequently have a clinical tone: witness this one written in the summer of 1955 that began with her chiding him for saying, "I wish I had a stronger heart for the work ahead."

> Don't for a moment think that my recognition of who you really are and of the great human being God meant you to be, is feminine sentimentality.... Whether you are elected President or not, you are bound to become the nation's outstanding leader if only you can overcome a deep psychopathic fear of your own greatness and destiny. What the origins of this emotional block may be I do not know since I have never had a chance to talk it over with you, but ever since we had our only meeting, I have allowed the passionate and disinterested sympathy I feel for you to stream out towards you. For I realize that whatever my reason, my political training and my wide connections can do for you—all this is secondary to your own need for love and for a faith in you that is far stronger than your own.[28]

Adlai's answer evaded the personal issue Agnes Meyer had identified. She was wrong. It wasn't a psychopathic fear of his own "greatness and destiny" that made him hesitate to grab for the ring. It was his equal readiness to "see someone else, and I would hope a better man, undertake the task.... which is the restoration of public interest government."

As time went on, she was less hesitant about telling him he was "a mother's boy." "He never once mentioned his father to me," Mrs. Meyer told Martin—whom she also told that he was a poor prospect for marriage to anyone at all. "He was very self-centered," she said, "and that made him careless of other people's feelings. If he thought about it, he was the kindest man in the world. Consciously he never wanted to hurt anyone—but unconsciously he hurt Tom, Dick and Harry.... No one ever adored him more than I—and no one was more critical of him. He was one of the most lovable and loyal friends I ever had.... I miss him more than anyone."

This relatively sparse sampling of the voluminous "evidence" of Adlai Stevenson's attachments with three of the women to whom he was closest is included in this account to provide a context within which the friendship he enjoyed with Eleanor Roosevelt may be understood. In 1957 he was 57 years old. It was seven years since his wife Ellen had sued him for divorce. Though her mental instability eventually made divorce inevitable, Adlai lifelong appeared to blame himself for his marriage's "failure." The soul-searching that Agnes Meyer had urged upon him was prompted by her conviction that his ambivalence about marriage was possibly the greatest obstacle to his pursuing the prize for which destiny had chosen him. Yet at the same time she doubted that he could ever achieve a compatible alliance with a mate. She and Eleanor shared that conviction and periodically sought each other's counsel on the subject.

Eleanor and Adlai cared deeply for each other, but neither would have thought of the other in a romantic way; support for this assertion is present throughout the record. (It should suffice that he rarely felt comfortable enough to call her by her first name.) Of the period here under consideration, there was the moment when Adlai escorted Eleanor to the airport following her devastatingly skillful performance at the 1956 convention. A reporter asked Adlai whether he was not going to kiss Mrs. Roosevelt goodbye. Both principals were insulted and bristled with anger. To be sure, there were several occasions when a possible alliance between them was mentioned, but usually only in a half-serious tone. There was the letter from a constituent in 1952 who suggested that Adlai "should marry Mrs. Roosevelt and put [her] on the ticket for Vice-President and you will go over big." There was the press conference in which he was asked if he was going to marry Eleanor, and Adlai's response about "the lady sixteen years his senior" was quick: "Oh, she is much too young to consider me!" Finally, as Porter McKeever recalls, "In at least two public speeches where she was present, he humorously proposed marriage with such grace and obviously sincere affection that her delight shone through her laughter." He concludes, "It is an injustice to describe their friendship as a mother-son relationship; the dimensions of their love and respect for each other were infinite."[29] For this writer, the relationship, when carefully examined over the entire course of its sixteen years, most closely resembles that of a loving and devoted older sister with an equally doting and respectful younger brother.

CHAPTER 11

THE 1957 CIVIL RIGHTS BILL

FOLLOWING ELECTION DAY IN NOVEMBER, Eleanor and Adlai went their separate ways: he to renew his connections with several of his former law clients with interests in Africa (whence he was planning a trip for the following summer), she to return to her lecture circuit commitments for the Colston Leigh agency and her work for the American Association for the United Nations. There were only infrequent contacts between them over the next several months.

In early January President Eisenhower sent to Congress legislation that embodied what came to be called "the Eisenhower Doctrine." Introduced as a joint resolution (of House and Senate), it would have authorized the president to use U.S. forces "as he deems necessary to secure and protect the territorial integrity and political independence" of Middle Eastern nations "requesting such aid against overt armed aggression from any nation controlled by international communism." Under questioning from the press, Secretary of State Dulles admitted that "we did not discuss [the 'Eisenhower Doctrine'] with the British or the French" before adopting it. He warned that "long delay or a sharp division" in Congress over the resolution's import "would be quite disastrous." There was a note of desperation in the secretary's plea.

The request provoked a response from the Democratic Advisory Committee that had a Stevensonian timbre. On January 5, it called the proposal "an effort to partially close the stable door after the horse is partially outside the stable." It charged that the president had a responsibility to deal with "the root problems of the Middle East...the problems which Mr. Eisenhower has brushed aside....the problems of Suez and relations between Israel and the Arab states." It blamed the administration's "bullying of our allies and placation of our enemies" for eroding "our position until we have sided with Communist Russia against free Britain and free France and we have sided with dictator-controlled Egypt against free Israel." Stevenson himself said the president was asking "for another military blank check." Democrats said that the proposal "could be adopted only after thorough Congressional scrutiny and debate." The DAC, it was clear, could truly serve the useful purpose Adlai had envisaged for it during the years the Democrats were out of power.

By mid-February of the new year he was still feeling drained of energy; he wrote to T.S. Matthews, "All I want is sun and peace and solitude and all I get is cold and snow and clatter."[1] The year 1957 for Adlai was nonetheless noteworthy for two flattering gestures of recognition, one of which pleased him enormously while the other caused him considerable discomfort. Oxford University was the source of the first: an invitation to receive an Honorary Doctor of Civil Law degree at Jesus College. According to his friend Barbara Ward (Lady Jackson), the ceremony had all the medieval pomp one could possibly have wished for, though "he complained of his mortarboard. On his first official occasion, he had to raise it 193 times in thirty minutes. 'And,' he added, 'I have arthritic fingers.'" She continued:

> The great doors at the end of the arena...opened once and a cautious face looked in. Through the crack, we could see the distant figure of the Governor, gorgeous in scarlet, standing beside the Public Orator and surrounded by a bedlam of press photographers. This only added to the hush and decorum within. The great doors swung open, the Proctors righted about and stamped slowly back followed by the Governor, looking pale and moved, and the Public Orator. There was absolute silence until the procession reached the open space before the throne. Then the Public Orator read out the citation, very gracefully, savoring every phrase (and why not, for he wrote it) and then the Governor advanced and climbed the excessively abrupt steps to the throne. The Vice-Chancellor...raised his mortarboard, then grasped the Governor by the hand and declared him Doctor Honoris Causa.
>
> Thereafter a really very surprising thing happened—for Oxford at least. The assembled audience raised the roof. They clapped, they stamped, they banged the benches and the hurricane went on for at least two minutes. Many of the deans were visibly surprised—and as visibly delighted....It was a wonderful demonstration of affection and respect and, I believe, unique in Oxford, at least in these last cynical, unemotional decades.
>
> The Governor then lectured for nearly an hour [His subject was Anglo-American relations] and was listened to with deep attention....He won all hearts at the beginning by referring to the saying that Oxford is reputed to be the home of Lost Causes. Whom, then, could they more fitly distinguish than the man who was probably the world's greatest living exponent of the Lost Cause.

> At the end, the ovation was as warm as at the start—a test, indeed, after
> 55 minutes of oratory…And the demonstration was all the more remarkable
> in that 1957 is not, alas, a year in which America is much loved in Britain.
> The Oxford occasion turned into a reaffirmation of our deeper links and only
> the Governor could have achieved this.[2]

Stevenson was as elated as he was humbled by the Oxford celebration.
Shortly thereafter he wrote Carol Evans describing the dinner at All Souls
College. After an effusive number of toasts, he decided he could "keep silent
no more: I struggled to my giddy feet and mumbled through the wine that I
had dined with the great, near and far, but this was the first time that I had
dined with the Warden of St. Anthony, the Principal of All Souls, and the
Master of Jesus!"[3]

A month-long business trip to several African countries occupied most of
June, followed by visits with friends in Europe before returning to his law
office in Chicago.

*   *   *

The other gesture in Adlai's direction came from President Eisenhower
himself, delivered by his secretary of state, John Foster Dulles. Stevenson
had been closely involved with Dulles during the early days of the United
Nations Preparatory Commission meetings in London, so he knew a good
deal about the man's proclivities in the conduct of foreign affairs. He had,
in fact, written and spoken forcefully and on numerous occasions about
what he considered the secretary's essential incompetence as the nation's
chief administrative officer in charge of U.S. relations with the rest of the
world. Yet in late October Dulles approached him—clearly on orders from
the president—with an invitation to become a special assistant to the president to advise on U.S. policy at the forthcoming Summit Meeting of NATO
in Paris. Stevenson and Dulles met on October 30 to discuss a six-page
"secret" memorandum outlining Stevenson's responsibilities if he accepted
the assignment; the persons to whom he would report; and the staffs he
would have at his disposal from the State and Defense Departments and
the Atomic Energy Commission, and other such matters. "I hope that your
response will be affirmative," Dulles wrote Stevenson. "It would symbolize
at home and abroad solidarity with respect to a sector of our international
policy where, I think, there cannot be any serious difference of opinion."[4]

Stevenson decided to decline the offer on the grounds that he questioned
whether "this responsibility should be assumed or could be performed by an
'opposition' leader…as a temporary member of the Executive Branch, no
matter how highly placed." "The responsibility for formulating foreign policy

and position," he wrote, "is for the President to do.... But," he said, "I do not want to leave it there." He would be willing "to review and discuss your proposals from time to time before they are put into final form... to undertake to make... a journey as a special envoy of the President" in advance of the NATO meeting. "And where we are in agreement, I will do such 'missionary' work as I can and give such policies all the support, private, public and political, as I can, both here and abroad." Twenty-four hours later, he sent Dulles a four-page "Preliminary Memorandum RE: U.S. Position at North Atlantic Treaty Council Meeting in December 1957," setting forth his recommendations for a strong policy stance. It included three sentences that underscored a fundamental conviction about U.S. foreign policy that he also knew to be at odds with the Eisenhower-Dulles position: "Collective economic development programs in the retarded countries [are] a responsibility and mechanism of defense that is of equivalent or greater importance than military strength. The main threat is *not military aggression* [italics in original], but subversion by propaganda, economic bribery and political penetration. Have we any common plans to counter such ambiguous aggressions?"[5]

*   *   *

With this approach to U.S. relations with other countries Eleanor Roosevelt was in total accord. She would have recognized that, in stating so clearly a fundamental conviction about those relations that differed from the geopolitical calculations then driving U.S. foreign policy, Stevenson had articulated a basic foreign policy divide between the Republican and Democratic philosophies of international relations. Her concurrence with his position is nowhere more evident than in an exchange she had with the King of Morocco when she visited that country in March.

> I had felt since our arrival that there was on the part of the Moroccans a greater warmth toward the United States than in other Arab countries but perhaps I did not fully understand it until we had talked with the Sultan. This attitude of friendship went back to the time during World War II when Franklin and Prime Minister Winston Churchill met at Casablanca. The French officials then ruling Morocco paid them a formal call, and when they had departed Franklin said:
> "Now we must see the Sultan."
> Mr. Churchill looked at him without much enthusiasm.
> "Why should we do that?" he asked. "We have seen the French."
> "We must see the Sultan," my husband replied, "because this is his country."
> So Franklin [invited] the Crown Prince and members of the Sultan's household to dinner. The Sultan and Franklin talked with great enthusiasm

about what might be done to improve conditions in Morocco after the war. My husband...believed that proper methods could do much to restore the fertility of desert areas in Morocco.

"You will doubtless find oil in your desert," he told the Sultan. "But when you do you must never turn all the concessions over to any foreign country. Keep control of a part of the oil, for I feel sure there are underground rivers under the Sahara. Once this area was the bread basket of the Mediterranean. It can be again if you keep control of some of your oil and have the power to pump the water to the surface."

It was this that the Sultan was thinking about when he said my husband gave him disinterested advice that convinced him of the friendship of the United States. His attitude of helpfulness had become known everywhere in Morocco and many persons told me that the assurance of the friendship of the United States was a kind of milestone in the Moroccan campaign for independence.[6]

Once home from her African journey, Eleanor's preoccupation, aside from her writing and radio or television appearances and entertaining the many guests who came to see her at Val-Kill—"My mother-in-law once remarked that I liked to 'keep a hotel', and I...do when I am at Hyde Park"—was her organizing work for the American Association for the United Nations (AAUN). There were thirty chapters across the United States when she assumed that responsibility in 1953; by 1960, when she would relinquish her post, there would be nearly two hundred and fifty. To accommodate her travel schedule she divided her time between Hyde Park and her New York City apartment. Stevenson would drop in occasionally to see her when he was in the Big Apple. Eleanor describes one such occasion in which Adlai was involved. It was on a day

when I had a rather busy schedule, but I firmly announced that I was reserving "a few quiet moments" before dinner for a chat with an old friend, Lady Reading, who had just arrived from England. The day was not far along, however, before another old friend, former Governor Adlai Stevenson of Illinois, called me on the telephone. He had just returned from a trip to Africa.

"I wondered if it would be all right if I dropped by and had just a few minutes' quiet talk with you before dinner," he said.

Of course, I told him, I should be delighted to see him and he and Lady Reading arrived about the same time. We had hardly settled down in the living room when the doorbell rang.

There were two young men in the hallway. One of them was wearing a bathrobe—and obviously nothing else. He was staying in the apartment above mine while the owner was away and he had accidentally been locked out.

"Oh, I forgot! I left the water running in the bathtub and it will overflow and flood the floor."

Yes, I thought, and it will all come down through my apartment ceiling! At that moment Governor Stevenson came to the door, saying that he could no longer stand the suspense and wanted to know what was wrong. When I explained, he rose to the emergency by dashing down to the basement and turning all the knobs he could find in an effort to shut off the water for the entire building. Meantime I sent around the corner to get a locksmith. By the time he arrived Governor Stevenson had acknowledged a certain lack of success as a plumber, but the locksmith was able to open the door of the boy's apartment before we were flooded out. It was all rather amusing but it did interfere with my "few quiet minutes" with my guests....I don't usually have many quiet minutes in the day.[7]

One reason for that last-mentioned fact was the many boards of which she was a member and the seriousness with which she took those responsibilities. Abram Sachar, founding president of Brandeis University in Waltham, Massachusetts, recalled an incident that demonstrated her fidelity:

I'll never forget the time she came in about five minutes late. The board had already been in session, and she addressed the chairman of the board: "Do you need me for a quorum today?" And he said, "Well, not really, but we're always glad to welcome you, and we hope that you can stay." She said, "I'm due in Algeria tomorrow, and I have to get off very soon." She had come in from Minnesota in a storm. She was due in Africa the next day. But she came. This sense of responsibility never left her. She was a marvelous board member.[8]

* * *

Of interest to both Eleanor and Adlai was the passage in the U.S. Senate of the "Civil Rights Bill of 1957." The House of Representatives had passed HR 6127 earlier in the year. It was a remarkably comprehensive bill, its Title III providing for the elimination of racial discrimination in all places of public accommodation throughout the nation—hotels, parks, restaurants, trains, buses—protection of voting rights for all, jury trial for alleged violations, and even the use of federal troops when required to enforce federal laws. There was no possibility in 1957 of such a bill passing the U.S. Senate and no one knew that better than its majority leader, Senator Lyndon Baines Johnson. As shown in chapter 7, section II, the senator from Texas had presidential ambitions and during his nine years in the Senate he had always had an eye out for the main chance.

In mid-December Jim Rowe, one of his closest advisers, wrote him two long memoranda describing the strategic realities he faced: It would be "almost impossible" for him to be nominated for the presidency in 1960,

Rowe wrote, unless he could prove to the country that he was not just a Southern, a "sectional" leader (his current image) but a national one. "The only way to do that," Rowe continued, is "by passing civil rights legislation." Johnson had received similar advice from *Washington Post* publisher Phil Graham. As Doris Kearns Goodwin observes: "The issue of civil rights had created a crisis of legitimacy for both the Senate and the Democratic Party,"[9] one that demanded of Johnson a tactical maneuver.

He decided first to eviscerate HR 6127 by removing its core Title III altogether. (It would become the core of the Civil Rights Act of 1964, again under LBJ's leadership.) He then set about securing senators' assent to substituting clauses guaranteeing voting rights and jury trials. There was no visible shred of idealism in the game that Johnson parlayed to success. At the time, he was seen as fully sharing the racist prejudices of his fellow Southerners. He described to Doris Kearns (Goodwin) how he secured his colleagues' agreement to a bill that early in the year no member of the U.S. Senate, had they been asked, would have given the slightest chance of passage.[10] He successfully won the confidence of his fellow Southerners by assuring them, first, that a civil rights bill was an absolute must, given the public pressure for action that had been building since the *Brown* decision; second, that his bill—which was a substitute for the measure introduced the previous year—had removed Title III, which Johnson called "the notorious troops-in-the-South provision;" and, third, that his bill provided that any alleged violation of an individual's voting rights could be settled by a trial by jury—and who would doubt that a Southern jury would always deliver a just verdict? ("I was able to show the reasonable Southerners that some progress was necessary," he said, "and that as long as they trusted me the progress would be slow and easy."[11]) Western Senators, in return for their support, could count on the Southerners' votes to fund their priority project: construction of the Hell's Canyon dam, and Northerners would be elated that the bill contained a guarantee for all citizens' voting rights, including the rights of blacks. Thus did the "Master of the Senate" garner the necessary votes for the bill's passage.

Eleanor Roosevelt had been following the complex political maneuvering of the Southern senators whose antipathy toward civil rights was legendary and virulent. She shared the conviction of the NAACP and most other liberals that the bill the House had already passed (HR 6127) was a "dream bill." But she was also realist enough to know that such a measure would be filibustered to death if it ever reached the floor. Learning of Johnson's proposed substitute, she became uncertain; her ambivalence was clear in her August 6 *My Day* column. Her column may have been suggested by Adlai who, on landing in New York from his African trip, had immediately sought her out. "Adlai Stevenson came to see me Tuesday" (the 6th), she told Joe Lash. "The trip has convinced him that we have to move on civil rights. It is one of those difficult decisions in which you know that the way you are voting may possibly injure the objective you are trying to attain," but she had concluded that "the civil rights bill with the [jury] amendment would be a small step forward and I hope it will become law."[12]

Finally on August 7, now sure that he had the votes to pass his "sanitized" bill, Johnson called for the ayes and nays. The vote was overwhelming: 72 to 18. It was the first legislation in the field of civil rights in eighty-two years. That fact alone led the *New York Times* to call the measure "incomparably the most significant action of any Congress in this century."

Stevenson was asked at a "mammoth press conference" for his view of the legislation. He would have preferred a stronger bill, he said, but he supported this one. Eleanor's verdict revealed her irritation with the hypocrisy involved in this legislative "triumph." She all but dismissed its significance as pabulum in the context of the gathering storm over civil rights: She thought Johnson and Richard Russell (D-Georgia), with the Southern senators' support, had "won a costly victory—because this fight for civil rights is not going to stop." The ferment in the country mirrored a global unrest, and "our people are not going to be satisfied with crumbs such as this civil rights bill has given them...but better pass it and see what we can achieve with even this slight change." The Republicans, she thought, would "do nothing and then will try to use it as an issue in the next campaign. Vice-President Richard Nixon and Senator Johnson both are trying to fool the people, white and colored people alike. It will be interesting to see how far they succeed."[13]

All the same, the bill *was* a major triumph for Johnson. It firmly anchored his position as the upper chamber's preeminent power broker. More importantly, as the *Washington Post* editorialized, "Mr. Johnson came out of the debate a national rather than a regional figure," the ultimate and indispensable objective mentioned by Jim Rowe in those December communications.

There was, though, an even greater significance in the majority leader's achievement. Robert Caro explains,

The deal had created a new reality in the Senate of the United States. For two decades, the dominant reality in the Senate had been its control by a coalition of southerners and conservative Republicans. In January, 1957, that coalition had been "knocked into bits." The South had found itself isolated, without allies. But then Johnson had brought new allies to the South's side.

In place of the southern-Republican coalition there was a southern-western coalition now.[14]

Johnson had thereby unquestionably created the precondition for any future liberal legislation in the field of civil rights. Commenting on the significance of his accomplishment as he himself saw it, he said,

> The real story of the Civil Rights Act is that five states left the Confederacy voluntarily—the healthiest thing that could have happened to this country in years. The ultra-liberal position would have left eleven states solid—cut off from the rest of the country, dividing the Nation in an hour of peril. But now—by opening a division between those Southerners who have always been uncomfortable at the denial of so basic a right as the right to vote, and those who are determined from unshakeable habit and prejudice to stand against everything for the Negro, we have passed a bill and have bought for ourselves needed time—time to reconcile the North and the South so we can present a united front in 1960.[15]

Stevenson wrote Johnson to commend his "extraordinary management of our Democratic majority," saying only that "the bill as it appears to be emerging has merits which, happily, seem to be better perceived now from day to day."

President Eisenhower signed the bill on September 9.

* * *

Its impact was instantaneous. When schools opened on September 3, Governor Orval Faubus, in defiance of a federal court order, sent Arkansas National Guard troops to prevent nine Negro students from attending Little Rock's Central High School. Faubus until then had earned a somewhat shaky reputation as a moderate governor but had become convinced that the absence of national leadership spelled the end of moderation. He had, therefore, switched to the strategy of resistance advocated by other Southern governors in the name of "interposition" of state versus federal authority. Hours later President Eisenhower ordered 101st Airborne troops to the scene at Little Rock's Central High School. Asked for a statement on the governor's initiative, Stevenson said,

> At this point the President had no choice. The combination of lawless violence and the Governor's irresponsible behavior have created a crisis which Arkansas is powerless to meet. Federal force must in this situation be used to put down force.

But this is only a temporary solution. We have suffered a national disaster and I hope the President will now mobilize the nation's conscience as he has mobilized its arms.[16]

President Eisenhower now suggested that a conference of Southern governors be held to find a solution to the crisis, but confrontation had already taken center stage. It was the first scene in what later came to be called the Civil Rights Movement; some would call it the opening chapter of America's second revolution.

CHAPTER 12

THE ALLIANCE LOOSENS

STEVENSON'S BRIEF ASSISTANCE TO SECRETARY DULLES in the latter's preparations for the NATO heads of state meetings in Paris scheduled for January 1958 had a public and a private consequence. It kept alive his public image as one of his generation's preeminent statesman-diplomats, simultaneously rekindling interest among politicians and pundits in the possibility of his taking another run for the presidency. Not surprisingly, it seemed to renew in Adlai himself a willingness to entertain such thoughts again. John B. Oakes of the *New York Times* wrote, "Whether Mr. Stevenson still has any political ambitions is anybody's guess. He gazes at you with amazement if you put the question, and it is hard to imagine so sensitive a man who went through what he went through twice wanting to do it a third time. However, any experienced politician will tell you that the Presidential virus is harder to get rid of than the Asian flu."[1]

By this time he was certainly an "experienced politician" and had, indeed, been unable to wholly dismiss such ambition. But if the flame was to be kept alive, he must give no slightest inkling of such interest. Should another such opportunity present itself, he would handle it adeptly; he had accumulated enough experience of the booby traps and landmines that could surround a declaration of neutrality to be able to tiptoe among such obstacles without springing them. Meanwhile, his only defensible stance would be one of incredulity when anyone, such as Oakes, would query him point blank.

The same week a letter arrived from New Delhi, India. Written on stationery of the U.S. Educational Foundation, it must have warmed Stevenson's heart. Seyom Brown, a graduate student at the institution, wrote that Stevenson's 1952 and 1956 campaigns had been "an inspiration to a generation of young intellectuals," demonstrating that "political activity in a democracy can still be a noble pursuit." Brown's enthusiasm was shared by significant numbers of his peers worldwide.

On the CBS program "Face the Nation" on September 8, Stevenson was asked what he thought the major issues would be in the 1958 congressional elections. Echoing Mrs. Roosevelt's speech at the previous year's party convention,[2] Stevenson spoke first of the inextricability of domestic needs with foreign policy issues. He thought the world had begun to realize that "great wealth and great poverty can't exist safely side by side indefinitely," and that the revolution against want and the revolution against foreign domination called for "an international authority that would bring 'the have and the have not nations' together to create a more equitable balance between the two, very much as we did under the Marshall Plan."[3]

It was a theme he would return to time and again throughout his public service career: Military "assistance" is never an adequate substitute for—and frequently may be an obstacle to—the economic and social development that people everywhere long for... and deserve.

As 1957 neared its end, the mood of reverie it encouraged stirred reflective moments, as is evident in a letter to Agnes Meyer: He would thank his "maker" in this season of beginning "for giving me such a brilliant, exciting and comforting friend who, despite her tolerance of his "frailties," had nourished his self-respect. She and "Eleanor R (she waltzed gaily & lightly at a dance the other night!) [had] a way of unconsciously reminding me of my limitations!" Nonetheless he admired them both: "You are indestructibly youthful not just because you are always learning but because you are also always brave."[4]

Writing to her again, a week before his speech to the Americans for Democratic Action annual Roosevelt dinner, he said he thought he would "concentrate on 'the other war'—economic-political penetration. Here, of course, is both our best opportunity to *really* help and do something constructive and at the same time our greatest danger." He concluded, "I had a visit with Eleanor Roosevelt the other night and found her keener than ever. What extraordinary gals you are!"[5]

Here is a brief excerpt from his speech at the Roosevelt Day dinner on January 31:

> Nations which were unwilling to join us in military pacts have had relatively little economic assistance.... We should know that they can preserve freedom and contribute to world order only by fulfilling the aspirations of their peoples for human dignity and a tolerable standard of living. For that they need help—loans and credits mostly—and ultimately they are likely to take it where they can get it. ...
>
> The Communist bloc have a clear-cut strategy for dealing with the surging nationalism of the new nations—keep it aimed forever against their old colonial masters and by skillful penetration and subversion to gradually chain these decisive regions to their victorious chariot.... a bold, sustained Western economic development effort is just as imperative, just as urgent,

as missiles and nuclear weapons. Deterioration of economic standards and failure of hope is the classical recipe for unrest, disorder and final war. So let us take care not to lose the earth while we are trying to win the sky.[6]

* * *

Adlai and Eleanor both visited the Soviet Union in 1958. For both it was their second trip. Provoked by Sputnik (the Soviets' unmanned satellite that had successfully circumnavigated the globe the previous October), they both paid special attention to the Soviet system of education. The clearly implied challenge to U.S. education, particularly in the sciences, was a blow to American pride and for a time shook the nation out of its complacency.

Stevenson's observations were syndicated in newspapers before appearing in book form.[7] Major conclusions derived from what he saw and heard convinced him that the Soviets had abandoned their old assumption that capitalism would fight its way out of its "war" with socialism; that when Khrushchev had warned, "We will bury you," he meant by proving his system superior to capitalism's *without* war. Most importantly he said, "Moscow will be more likely to talk seriously if the Western alliance is vital and viable, the residual colonial problems being dealt with, and above all the free world making a concerted effort to unite the advanced and retarded areas in common economic enterprises."

Two weeks after his return, the media reported a major Eisenhower move to suspend U.S. nuclear bomb testing for two years provided the Soviets would agree to cease production of plutonium for military purposes. Though slightly more limited than Stevenson's original suggestion, it was widely seen as a vindication of his proposal that the president had originally labeled "a theatrical gesture."

Eleanor Roosevelt had been preparing herself for her second trip to the U.S.S.R. months before she and the Gurewitsches departed the United States. Alarmed by Sputnik's implications for the U.S. educational system, she devoted her May 24 *My Day* column to that topic. She lamented the shelving of a proposed federal aid to education bill and urged "the parents of the country" to register their protest "through every organization at their command" at Congress' attitude that arresting the deterioration of schools isn't "worth paying for." "If we do not pay for children in good schools," she warned, "then we are going to pay for them in prisons and mental hospitals."

In an early June speech at Michigan State University, Stevenson urged "the free nations" "to achieve a functioning, expanding free world trading system." ER supported his plea in her June 11 column, suggesting with her characteristic foresight that at the time U.S. representatives were negotiating for broader world trade, changing our own economy would require "retraining our people, bringing in new industries." Stevenson had suggested that declaration of "an international medical research and health year" would encourage such expansion. Eleanor wondered aloud: "Will the present Administration dare to accept these ideas from a Democratic leader or will it feel it must persist in doing nothing?" There was no evidence that the administration was listening.

Returning from her second trip to the Soviet Union, she, like Stevenson, was moved by that government's impressive record. In forty years illiteracy had been reduced from 90 percent to less than 10 percent. Modest but decent housing was now provided for a great portion of the populace, for 2 million in Moscow alone. Furthermore,

> The leaders of the Soviets can say to...the masses of people in Asia, Africa and parts of Latin America: "Our people were once hungry, too, not only for food but for health and education, for knowledge and for hope for the future. Look at what we have done in forty years. We can help you."

But she came back convinced, as was Stevenson before her, that (as he wrote) "Russia is not the largest question mark in America's future. It is number two. Our number one problem is China—and so is Russia's." Eleanor added to this: "Yet the only way we have found to cope with [China's] growing threat is to ignore their political existence, by which they lose face and feel bitterness, and to refuse to trade with them, by which we force them to build up their own ability to produce the very things they might buy from us, thus acting as a spur to their industrialization." The near-unanimity of perception of these two farsighted individuals is notable, though it failed to win the White House for Stevenson.

*   *   *

The year 1958 was a landmark period in Eleanor Roosevelt's interior life, though few people outside her closest circle would have recognized it as such. On February 23, David Gurewitsch and Edna Perkel became husband and wife. Eleanor had been doing her best over the previous year to make the emotional shift that change in status implied for herself as well as for Dr. Gurewitsch. It had not been easy but, realist that she was, she now extended herself to include them both in social events, and in separate notes to either of them, to mention the other with fondness. A note to "Edna dear" the day following the wedding set the tone:

> I have always loved doing anything I could for David and now I shall love doing anything I can for you both. I never want to be a burden, but it is a

great joy to me to feel close to the few people I really love and to be able to do anything for them. I need you both very much, but don't let me be a nuisance for David and you both need time alone in your own home.[8]

Eleanor Roosevelt seemed to require for her sense of personal security the presence in her life of a person (or persons) who would accept and affirm her unconditionally regardless of her shortcomings, and who shared her conviction that people who have been blessed by advantages—economic, social, educational—should give back to the society that afforded them those advantages. In her early married life in Hyde Park, Marion Dickerman and Nancy Cook filled that role for her, until Val-Kill Industries disbanded. Lorena Hickok appeared on her horizon shortly thereafter and that friendship was a long, deep, and stormy one. Joe Lash, then head of the American Student Union and later ER's biographer, from 1939 came to occupy a unique place in her affections. Twenty-five years her junior, he—and later his wife, Trude—lived in the White House at various periods, and then nearby her Hyde Park home, Val-Kill, as he became one of her closest confidants and advisers. (The Joseph Lash Papers, throughout which Eleanor Roosevelt figures prominently, fill more than fifty boxes at the Franklin D. Roosevelt Library at Hyde Park, New York.)

On April 12, 1959, after an emotional evening with Mrs. Roosevelt and sixteen family members and friends, Joe Lash wrote a poignant paragraph in his journal.[9] It read,

> I feel sorry for Mrs. R. I have felt all along that she turned to David because Trude and I were so often unavailable when she needed us in the postwar years or when she thought we ought to be there. While she recognized how hard her children made it for us [the Roosevelt children disapproved of their mother's relationship with this radical young man], she resented our building our own lives....I understood her need for someone like David, but I must say that being thrust aside for David was one of the hardest things to bear these past ten years....All the special things she did for us were stopped and done for David, often, of course, in our presence.

By summer ER and the Gurewitsches would be planning a joint purchase of the brownstone house at 55 East 74th Street (nine city blocks north of the two connecting houses her mother-in-law, Sara Delano Roosevelt, had built in 1907–1908 for herself and, three years after they were married, for Franklin and Eleanor.)[10] For her remaining years Eleanor would be "in a house with someone I know."

During the early months of 1958 she had begun to distance herself a bit from Adlai. It wasn't that she had lost confidence in his intellectual power: Of all the major actors on the international stage, he was someone she considered to have the broadest and deepest understanding of the currents running in world affairs. That conviction would guide her efforts in future months to secure him a position of major influence at the top of the nation's policymaking establishment. Nor did she allow her assessment of political reality to dampen her personal affection for Adlai and her delight in his company whenever they could manage an exchange of experiences and views.

But she had come to believe that he lacked the ability to communicate convincingly with the proverbial "man—and woman—in the street." She had, therefore, decided that if the "Presidential virus" once more came to possess him, he would fail again, and that for the good of the Democratic Party she was obliged to signal her convictions. The vehicle she chose was the *Saturday Evening Post* whose edition of March 8, 1958 carried an article, portions of which were later incorporated in her *Autobiography* in a section titled "On My Own." The following paragraph could not have pleased Adlai when he read it, knowing that some 350,000 other pairs of eyes had probably read it too. After describing his paying a call on her to ask whether she didn't think there were "others who would do better than [himself] as leader of our party," Eleanor stated bluntly that she knew of no one so supremely qualified as he. She then wrote,

> But I could tell there was some other question he really wanted to ask me. And finally he said, "Will you tell me something? You and Franklin had very much the same kind of background when you were growing up that I did. Yet both of you were always very much more at home in talking with the people than I am. What is it that makes this difference?"
>
> It seemed to me that Governor Stevenson, in his humility, had put his finger on a problem in his own political career. It was an intelligent kind of self-criticism that would never have been possible for most politicians.
>
> (The above and immediately following accounts are left out of the published edition of Mrs. Roosevelt's *Autobiography*.)

She then described how Franklin had grown up and lived in upstate New York's Dutchess County most of his life until he ran for governor of that state. He had ridden his pony "everywhere," come to know his family's neighbors and friends, and, when he got into politics, driven all over the state. "He listened to the people and, most important of all, he got the 'feel' of the people." Stevenson, she said, should do likewise: travel the various parts of the country, accompanied always by an individual who knew the local people, and staying "in each area until you can feel what they are feeling." Stevenson, she wrote, replied, " 'I don't know whether I can ever do that' " and, she wrote, "As it turned out, he didn't try."[11]

The term "egghead" had surfaced in the press during the 1952 election campaign. It was employed at the time by some mudslingers of the type that seem to besmirch most American political campaigns—prominently in that contest by Richard Nixon—to bolster the claim that Stevenson's speeches were too high-flown to be understood by ordinary folk The paragraph below can be understood in two ways: On the one hand, after close reading one might conclude—especially given the context furnished by the preceding account—that by subtle indirection, Mrs. Roosevelt is dissociating herself, however slightly, from the man who was "her" candidate only months earlier—and would be again. On the other, she is offering a defense of Stevenson's superior qualifications for the job of either president or secretary of state:

> I do not believe I qualify as an Egghead. I always remember the time when a young man made a study of American columnists for his college thesis and concluded that a reader should have at least 2 years of college to understand the columns of Walter Lippmann and Arthur Krock [two prominent writers whose columns appeared regularly in the *New York Times*.] But, he added, you need only a fifth-grade education to understand Mrs. Roosevelt's columns! So I am not an Egghead but I am in favor of Eggheads if that means the application of our best intellects to the problems of government. I believe most voters feel the same way....I don't believe the voters want their candidates to be dumb.[12]

As late as November, according to Joseph Lash's account of a social evening,

> Mrs. R. said she was minded to support Bill [William O.] Douglas, [Supreme Court Associate Justice] [for president] in '60 because he was the only one willing to speak to Americans frankly on China....On Adlai Mrs. R. came back to her fear that he did not communicate with people. She wanted him as Secretary of State. Anna said he was unable to make decisions. She told of going to him in 1956 along with Mrs. R. and Tom Finletter and Stevenson explained to them that he stayed up until 3 and 4 a.m. polishing his speeches. Mrs. R. counseled him gently, "Governor, not every speech has to be a Gettysburg address. It is more important what you say."[13]

The final shard of evidence of Eleanor's loosening her bond with Adlai Stevenson even as she drew tighter the bond with David and Edna is found on the dedication page of her (separately published) "On My Own." (It was omitted from the *Autobiography*.)

> Now that I near the end of my active life, I would like to dedicate this book to all those who have worked with me, one of whom [Malvina Thompson] is

no longer living, except as she lives in my memory. I am grateful to them and to my children for allowing me to live freely, and to my close friends. I list them here below in the hope that this book will bring them a few interesting hours.

> Malvina Thompson
> Maureen Corr
> Anna Roosevelt Halsted
> James Roosevelt
> Elliott Roosevelt
> Franklin D. Roosevelt, Jr.
> John A. Roosevelt
> David and Edna Gurewitsch
> Joe and Trude Lash

It seems noteworthy that the name of Adlai Stevenson was not included in this list. Whatever that omission's significance, and whatever the import of the other signs of ER's waning enthusiasm for his political prospects that have been examined in this chapter, he would not allow their friendship to be affected. On December 12 he penned ER a note:

> On the eve of another departure from Chicago, I am reminded that I shall miss you here next week. But I am going to see you in New York at the dance if I have to come disguised as a waiter. Love, Adlai

CHAPTER 13

END OF THE ALLIANCE

THE BY-ELECTION IN NOVEMBER 1958 gave the Democrats a nationwide sweep: 48 new House seats landed in the Democratic column, giving that party a margin of 281 to 154, while in the Senate the Democrats gained 15 new seats for a majority of 64 to 34 Republican seats. Democrats also took six new governorships.

On November 28, the Motion Picture Pioneers sponsored a dinner honoring two of their number, Robert S. Benjamin and Arthur B. Krim of United Artists. Harry Belafonte sang and Stevenson and Bob Hope were the two invited speakers. Adlai was in top form that evening. Beginning his talk[1] with a veiled allusion to the recent blacklisting of numerous Hollywood actors, directors, and producers, he wondered out loud "whether the word is 'pioneers' or 'survivors'" and recalled a previous occasion, a decade earlier, when he'd been invited to speak to this same group:

> You sandwiched me in between Jack Benny and Fred Allen [two stand-up comics of the period]. At that time I think it was Fred Allen who spoke first; and then it was my turn. I had to tell the simple truth that during dinner he was so exquisite when he spoke people stood on their chairs, threw their napkins in the air, hollered and shouted, and then the master of ceremonies said: "Now we have another speaker, Governor Stevenson of Illinois." And I got up and I said but the simple truth, that during dinner Mr. Allen had said to me: "What are you going to say?" and I said: "Well, I have prepared a manuscript," and he said: "Let me see it." "Gentlemen, you have just heard my manuscript. As far as his was concerned. I read it and I can't remember a word of it." And now you've done it to me again, and I'm getting suspicious.

He went on in this vein for twenty minutes or more before he reached the one serious note of his entire speech; it was a plea for "the international communion of the arts." Cultural exchanges, he said, "have been of enormous value to us."

I believe, like you, that if people can laugh together that is the first step, perhaps, toward living together. And certainly this is the most important unfinished business of the generation in which we live. I think it is time we all stopped shivering with fear about what is going to happen to us and started thinking about what we are going to make happen to us....All of us who are unafraid of translating goodwill into action can do much to bring to reality the golden promise of this century.

In mid-January, he delivered the first annual A. Powell Davies memorial lecture at Constitution Hall in Washington D.C. to an audience of 4,000 people.[2] The title of his address was "The Political Relevance of Moral Principle." The dynamism he had witnessed among the Russian people on his recent visit there and the contrast he felt on his return was still gnawing at his conscience. Such dynamism stood in sharp opposition to "our foolish languor."

Tyranny is the normal pattern of government. It is only by intense thought, by great effort, by burning idealism and unlimited sacrifice that freedom has prevailed as a system of government. And the efforts which were first necessary to create it are fully as necessary to sustain it in our own day.

Most of the major problems of our day present themselves in moral terms. [He proffered two instances.] At least five million families still live in squalid but remediable poverty. They depend, for remedies, upon the alert conscience of the majority....We shall have the drive...to wipe poverty out of this rich land only if the well-to-do majority of today does not repeat the selfish indifference which, in many communities has been the epitaph of yesterday's wealthy élite. [His other example was] the rights and status of our colored citizens. It is our major role to create a society in which all men can hold up their heads as equals...[and] resist in the core of their being the moral evil of treating any of God's children as essentially inferior.

In June he visited friends in England and then boarded the *Flying Clipper,* William Benton's 200' yacht, in the Mediterranean for a genuine vacation. On July 25, he sent ER a postcard from France. He had had "three idle weeks" on Bill Benton's "lovely yacht with Adlai and Nancy, Bill Benton's family and some friends—and all we've missed is you!" He thought he was now truly "relaxed at last, or perhaps 'decomposed' is a better word."

Eleanor was delighted. It had been some weeks since they were in touch. It was "very exciting" to hear from him and to know he was having a good time. She doubted, though, that she would be "the perfect addition" to his party, as she had "never had Franklin's [enjoyment] of the ocean even when it is fairly calm."[3]

As his cruise concluded, the BBC had scheduled an interview with Stevenson. Asked what he thought his contribution to his generation had been, Adlai replied, "I should like most to be remembered for having made some contribution to a higher level of political dialogue in the United States than I found when I came, at the top level." (That wish was freely granted by many following his death.) More succinctly, when asked what he would choose for his epitaph, he thought a moment and then said, "He disturbed the peace of his generation."

The year was marked by sporadic and increasingly insistent comment that Stevenson should run, would run, would need to be persuaded to run, and could not possibly win if he ran for president one more time. As we have seen, Eleanor had concluded after his 1956 defeat that he lacked the requisite "common touch" as well as "fire in the belly" for victory. During most of this year she would hold to that view and cling to the hope that he might serve as secretary of state in a future Democratic administration.

As summer doldrums gave way to autumn's increased tempo, the political jockeying for recognition and for public favor began likewise to increase. Senator John F. Kennedy was emerging as a "dark horse" presidential candidate. This did not please Eleanor Roosevelt. Ever since his equivocation, as she saw it, over Joseph McCarthy's destructive campaign against supposed "Communists in government," she had concluded that whenever principle and power were weighed in the balance, Kennedy would choose the path to power. With near-venom she had given vent to her feelings on ABC-TV the previous December, stating that although he had written a book, *Profiles in Courage*, she "would hesitate to place the difficult decisions that the next President will make with someone who understands what courage is and admires it but has not quite the independence to have it."[4] Joe Lash thought that "somewhere deep in her subconscious was an anti-Catholicism which was a part of her Protestant heritage."[5]

By November she had become convinced that Stevenson was the sole Democrat with the stature to do justice to the exalted position of president. She might have had second thoughts about his readiness for the office had she known of a dinner party Adlai hosted the month before. Porter McKeever tells the story:[6]

> Sekou Touré, the president of Guinea, was on an official visit and Adlai, as a consequence of his earlier contacts, ... invited the president and his party to a dinner at Libertyville. He called Viola, his cook, to tell her only that eighteen guests would arrive for dinner at six-thirty. Later he called back to say there would be twenty-eight and she should get some more food. She was making beef Stroganoff and decided it could be expanded by adding ham that she had on hand. Adlai was delayed at the office and the guests arrived before he did. When Viola answered the doorbell, she was confronted by a group of people in flowing robes. It was the night before Halloween, and thinking that they were trick-or-treaters, she passed around fruit, candy and peanuts, and shut the door. The doorbell rang again; this time a State Department escort

explained that these were the expected guests. With embarrassed warmth, Viola invited them in and asked for their hats, which, as Moslems, they were not prepared to part with. Shortly thereafter, Adlai rushed in with Bill Blair and Newt Minow, who has given this account of what happened next:

Touré said, "What a quaint American custom to serve guests nuts and apples at the door before dinner."... The next thing that went wrong was Mrs. Touré. I heard a scream—I looked around—her dress had fallen off. It was held up by one strap and the strap broke. She was naked to the waist.... She rushed to the bathroom. The Governor was trying to jolly everyone along. We went into dinner. There was a lot of excited conversation in French—I can't speak French. I heard somebody say something about pork. The question was: Is there any ham in the stew? The Gov (knowing Muslims can not eat pork) said, "Oh no—this is beef Stroganoff." Just then the girl from the State Department said, "Governor Stevenson, this ham is absolutely delicious."

At this point the doorbell rang. It was more trick-or-treat—real this time—Marshall Field and his kids came in flowing robes. Viola invited them in, thinking they were more guests. They joined the party. I tried to save the evening. There was a very good looking Negro who spoke English. I said to him, "You speak English beautifully." He looked at me and said, "Why not? I'm the United States Ambassador to Guinea."

On December 7, the Democratic Advisory Committee held a dinner at the Waldorf Astoria honoring Mrs. Roosevelt. There she and former president Harry Truman engaged in a reprise of their 1956 convention argument about the future of the Democratic Party. This time the focus was not on youth versus experience, but rather liberal versus the party power leaders' Democratic philosophy and conviction. As in 1956 at Chicago, Mr. Truman preceded the First Lady on the program. His remarks excoriated people he called "hothouse liberals," self-appointed purveyors of a form of liberalism that alienated voters within the party as well as outside and that "paved the way for reaction." The virulence of his remarks sent shock waves through the crowd; clearly his target was (still) Stevenson and the growing sentiment within much of the country that Adlai would be the Democratic Party's strongest and, therefore, logical candidate.

Eleanor Roosevelt, following, stood before the microphone smiling and announced that she was "going to differ with Mr. Truman a little bit tonight.. He doesn't like certain kinds of liberalism. I welcome every kind of liberal that begins to learn by coming into our party what it is to work on being a liberal." She said, older people in the party, like Mr. Truman and herself (they were both seventy-five, she pointed out), "have something to learn from liberals that are younger...because they may be conscious of new things that we have to learn." She hoped a Democrat would be elected in 1960, one who would "bring to the people of the world the thing they wish for most, which is peace and an opportunity to make life better...at home and abroad."[7]

A fortnight later, she wrote Anna: "At the dinner the Dem. Advisory Com. gave for me, Mr. Truman & I had 'a little difference' again. I thought I was gentle but the papers played it up. Adlai's speech seemed much more mature than any of the candidates."

The dominant theme of that speech had been that

> in the most radical and revolutionary epoch of man's history, the dominant concerns of our leadership have been almost wholly defensive.... Our foreign policy has been dominated by fear of communism, our domestic policy by fear of inflation. Economic assistance programs have been "sold" to the American people chiefly as a means of checking the communists, never as our creative part in extending our technological revolution to the rest of mankind.... Our sense of urgency is yet not sufficient to overrule our fears that... in spite of having a Gross National Product of almost $500 billion and a per capita income almost twice as high as any other country's, we are staring bankruptcy in the face.

It was a plea for courage, hard work, and the determination that "as science and technology bring the nations inescapably together, freedom, not tyranny, will be the organizing principle of the society of man."[8]

His tribute to ER was graceful and moving:

> How blessed we are that our beloved guest of honor is the representative by whom we are proudest to have posterity judge us—whether we deserve it or not!... There is a prophetic story told about her when she was five years old. While visiting Sorrento with her family, she went for a donkey ride (perhaps that was prophetic, too!). When she saw that the feet of the little boy who led her donkey were sore and tender she jumped off and put him on and walked home. From that day to this...she has walked with the less fortunate, and devoted her enormous talents and energies to working for justice, happiness and harmony for all humanity. ...
>
> I myself have seen people in the streets of Europe in the hard, cold, hungry days after the war doff their hats, bare their heads, and kneel, as she passed by.... Her courage has inspired us, her honesty and simplicity have humbled us, and her compassion has warmed the heart of the world.... We may safely predict at the age of seventy-five that she will never grow old, because, as the poet said, the wise never grow old; their minds are nursed by living by the bold light of day.[9]

CHAPTER 14

TRANSITION

THERE WAS A CODA TO STEVENSON'S RECITAL OF Eleanor Roosevelt's virtues in that after-dinner speech December 7 that caused the honoree's eyes to dance and the crowd to cheer. Nor was its political implication lost on any of the seven aspiring presidential candidates present. As Joe Lash tells it: "He recalled that in 1952 he had come to a similar rally in New York." Since he was insisting at that time that he was a candidate only for reelection as governor of Illinois and not for the Democratic presidential nomination, he had ducked the issue by proposing marriage to Mrs. FDR. Although she had not accepted him, he remained, he went on, "a patient man and still available."[1]

The key was still to remain aloof, above the battle that was already forming as Stevenson-for-President committees were beginning, independently of one another, to spring up across the country. Another flag in the wind caught the attention of a few alert reporters: William Attwood, the *LOOK* magazine editor who had accompanied Adlai on his 1953 trip through Europe, the Middle East, and Asia, had been granted a leave of absence from his magazine: "not to help him get the nomination but to help defeat Nixon," he said coyly.[2] It was as though a distant drumbeat had begun to be heard in the land. It would persist until it reached a crashing crescendo at the Democratic National Convention in July.

On January 18, Eleanor sent Adlai an urgent note about an issue they both considered their generation's most urgent responsibility, namely, nuclear testing. U.S. ambassador to the UN James J. Wadsworth[3] was that afternoon bound for Geneva and an international conference on the issue. Wadsworth, she reported, was "very discouraged" about his government's position on the issue. As a knowledgeable scientist—he later became President Kennedy's science adviser—he felt "very strongly that we must have a treaty now, even though it might not be a foolproof one." Research about safeguards was proceeding apace, which convinced him that "by the time [a treaty] was in operation we probably would have the technical advances which would make even underground testing secure." Writing that "polls show that 70% of our people want this," she urged Adlai to underscore the importance of such a treaty at the upcoming Americans for Democratic Action dinner.

Later on that month, an article by Stevenson appeared in the magazine *Foreign Affairs*,[4] in which he made precisely such a plea:

> Fear [between the United States and the U.S.S.R.] will not vanish until the arms race is arrested....The recent proposal by some of our leaders that the United States resume underground nuclear tests, just when the first break in the arms deadlock seems possible, shocked me....We should extend our test suspension so long as negotiations continue in good faith and Russia maintains a similar suspension....Conventional and nuclear suspension must go hand in hand...and...progress at each stage must be subject to effective international control....Meanwhile, pending the disarmament millennium, we must...make good the deficiencies in our defenses to keep at least an equality of strength with the Russians.

Syracuse University's Stuart Gerry Brown commended him on the piece, calling it "your own strongest foreign policy line."[5]

A plaintive letter to Agnes Meyer a few days later read, "Our beloved Eleanor was in San Francisco the same time I was speaking and then passed through here [Chicago]. Helen Benton reports she looked pale and tired at a party Elliott insisted on having for her when she should have had rest."[6]

Eleanor's acerbic *My Day* column for February 1 alluded to the concern she'd written him about several days earlier:

> I had the pleasure [at the Americans for Democratic Action dinner] of presenting the ADA citation to Adlai Stevenson, praising him for his foresight in his campaign four years ago when he asked that we negotiate to ban nuclear tests. The Republican standard bearer [Richard Nixon] in the coming presidential campaign called it "treasonable nonsense" at that time, but it has become part of his own party's program. He will probably be praising the work that his party has begun to do and, with his usual facility, he will forget that he ever opposed it or that Adlai Stevenson advocated it in the campaign four years ago and was given a citation because of his foresight. Mr. Nixon never has anything but hindsight.

Stevenson had cleared his calendar of all commitments for the three weeks ending March 16 for "a self-education trip" to Latin America. It was the one remaining part of the world he had visited only cursorily until now. To absent himself from the charade he'd chosen to play during the months leading up to the 1960 convention also seemed a prudent decision. Before departing, however, he decided to seek another meeting with

Eleanor. She knew him well enough to suspect his mission: she summoned David and Edna for the hour Adlai would arrive. "He's really coming," she told Edna, "in the hope that I will persuade him to run for President. I will not persuade him. I believe that anyone who needs to be urged should not run."[7] She would maintain her hands-off position on his "non-candidacy" for most of the first five months of this election year, even as Stevenson-for-President committees continued to mushroom in state after state and, unbeknownst to Adlai, a secret national "draft" office was opened in the nation's capital. It was directed by Oklahoma senator Mike Monroney and Adlai's good friend and former law partner George Ball. A month before the convention itself, that professionally conducted campaign would merge with the wholly volunteer movement to produce a monumental presence at the convention.

Her attention now fixed on the forthcoming battle for the presidential nomination. Eleanor wrote Adlai in March, suggesting that he appear on her "Prospects of Mankind" program originating from the Brandeis University campus. "I realize the pressures you are under just now," she wrote, "but I am most anxious that your ideas be given full expression on this program which reaches a different, more specialized audience than the usual commercial television channels." He would appear on her last such program of the season on June 5.

Her My Day columns, appearing, at the time, five days a week in fifty papers throughout the country, for the remainder of June and early July became an engine of the draft campaign. Her July 5 column commented, "It seems obvious to me that more and more people are joining the bandwagon for Stevenson"; next day, "A Stevenson-Kennedy ticket, with the men they would draw around them, would give confidence to the world in a way that no other ticket I can think of would do." On July 7, though, she said flatly that she was "not coming out for any candidate until the national convention." It was a vow she would break only a few days later. Aware that this would be Adlai's—as well as her own—"last hurrah," she was acting a bit erratically as the convention date approached.

A week following the Eleanor–Adlai "Prospects" program, Joe Lash noted in his diary that he and his wife Trude

> had dinner alone with Mrs. R after she came down from H[yde] P[ark]. Sam and Dorothy Rosenman, the Morgenthaus, [Isidore] Lubins and Averell Harriman there ... tried to smoke her out on a presidential candidate. ... She refused to be drawn out. Dorothy Rosenman then said that women stuck to Adlai. ... they either wanted to marry or protect him. Wasn't Mrs. R's attitude the protective one? No, she replied, he did not interest her at all as a woman, that it was his mind that interested her.[8]

Whether as a result of Stevenson's comments during that June 5 "Prospects" program, or a post-program conversation, Mrs. Roosevelt decided there was simply no candidate within Democratic Party ranks who could provide the caliber of leadership of Adlai Stevenson. Despite her June 7 statement about withholding her decision on a candidate, on June 10 she called a press conference to announce she could stay silent no longer. The precipitating reason, she said, was the breakdown of the heads of state summit conference at Paris. That conference, scheduled for May 5, was summarily scuttled by Premier Khrushchev after the Soviets downed a U-2 spy plane over interior Russia. President Eisenhower had first declared that the plane was a weather research aircraft that had mistakenly trespassed Soviet air space. Khrushchev angrily countered that its pilot, Francis Gary Powers, had been captured and had confessed that he was engaged in photographic espionage. Photographs of Powers and his plane's sophisticated equipment were sent over the international wire services to prove the point. Eisenhower nonetheless once more equivocated about the program Powers was a part of, conceding the truth only after the world had concluded that the U.S. president was lying.

Alarmed at this development, Mrs. Roosevelt reversed her previous determination to endorse no candidate until the convention.[9] She was concerned that Kennedy, in addition to having prevaricated about Joseph McCarthy, lacked Stevenson's experience in international affairs. This was simply too dangerous a world for the president of the United States to be a man without extensive international experience and knowledge. She admitted the Massachusetts senator was currently the clear front-runner, but her mail, she said, was practically unanimous that "the position in the world now requires maturity, it requires experience, and the only man meeting the requirements since the failure of the Summit is Adlai E. Stevenson." She hoped Kennedy would accept the vice presidential nomination on a Stevenson-Kennedy ticket.[10]

Her endorsement served to loosen Adlai's hold on his neutral posture. Writing her the same day, he averred that her initiative had left him "a little shaken...but more of that later." A letter from Mary Lasker had raised another concern: namely that Mrs. Roosevelt was not planning to go to the convention. "While I doubt very much if I become involved out there," he wrote, "I would think as a Democrat that your presence is important, symbolically and actually. Moreover, I hope you will reconsider and plan to be there."

He was suddenly reenergized by her change of heart. At the same time, however, he felt hobbled by a statement he had made following his defeat in 1956 indicating that he would not again seek the office of presidency. Porter McKeever reports that "He came under increasing pressure, if not to declare himself, then to seek support quietly from key leaders in key delegations.

Pressed by Finletter to make a direct bid, with uncharacteristic petulance he replied, '*You* made me put out that damned statement. . . . And now you want me to break my word.' "[11]

He felt "heisted by his own petard," knowing full well that the media would revel in the red meat his reversing himself would give them if he now acted on Finletter's advice. He would keep to his aloof posture, hard as it was to do so. But over the next month he was constantly tempted to abandon that role.

Eleanor increased the pressure, three days following her press conference, with a follow-up statement noting that two leading intellectual leaders, Henry Steele Commager and Arthur Schlesinger, Jr., having apparently concluded—she felt prematurely—that Stevenson would not "grasp the nettle," had begun to work for Kennedy's nomination. National Chairman Paul Butler, she wrote, was apparently equally confused. She had, therefore, asked Stevenson to clarify his position and he had responded.

I quote his statement here:

> I have, as you know, taken no part in Presidential politics for the past three years. And I do not now intend to try to influence the nomination in any way by "endorsing" anyone or trying to "stop" anyone, or by seeking it myself.
>
> I have not made and will not make any "deals" with anyone. I am not, as you recognize in your statement, a "declared candidate." This leaves only the question, again in your terms, of "shirking public responsibility."
>
> I have declined repeatedly to comment on questions about a "draft." I think I have made it clear in my public life, however, that I will serve my country and my party whenever called upon.

Her statement continued:

> From this statement I think you will find it clear that he is a candidate, since there is a sizeable number of people who are asking him to accept the responsibility of being the candidate for the Democratic Party in the next Convention. . . . I stress again his words: "I think I have made it clear in my public life, however, that I would serve my country and my party whenever called upon."[12]

He wrote her that same day, June 13:

> I am anxious about your reaction to my statement that "I am not a candidate." Obviously this is what I had to say, because it is true, and to be consistent with all I have said for the past three and a half years—i.e., that I will not seek the nomination at the convention. I suppose the confusion arises over availability to serve if called upon and being a candidate, which means to seek, if my understanding of the word is correct. I do not want people to feel I have altered my position of not seeking and yet readiness to serve if called upon.

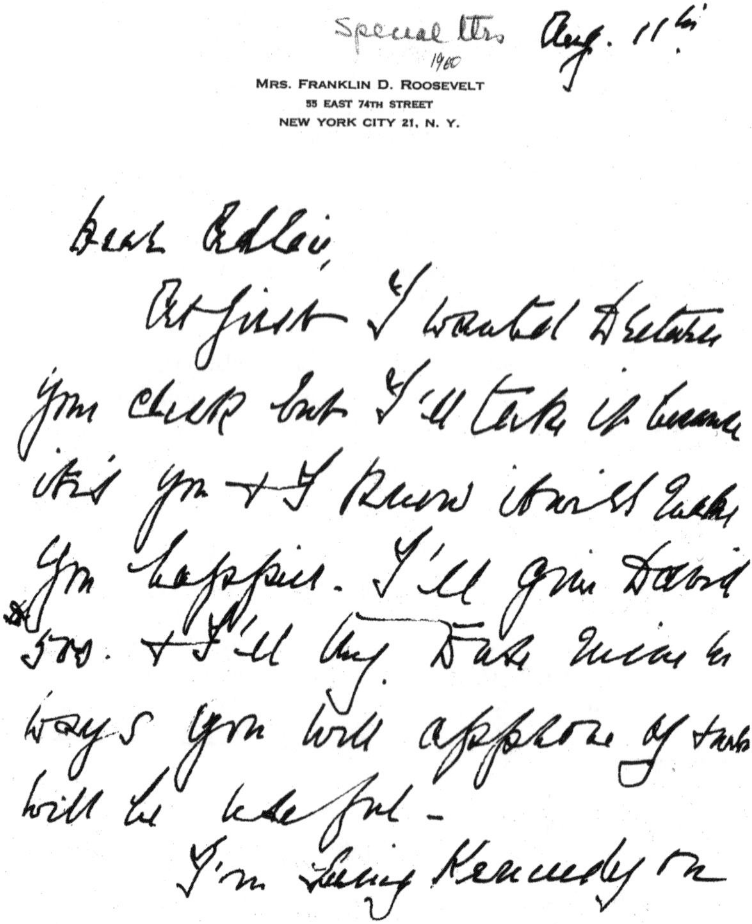

Special ltrs
1960
Aug. 11th

MRS. FRANKLIN D. ROOSEVELT
55 EAST 74TH STREET
NEW YORK CITY 21, N. Y.

Dear Adlai,
At first I wanted to return your check but I'll take it because it's you & I know it will make you happier. I'll give David $500. & I'll buy [illegible] in ways you will approve of that will be useful –
I'm leaving Kennedy on

"Unfortunately my handwriting is so bad these days that nobody can read it"

He ended saying that this was a communication "not for the public eye" and signed off "With all my thanks and much love, Yours, Adlai."[13] His euphoria extended over another week, addressing a brief note to her on the 18th as "Dear Eleanor"—a radical departure from the formal "Dear Mrs. Roosevelt" that had been his habit from the time they met fourteen years earlier. (He recovered his composure the next day and returned to the more formal "Mrs. Roosevelt.") A *New York Times* headline June 13 trumpeted, "Stevenson: Not Candidate. Mrs. Roosevelt: Yes, He Is."

She now saw that her activity on Adlai's behalf had torpedoed her earlier decision not to attend the convention. "Politics are very active," she wrote

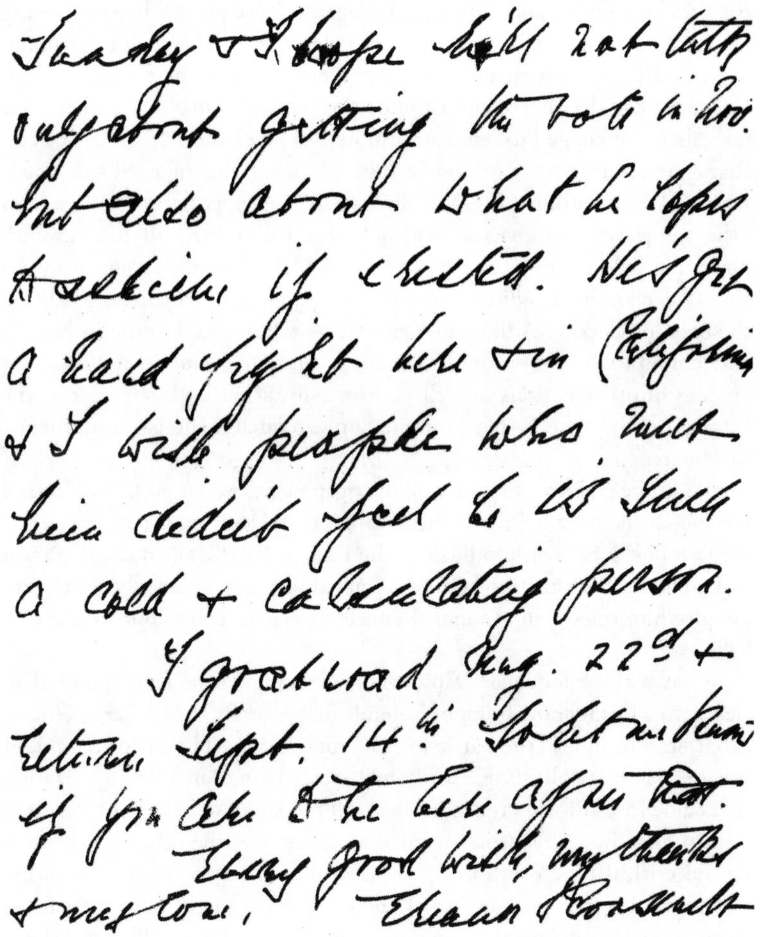
Tuesday & I hope he'll not talk only about getting the vote in Nov. but also about what he hopes to achieve if elected. He's got a hard fight here & in California & I wish people who meet him didn't feel he is such a cold & calculating person.
I go abroad Aug. 22d & return Sept. 14th. Do let me know if you are to be here after that.
Every good wish, my thanks & my love,
Eleanor Roosevelt

Anna, "because I decided to come out for Stevenson & now I have to go out to the convention."[14] She wasn't looking forward to the battle she knew would have to be fought there.

* * *

July 11 was a Monday. Though the convention proper would not officially begin until Chairman Rayburn banged his gavel at 5:00 p.m. that afternoon, State delegations and party committees had meetings scheduled for the previous Friday and Saturday. Delegates consequently began arriving at Los Angeles hotels as early as Thursday the 7th. To avoid dramatizing her difference with her sons who were working for Kennedy, Mrs. Roosevelt had decided to come to Los Angeles on Sunday. Once there, she nonetheless managed to replicate almost 100 percent the frenzied activity that characterized her work on Stevenson's behalf during the Democratic National Convention of 1956. She urged governors, labor leaders, and other political operatives to withhold endorsing JFK till the eleventh hour; she held a press conference at which she hoped Stevenson might finally declare his candidacy; she visited eleven state caucuses to talk up the case for electing Adlai and Kennedy as a team, explaining in her *My Day* column why they would reassure not just the American public but citizens of other nations as well. At the convention itself she gave a stirring seconding speech that prompted an extended demonstration for her candidate.

But in the end it was to no avail. Delegates gave Stevenson himself one of the longest and most boisterous demonstrations in Democratic Party history—given, at that, for a "non-candidate"; John Bartlow Martin said it lasted "almost half an hour." But that was "what delegates always give a man when they cannot give him votes—an ovation." Kennedy swept the convention on the first ballot.

What really happened? Why, when so many of the signs pointed so clearly to a Democratic upset of Republican power in November 1960, did Adlai Stevenson lose the battle for the nomination? The major reason, of course, was that John F. Kennedy had created a nationwide organization that came to California that summer well prepared to deliver the nomination to him. But Stevenson's studied aloofness was the other. There were several critical junctures during the two days prior to the actual voting when even his slightest gesture of encouragement might have sufficed to create a nearly unstoppable juggernaut for his candidacy. The questions, however, were: Would he make the move? Would he accept the fact that support for him was so strong that a refusal to respond accordingly would be tantamount to scorn of the public will?

One need not review the entire drama that unfolded over that fateful week,[15] just two emotional outbursts from two of Stevenson's most ardent supporters convey the temper and mood of the thousands who had become involved in his extraordinary movement for "a new America." Sunday night Pennsylvania governor David L. Lawrence, who held Stevenson in highest regard, invited him to meet with a half dozen of the Pennsylvania delegates. Lawrence hoped to hear from Adlai that he was now, indeed, willing to declare himself a candidate. Russell Hemenway, who as one of the leaders in the "draft" movement was present, reported that if Adlai refused,

> in the morning he [Lawrence] was appearing on the *Today Show*... to tell the world Pennsylvania was going for Jack Kennedy. And Adlai said to Lawrence: "Do what you have to do, Dave."
> And Bill Wirtz who was there, asked Adlai, "Governor, are you sure that's the message you want to give Governor Lawrence?" And Adlai said it was.
> Christ, Adlai could've said anything but that and he would've stopped Pennsylvania from going to Kennedy. David Lawrence was the ace in the hole and we let him go. You know something? That might have been a watershed in American history. Think of it! No Vietnam War![16]

Another occasion when Adlai might have changed the convention's outcome came on Tuesday night when he decided to attend as a "non-candidate" Illinois delegate. The draft committee had everything arranged for a huge demonstration. Stevenson was surrounded as he entered the arena and had to force his way to the rostrum. Once there, he delivered a body blow to his own cause: "After going back and forth through the Biltmore today, I know who's going to be the nominee of this convention—the last man to survive." Agnes Meyer, a prime mover in planning that event, recalled what happened next:

> We had worked so hard for the nomination. He came in on the floor. Mrs. Roosevelt and I sat there—we and [Tom] Finletter had worked for the demonstration—we had the applause there—but then he went up on the platform and throws [*sic*] it out the window. He could have swept that Convention. I could have murdered him....I could see Bobby [Kennedy] running around on the floor trying to hold his delegates. Either he [Stevenson] should have had a decent speech ready or stepped off the floor. He should have told us he wouldn't fight. He always wanted to be President but he was not willing to fight for it.[17]
> [Anna] Rosenberg remembered seeing Mrs. Roosevelt "standing with Senator [A.S. Mike] Monroney and the tears were falling down her face when she realized that it wasn't going to be Stevenson."[18]

He had taken to its farthest extremity the point of principle—namely, that no mere mortal should be so arrogant as to "seek" the power inherent in the office of the U.S. presidency. But the nationwide acclaim, attested by the spontaneous emergence in nearly every state of "Stevenson-for-President" committees; the more than a million signatures on petitions urging him to announce; and now the tremendous outpouring of enthusiasm and affection of delegates from all across the country—these, combined with the unprecedented admiration that had greeted him wherever he went in his travels abroad (and this at a time when Vice President Richard Nixon, visiting Venezuela, was the target of a violent, rock-throwing crowd that forced him to flee the country), should certainly have been interpreted by the man himself as the near-universal approval it, in fact, was? Yet he would not find within himself the strength—or was it the will?—to bow and say, "Here am I. Send me."

Or was Stevenson's actual objective all along—whether he acknowledged it to himself or not—the office of secretary of state? He did, after all, see himself far more as a statesman than as a politician. A definitive answer to this question will likely forever elude us. According to Elliott Roosevelt's rather melodramatic verdict, what was nonetheless "tormentingly clear" was that

> the out-of-hand rejection of Adlai...was her defeat, too. The influence she exercised as a public figure...counted for nothing now in the party she had served all her adult life. Her pleas had gone unheard. She had put her heart and soul into a fight for Stevenson, and she had lost. She could dream no longer of ushering into the White House the one man she trusted completely to hold to the course set by Father and, in his image, continue striving to build a braver America and a more hopeful world. She realized at last that she was growing too old to carry the standard of FDR.[19]

* * *

It was a somewhat premature pronouncement on his mother's political demise, but she did leave Los Angeles the day after the decisive vote, angry and disheartened. She was still uneasy about Kennedy and not at all pleased with the role she had played over the past few days. She was furious with Adlai. His refusal to fight for the nomination when she herself had gone all out for him had left her in an untenable position. Moreover she had probably deepened the gulf between herself and the new party standard bearer, thereby damaging Adlai's chances for the secretary of state position. Did that not mean, as Elliott thought, that her influence in party politics had been dealt a mortal blow at this pivotal moment in world affairs? Asked for a meeting, she told Kennedy that he had enough to worry about without bothering to see her, but that if he insisted, her son Franklin Jr. would handle any future communication between them.

Stevenson himself had helped create the rift that now yawned between himself and the party's new titular head. In May the two men had met at Stevenson's Libertyville farm but the session had not gone well. Kennedy came away feeling that Adlai was not forthcoming or frank about his plans, while "the Gov," according to Arthur Schlesinger, saw Kennedy as "a young man pushing too hard who should await his turn."[20]

From the senator's earliest expression of his presidential ambition, Stevenson felt he had met Kennedy's expectations more than half way. He had unburdened himself to Arthur Schlesinger in early June: He had "always felt in a way responsible for Jack's recent political progress." As evidence he pointed to his having asked Jack to be his vice presidential candidate in 1956—"or at least I wanted him to have every chance to be my vice-presidential candidate," his asking Jack to nominate him. In short he felt he had "launched him on the national scene" and "with all this in mind, I have found the talk from his camp, albeit not from him, quite aggravating."[21]

That perception persisted up to and during the convention. Then came the final blows. Kennedy was incensed by Stevenson's refusal to call off his supporters when it became crystal clear that he could not be nominated. When he also refused the senator's request to give the nominating speech for him as turnabout for the same favor he had bestowed on the governor four years earlier, that was the final straw: The stage was set for difficult dialogue between the two men even before the curtain rang down on the convention on July 15.

They met at the Kennedy compound in Hyannis Port a fortnight later, he wrote Eleanor, for "a long and frequently interrupted talk." (His pique was still showing.)

> He wanted suggestions on how to meet the youth and inexperience charge and asked me to campaign for him which I will do, of course, if not as much as his managers may want. There was no hint of his plans about the State Department and I said nothing. . . . His interest and concentration seemed to be on organization not ideas at this stage, which I suppose is proper.

She wrote back that she would be "seeing Kennedy on Sunday and I hope he'll not talk only about getting the vote in November, but also about what he hopes to achieve if elected. He's got a hard fight here and in California & I wish people who meet him didn't feel he is such a cold and calculating person."

Kennedy had gently but persistently pursued ER till she finally granted an interview at her Val-Kill cottage. The day before their meeting, a beloved grandchild, the John Roosevelts' daughter Sally, was killed in a riding accident. Kennedy suggested postponing the visit, but she told him to come. She wrote Trude and Joe Lash, "I can hardly realize that I'll never see her run into the house or ride by again." The successful candidate would come with the determination not just to disabuse his hostess of her negative opinion of his courage, but to secure her active collaboration in his campaign. He wanted her to join New York's senior senator Herbert Lehman as honorary co-chair of the New York State organization, to write a *My Day* column setting out her reasons for endorsing him, and, if her energy held, to do as many speeches on his behalf as possible.

Having succeeded in achieving the entirely private tête-à-tête each had hoped for—and each was uneasy about—they emerged after an hour's talk, wreathed in smiles. The senator had apparently put to rest any doubts—and there were many—she had been harboring. Or so it appeared as the cameras flashed and the two kept smiling. But appearances were deceiving. When they joined the small family group in the next room who during the hour had been hosting Pierre Salinger (later JFK's press secretary) and Bill Walton (manager of Kennedy's New York City campaign), Mrs. Roosevelt reviewed briefly the gist of her discussion with Kennedy before bringing her hearers up short with a comment: "I have come to believe Governor Stevenson does not have some of the characteristics I thought he had."[22] Though she may already have confided in the Gurewitsches and the Lashes, her comment took the others aback. Till that moment she had shared her doubts only with her most intimate circle.

Later that day she reported to Stevenson by phone the substance of the hour's exchange. Her notes about that call,[23] which she sent to Ruth Field, record the following:

> I did not ask the Senator for any definite promise as I felt this would be almost impossible. But I told him that he needed the Stevenson votes in New York and California and that he had to carry these two states or he would be in trouble because he probably could not hold the solid South....I felt that he had to prove by...appearing on the same platforms, and perhaps by references and quotation, that there was close cooperation....He agreed and said he would try to do this....
>
> He said he thought Adlai was the best man for the Secretary of State post....
>
> I have no promises from him, but I have the distinct feeling that he is planning to work closely with Adlai...

As per her agreement with Kennedy, her August 17 column glowed with flattering comments about her erstwhile thorny acquaintance, even while she continued to press Adlai's case: She felt it important that the two men "should have a good relationship...thereby demonstrating that they could work well together in the future—even though Mr. Stevenson has a more judicial and reflective type of mind." She was "pleased to learn that the Senator already had made plans along these lines."

That, though, was as much water as she would publicly commit to carrying for "the Gov." Her disillusionment over his behavior in Los Angeles was deep and there seems little question that convention week had shaken her confidence in herself as well as in him. But she would "soldier on." Her August 17 column continued:

> I think Senator Kennedy is anxious to learn. I think he is hospitable to new ideas. He is hard-headed. He calculates the political effect of every move. I left my conversation with him feeling that here was a man who wants to

leave a record of not only having helped his countrymen, but having helped humanity as a whole....After [the] visit I telephoned my acceptance to serve with Mr. [Herbert] Lehman, [New York senior senator] as honorary chairman of the Democratic Citizens Committee of New York...for I have come to the conclusion that the people will have in John F. Kennedy, if he is elected, a good President.

It may have seemed to many an abrupt, almost impulsive transfer of loyalty. But Eleanor Roosevelt was one of her generation's most sophisticated and—contrary to the convictions of some—least sentimental politicians on the American stage. Her friend Adlai had, to all intents and purposes, refused the crown when his party had offered it to him. It was a cause for which she had risked her own credibility, yet to no avail. There was nothing for it but to accept the fact that he would never fulfill the extravagant hopes she had nurtured for him ever since those long-ago days in London when they were laboring side by side to bring the fledgling United Nations to birth.

That emphatically did not mean that she would allow her disappointment to undermine her conviction that his voice should have a prominent role in the new administration she expected to take the reins of power in January. If Adlai couldn't bring himself to claim the power he had clearly been offered, such diffidence would surely not inhibit his aggressive reach for the position of secretary of state. She would now do what she could to aid and abet that cause.

Unlike Stevenson, Kennedy had shown himself amply endowed with the one indispensable quality a successful politician requires. As Richard Reeves has written, he "had shown that the most important qualification for the most powerful job in the world was wanting it. When he was asked early in the [1960] campaign why he thought he was qualified to be President, he answered: 'I look around me at the others in the race, and I say to myself, Well, if they think they can do it, why not me? That's the answer. And I think it's enough.'"[24]

At this juncture it was *not* enough for Eleanor Roosevelt. The young contender would still have to prove himself in her eyes. But she had been reassured by his responses to her hard questions over the previous hour. And he had demonstrated considerable political skills prior to Los Angeles on the campaign trail. She would throw in her lot with the young Massachusetts senator and keep her eyes open.

PART III

CHAPTER 1

ELEANOR, ADLAI, AND J.F.K.

A TRIP TO FAVORITE EUROPEAN HAUNTS—museums, restaurants, inspiring natural scenes—with people she loved was a tried and true prescription for Eleanor Roosevelt to purge the bile from her system. She had planned such a venture in August with her secretary, Maureen Corr, as well as David, Edna, and Grania Gurewitsch. The itinerary included Switzerland, London, Paris, Warsaw (for a meeting of the World Federation of United Nations Associations), London again, and Paris before the journey home, where, one more time, she would lend her prodigious power to a presidential election campaign.

Her energy level would not quite measure up, however, to the whirlwind months she gave Adlai Stevenson's 1956 campaign. There was a reason for that difference: In early 1960 David Gurewitsch had diagnosed a blood disease he called aplastic anemia. There was fear that it might be leukemia or a different form of blood disease, but by July at least the possibility of cancer had been ruled out.* Whatever it was, it would gradually deplete Mrs. Roosevelt's energies over the remaining months of her life. Her characteristic response to the news was to dismiss it out of hand. She would take her pills "to please David" and carry on, even though she recognized that her ability to maintain her customary pace had noticeably diminished.

Anna and Jim Halsted returned home from Iran in August to prepare for their next move, this time to Lexington, Kentucky, where Jim would become assistant dean of the university's new medical school. He and Anna would both be intimately involved in Mrs. Roosevelt's remaining months of life, which added an unfortunately contentious note to ER's care. Anna and Jim thought David's training in "rehabilitative medicine" inadequate

*The final diagnosis was tuberculosis of the bone marrow

to Mrs. Roosevelt's need, "Nor," writes Joseph Lash, "did David have high regard for Jim as a doctor."[1] He felt David should have sought the collaboration of a specialist. The gulf between them introduced an unnecessary strain on the patient who was caught in the middle. From a medical standpoint, however, Jim Halsted later said, "It probably wouldn't have made much difference—probably didn't make any difference."

Adlai wrote from Libertyville:

> I've heard the sad news about your granddaughter and send you this belated note of sympathy and love. With all you have to bear and do this further misery—just when you should be feeling peaceful and relaxed—seems grossly unfair.
>
> You have more love and devotion than any one alive, and I know that sustains you. I only wish that mine could somehow comfort you and ease your burdens. I like to think that you would promptly let me know where and when I could ever help—because I love you very much.[2]

A week before Election Day, Stevenson gave a rousing speech for Kennedy at a rally in Los Angeles. In his peroration he, perhaps unwittingly, summed up what many perceived as the crucial difference between himself and the Democratic Party's chosen candidate: "Do you remember," he asked, "that in classical times when Cicero had finished speaking, the people said, 'How well he spoke'—but when Demosthenes had finished speaking, the people said, 'Let us march.'" And with those words he presented "the next President of the United States, John F. Kennedy."[3]

November 8 produced one of the closest margins of victory in U.S. history. Of the 69 million votes cast, Kennedy edged out Nixon by a mere 120,000 votes. The margin was 49.71 percent to 49.55 for Nixon. The electoral margin was broader: 303 to 219, but it was clear that Kennedy would be a minority president. Nonetheless, as his confidence in a November victory grew over the summer and early fall, he lost no time assembling the team with whom he would conduct the first chapter of his thousand-day tenure in the White House.

At the same time, Stevenson was agonizing over whether he would be offered the post he now wanted more than anything else: that of secretary of state. He was convinced—and a great number of informed people agreed with him—that it was the one office for which he was better qualified than any individual on the United States or the world stage at the time. (Martin says, "Ruth Field thought Stevenson lifelong had seen himself as Secretary, not as President.")[4] He labored diligently for it over the summer and fall. Kennedy invited him to prepare a report on U.S. foreign policy priorities in the new administration. Stevenson asked his friend George Ball and several others to join a taskforce to prepare the report. Among these were Senator J.

William Fulbright, chairman of the Senate Foreign Relations Committee; Chester Bowles, a former member of the Finletter Group and later appointed by Kennedy under-secretary of state; and Tom Finletter himself. The final report ran to 150 pages. Looking it through, Kennedy exclaimed: "Very good. Terrific. This is excellent. Just what I needed."[5]

Stevenson prepared a profile of himself, his experience, and his qualifications for the secretary's job, in which he described at some length his "decisiveness, competence, influence abroad and position at home" and added the "60 to 75 speeches" made on JFK's behalf during the recent campaign, his invitation to Kennedy to deliver the nomination speech for him at the 1956 convention, and his giving the delegates their choice of the vice presidential candidate, providing an opportunity thereby for Kennedy to be chosen.

But there was silence from the Kennedy team. Word finally came from Bill Blair, who had been given an interview by Kennedy, that "the Gov" would be offered his choice of attorney general, ambassador to the United Kingdom, or ambassador to the United Nations. Adlai was devastated. His expertise was in making policy, not implementing policy made by others. Half-convinced by a dozen or more of his closest associates, ER among them, that the UN post would put him at the very center of policymaking on the international front, Stevenson decided to give Kennedy's offer his reluctant consideration. He would accept the position provided he would be made a full member of the cabinet, could attend "important meetings" of the National Security Council, and would be "in the mainstream of policy-making"—this latter a concern that in future would be too often disregarded by his superiors, to his great distress.

On December 8, the president-elect, as he had been doing with other appointees, summoned Stevenson to his Georgetown home for a press conference where he described Stevenson as a man who "has always answered the call of duty on every other occasion in his life, and I am hopeful that he will find it possible to serve the United States in this most vital position."[6]

What happened next almost guaranteed that the relationship between the two men would continue to be a difficult one. Instead of, as expected, graciously accepting the post, Stevenson thanked the president for his confidence, said he wanted to help, and averred that "the United Nations is the very center of our foreign policy and its effectiveness is indispensable to the peace and security of the world." There were still, however, some concerns he wanted to discuss further with the president-elect. A reporter asked whether that meant that he had not yet made up his mind about the position. "I have not accepted it pending a further talk,"[7] Stevenson replied. It was an embarrassing moment for Kennedy. His brother Bobby, Kennedy's campaign manager, was apoplectic. (A year later, having seen Adlai perform as UN ambassador, he said, "He did not make mistakes. He represented in an articulate way the United States in foreign eyes as well as could be. He was the best Ambassador we could have had there.")[8]

Finally, on December 12, Stevenson called a press conference and announced his acceptance of the appointment. Next day he flew to New York to start organizing the U.S. Mission to the UN. He would report directly to the assistant secretary of state for international organizations (or IO, as it was known among governmental employees). He would occupy an eighteen-room suite on the forty-second floor of the Waldorf-Astoria Towers, just blocks from the UN building complex on Manhattan's East River. A letter came from Eleanor Roosevelt, congratulating him on his appointment: "We need your voice there and I know your return will be greeted with enthusiasm by all the other delegates."

For most of 1961 and early 1962 ER managed to maintain a vigorous lifestyle. She had been traveling extensively since Election Day for the AAUN and for her lecture agency, Colston Leigh. A letter to Lorena Hickok revealed that even though she was keeping close to her yesteryear rhythm, she was anticipating slowing down:

> I got home from Boston late last night & Maureen [Corr] & I leave at 7 a.m. tomorrow for Ogden, Utah then L.A., Palm Springs, L.A. again & home Friday a.m. Next week end back to Boston. My long trips will all be over, however.[9]

One of Stevenson's first acts as ambassador was to inquire of John Kennedy if he might invite Mrs. Roosevelt to be a member of the U.S. delegation to the General Assembly. Kennedy approved and suggested that Stevenson make the selection of the entire delegation. The president-elect, honoring her request, did not suggest Mrs. Roosevelt for the UN's Human Rights Commission; that office would be filled, with distinction, by Marietta Tree.

Once again the correspondence began to flow between the two leading figures of this story. From now until her death the focus of them both was on the international stage, the search for talent among the many able men and women seeking positions in a variety of UN agencies, and the formulation of U.S. policy in what both considered—second only to the United States itself—the most important organization in the world. Typical was a letter from Eleanor to Adlai three days before Christmas, 1960, giving him a list of "really able women." She had checked the ones she thought he would find "best to work with," left others of evident ability unchecked; they were persons she thought might "ask for different things but for heaven's sake don't let them get anything. They will be a nuisance to you right along."[10]

She was back in a role she hugely enjoyed and knew she could be useful in—one that allowed her to live her personal creed. The year 1960 saw the publication of her book *You Learn by Living*. In it she had asked herself what the "most important requirements" for happiness were and answered her own question: "a feeling that you have been honest with yourself and those around you; a feeling that you have done the best you could both in your personal life and in your work; and the ability to love others." Reflecting on that triad after the book came out, she added a fourth requirement: "the feeling that you are, in some way, useful. Usefulness, [she said], whatever form it takes, is the price we should pay for the air we breathe and the food we eat and the privilege of being alive."[11]

In that spirit she accepted several tasks for President Kennedy, among them, advisor to the Peace Corps, member of the "Tractors for Cuba" team, and chair of the Commission on the Status of Women. Both she and Stevenson seemed to thrive under responsibilities even a fraction of whose weight would prove too much for most "normal" human beings. At this stage in their friendship, however, it must be acknowledged that that impulse stood in the way of the relationship's further ripening.

Early in the new year she arranged a reception for Adlai at the headquarters of the American Association for the United Nations. She wanted to solidify the new ambassador's interest in and concern for the organization's objective, which had been her cause ever since she had left the UN when Eisenhower became U.S. president. There was another matter on her mind, as well. The AAUN was one of two very large organizations whose sole intention was to educate the U.S. public about the purposes, programs, and emerging problems of the United Nations. The other was the U.S. Committee for the United Nations. The two differed mainly in their organizational structure: The committee's executive, by charter, was named by the president of the United States, which gave it a quasi-governmental tone, while the AAUN was a typical grass-roots voluntary organization.[12] Recently President Kennedy had asked ER to sound out Robert S. Benjamin about his willingness to take the helm at the committee. Benjamin was then chairman of United Artists Corporation's finance committee. He was a loyal Democrat and had been a major fund-raiser in all three of Adlai's presidential campaigns. According to his testimony,[13] he "didn't know what the organization was, but agreed to take it on."

Stevenson, meanwhile, had not been in his ambassadorial position long before he was accepting invitations throughout the country to speak about the UN's structure and hopes for the future. He was convinced that a large part of its success or failure would depend on its support by the American public. Benjamin said that all too frequently Stevenson was asked, following a lecture, "Which organization do I support? And do I support both? Isn't this one cause?" and other such questions. Adlai "was impatient: 'Let's end that competition. This is a case where competition doesn't help, it confuses.'" It was characteristic of ER that the reception for Adlai was arranged, in part, to provide an opportunity to move toward resolution of this problem. The occasion would also provide a chance for her to enjoy his company (even though having to share it with others); such an opportunity had been rare, indeed, at the USUN Mission.

By February Agnes Meyer was already beginning to worry that Adlai would find his role at the UN so lacking in opportunities to formulate policy or otherwise shape events, particularly in crisis situations, that he might one day impulsively throw up his hands and resign. The UN, of course, had been created precisely as the agency to which seemingly insoluble problems

With John Foster Dulles at the UN

should be referred before they escalated into full-scale conflict, as Adlai knew full well; after all, he had helped design it that way. Mrs. Meyer wrote him that Eleanor had paid her a visit and

> said that you had already transformed the UN attitude toward you and the U.S. by visits, friendliness, etc. She got this from many different sources.... Now please promise me that if you are ever tempted to resign, you will talk it over with Eleanor before doing anything.... She is steady, wise and just as devoted to you as I am.[14]

Merriment at the UN

A quiet moment at the UN

Adlai had, indeed, surprised even his severest critics by the aggressive and enlightened way he had approached his new responsibilities. The *New York Times*' Mary McGrory reported on March 9 that he had "entertained at lunch or dinner every chief of the 97 missions represented at the U.N. He has courted Afro-Asian nations with a fervor and industry unprecedented in American history, seeking them out at their homes and offices before they could come to him. One small new nation told him emotionally, 'You are the first United States delegate we have seen. Before, all we ever saw were junior representatives, when your country wanted us to vote for something. But you come and ask us what you can do for us.'"

She continued, quoting the ambassador:

I regard the U.N. not as an arena for conflict, but as an area for working out agreements, not for extending the cold war but for furthering peace. I refuse to engage in a competition of vindictive statements, although I must admit the provocation is sometimes extreme.

This latter comment came in response to the most serious crisis that had confronted the young organization since its founding. The Soviet Union had apparently decided that U.S. preoccupation with change of administrations in Washington D.C. provided an opening for undermining the authority of the UN itself. Bringing down the agency's highly capable secretary general, Dag Hammarskjold himself, would be their first priority. Failing that, they would propose an impossibly lopsided disarmament scheme the United States would be embarrassed to oppose. Stevenson arrived on the scene in the midst of intensely provocative behavior in the General Assembly of Soviet ambassador Andrei Gromyko and his deputy, Valerian Zorin. Both men had been pressing for Hammarskjold's removal in favor of a "troika" at the organization's helm, a proposal the United States saw as a brazen attempt to destroy the UN itself. To give both parties to the "cold war" a chance to cool off, Stevenson told the assembly, "We think a period of relative quiet would contribute to a better international climate for serious negotiation on such vital subjects as disarmament." His proposal to pare the agenda to only "essential" questions secured majority approval. It was an astute move that neutralized the Soviets' manipulative ploys.

He took advantage of the ensuing temporary lull to write the Nobel Committee a letter proposing Eleanor Roosevelt for its celebrated Peace Prize. He emphasized the unique service to world peace enshrined in the Universal Declaration of Human Rights that ER had piloted to unanimous approval in the General Assembly

> without any dissenting vote. That Declaration remains today, after more than twelve years, the world's most authoritative and widely accepted standard of the political, economic and social rights of man...a significant step toward the universal standard of justice which is a precondition of world peace.

Unfortunately his letter was too late for the committee's decision. A year later he wrote again, but ER died before the committee could act, and its terms of reference disallowed posthumous awards.

A major issue involving the dissolution of colonial empires was brought before the General Assembly in December 1960 by leaders of forty-three Asian and African nations. USUN and U.S. State Department personnel had provided advice and counsel on the resolution's legal phrasing. It stated that "all peoples have the right of self-determination" and that "immediate steps shall be taken" in all non-self-governing territories "to transfer all power to the people of these Territories, without any conditions or reservations, in accordance with their freely expressed will." The measure had been discussed during the latter days of the Eisenhower administration. Eisenhower had instructed the U.S. delegation to abstain from voting on that occasion and a sufficient number of other delegations followed the U.S. lead to deprive the measure of passage. Now, in March 1961 Stevenson cast a favorable U.S. vote on its behalf, prompting a substantial majority of other nations to follow suit. That single vote denied the Soviets an issue on which they had taunted and vilified the United States almost from the beginning of the UN's life.

The Russians responded enigmatically: Ambassador Gromyko sent Stevenson a basket of Russian caviar, cheese, and brandy and within a few days Valerian Zorin invited Adlai to attend a concert by the Moiseyev Ballet troupe. On April 6, Eleanor sent Adlai a note that seemed to confirm that the American ambassador's stand had won the momentary admiration of his Soviet counterparts:

> The Deputy Foreign Minister, Mr. Josef Winiewicz who has been heading the Polish Delegation is returning to his country on Monday. He asked to see me to say goodbye.... I could not understand his insistence on seeing me but decided that his real reason was to tell me, which he did before leaving, that their group felt a great change in atmosphere, that Mr. Gromyko had left deeply impressed by the greater possibility of negotiation and that they hoped for a change, that while as yet they have only been able to talk in a narrow area that this area would grow. I took it for granted that this was meant to be passed on and so I do so[15]

Less than a month later another crisis of even graver consequence for U.S international relations roared onto the stage of the General Assembly. It grew from what was later learned to be a CIA plan conceived by the Eisenhower administration—and agreed to by Kennedy—to foment a revolution among the Cuban people against their Communist leader, Fidel Castro. Accordingly, on April 17, eight B-26 planes bearing the crudely fabricated insignia of the Cuban Air Force bombed three airfields on the island, while simultaneously a flotilla of 1,400 men (most of them Cuban expatriates and "only about 135 of them soldiers"[16]) headed north from Nicaragua for Cuba's Bay of Pigs. Only a week before, hoping to discourage reporters who were on the trail of the story, President Kennedy had told a press conference, "There will not be, under any conditions, an intervention in Cuba by U.S. Armed Forces." A week before that he had told his cabinet that "he wished Stevenson to be fully informed, and that nothing said at the U.N. should be less than the truth, even if it could not be the full truth." He had earlier told Arthur Schlesinger, "The integrity and credibility of Adlai Stevenson constitute one of our great national assets. I don't want anything to be done which might jeopardize that."[17]

But Stevenson was not adequately informed by Kennedy's advisors. Indeed, both he and the State Department were kept "out of the loop" by the CIA and the joint chiefs of staff as to the full nature of the invasion fiasco. The U.S. ambassador was thus allowed to present to the UN's Political Committee as fact the CIA's limp cover story. Jane Dick later told of meeting Adlai in a Waldorf elevator: "I was shocked by his appearance," she wrote. "He looked dazedly right through me, apparently not seeing me." She accompanied him to the embassy suite. "You heard my speech today?" he asked. "Well, I did not tell the whole truth, I did not know the whole truth. I took this job at the President's request on the understanding that I would be consulted and kept fully informed on everything. Now my credibility has been compromised, and therefore my usefulness. Yet how can I resign at this moment and make things worse for the President?"[18] Stevenson's stature was such that the vast majority of delegates as well as of the world's press saw through the entire charade and placed responsibility squarely on the U.S. government rather than on Stevenson. He wrote Agnes Meyer, "The Cuba absurdity made me sick for a week while I had to indignantly defend the U.S. (and got finally a harmless resolution) but I've been surprised how little it seems to have affected my *personal* regard"[19] (italics in original). Informed opinion varies concerning the relationship between this reckless scheme and the Cuban missile crisis that erupted eighteen months later, but it seems clear that as of this date the new administration's foreign policy priorities had not yet been established.

Eleanor's illness ebbed and flowed over the remaining months of her life. For periods it would seem to interfere very little with her normally intense pace of living and then would suddenly lay her low. Though progressing slowly, it was nonetheless pulling her down.

> To all intents and purposes [she wrote Adlai] I am marooned at Hyde Park till Wednesday afternoon with the flu. Actually, I don't have the flu but Phlebitis! I didn't want to talk about it and thought the 'flu a good excuse.
>
> If there is a delegation meeting Thursday or Friday, I will try to come but I think I should probably be at home with my two old legs in the air! I am sorry to be such a useless assistant but this is how it is, and I have two contracts for a lecture trip from Saturday morning until Friday of next week.... You will just have to write me off your list of assistants at the UN session. I apologize and am deeply regretful but there seems to be no other way out.[20]

Two days later she wrote again to say she was formally submitting her resignation, though she knew that resignations at the conclusion of the session would be automatic. She then asked whether he could join herself and Clark Eichelberger (AAUN executive director) at lunch on April 25, saying he was "most anxious to have a talk with you." She commended Stevenson on having done "a marvelous job" of handling "the many difficult situations."[21] She then wrote President Kennedy as the Special Session ended: "I don't think I have been very useful but I think I accomplished what Adlai wanted in just appearing at the U.N."

Several months of work had preceded Kennedy's proposal in March of an "Alliance for Progress" between the United States and the nations of South America. Now the president turned to Stevenson to ask him to explain the program to our south-of-the-border neighbors. A letter from Stuart Gerry Brown thought it "a tough assignment" and opined, "After the intolerable position you were put in on the Cuba business you must look forward to your visit with mixed emotion."[22] It was true, the mission would go forward under the cloud of the Bay of Pigs fiasco but, as Adlai told Barbara Ward the end of May, "We have things pretty well turned around now so that the objective is groundwork for the 'Alliance for Progress' conference in Montevideo in July, and economic and social cooperation with the political reprisals against Castro muted....The emphasis will be on the future, not on the past."[23] In actuality, a major purpose of the trip, in addition to laying a foundation for economic cooperation throughout the hemisphere, was to persuade his hearers and governmental leaders that "the Cuban problem is not a bilateral one [between Cuba and the United States]. The real concern is the establishment of a beachhead for Communist penetration and subversion throughout the hemisphere."[24] Between June 4 and 22 he visited ten South American capitals and everywhere was met with enthusiastic response from his hearers. On his return he reported to the president "unanimous and intense interest" in the proposals wherever he went; the mission had made "the most favorable impression in Latin America since Franklin Roosevelt's announcement of the 'Good Neighbor' policy."[25] He wrote William Benton,

> It went extremely well, but the pace was fearful—17,000 miles, 10 cities, 18 days—and God knows how many speeches, appearances, receptions and thousands of words of cables. I think on the whole we are well out of it.[26]

Adlai and Eleanor shared the conviction that in a world in which the know-how to produce atomic bombs capable of cataclysmic human and environmental damage could not be controlled, steps toward disarmament should be the highest international priority. When Adlai made that concern the centerpiece of his annual address to the UN's Economic and Social Council meeting in Geneva, ER wrote an appreciative column.[27] A major argument, she wrote, against disarmament has historically been that the U.S. economy "could not stand giving up the continuation of full military production." Stevenson, she wrote, had spoken directly to this concern:

> He said that an accord to limit arms would provide the opportunity to turn "our resources from production of instruments of death to the production of

the manifold things we need for a better life for our own citizens and for the citizens of other nations."

In his speech he recognized the fact that a changeover period that comes abruptly nearly always causes a time of disruption, but if it is planned for it can be accomplished very quickly and the difficulties can be minimized. ...

Mr. Stevenson said such plans are really being considered in Washington. I hope they will be carried out to the point where business, particularly the business of mass production for war, will know exactly step by step what they will be able to do and what world needs they will begin to fill. I don't believe we have reached the point of pinpointing what our great industries could do if they turned their energies from military production to meet certain basic needs throughout the world. ...

To many of the representatives of the 18 countries present...it must have given great hope that even though we are telling our Soviet adversaries that we will take stock of our military situation and prevent any deterioration that will tempt them to such acts in the Berlin crisis as might lead to war, nevertheless our aim and objective is—and will always be-peaceful accommodation and development for the good of the human race as a whole.

It had been some time since she and Adlai had managed a meeting, both being heavily committed at the UN. A chance encounter in late August 1961 thus provided a pleasant surprise. Stevenson, she wrote in her September 1 column, was stumping for "young Harry Sedgwick, who is running for one of the local district leader offices. It was as usual a pleasure to listen to him," and she thought the occasion had given him "an amusing interlude from the more serious business of the special session of the UN."

Anticipating the new session of the UN General Assembly, Stevenson again invited ER to accept the post of "Special Advisor to the USUN Delegation," suggesting her duties would be "at [her] discretion." She declined on the basis of her waning strength. But, says Joe Lash, "She proceeded to move about the country characteristically, flying to Newfoundland at the President's request, making speeches for Colston Leigh and the AAUN on the West Coast, in the Rockies, the Midwest, and the South." Had she secretly hoped Adlai would insist she serve on the delegation?[28]

She was also campaigning for John Kennedy. Anna and Jim saw her on the Jack Paar and the Dave Garroway shows. "Not the most desirable hours for you to be working," Anna wrote her mother on Election Day, "I'm so hoping that after today you will cut down drastically on your schedule."[29] ER's voluminous file at FBI headquarters in Washington D.C. contains a report on her speaking on October 27 on behalf of Kennedy's candidacy to a Miami crowd of 9,000 to sequester atomic weapons with the United Nations.[30] The report in the October 28 *Miami Herald* read,

> "The world's atomic energy—including the super hydrogen bombs—should be turned over to the United Nations to be used toward universal peace," Mrs. Eleanor Roosevelt declared in Miami Thursday. "If that [atomic energy] stays in the hands of individual nations," she warned, "we will never be secure. ..."
>
> Mrs. Roosevelt described the United States and Russia as being deadlocked in "the most dangerous game of poker that could be played." But she added hopefully: "In the United Nations, what the Soviets are slowly doing is turning the whole world against them."

The reporter noted that "approximately 50 to 60 individuals" picketed the program and identified themselves as members of the Florida States Rights Party, Americans for Action Group, and the John Birch Society and that "except for an exchange of insults the demonstration was orderly."

She did manage to attend when Kennedy addressed the General Assembly's opening session in September (and sat with Jackie and other members of the Kennedy family), but on September 12 she wrote to express regret that she wouldn't be seeing Adlai soon again. "Dr. Gurewitsch insists that I rest in bed as much as possible for the next few days. I'm terribly cross but there is nothing I can do." Two weeks later she sent Adlai a note: "It was lovely to see you again last night."

She kept in nearly continuous touch with him all fall, but most of their communication concerned UN business. Her mail still ran to several hundred letters a week, she kept writing her newspaper column, and rarely was there a week without a treatise on some issue of formidable international moment its author knew Mrs. Roosevelt considered of critical urgency. "Here's another of these horrible things that should be read by someone interested in Latin America," she wrote Adlai, attaching a ten-page analysis of business conditions in South America "with apologies for bothering you."

A fortnight later she asked Adlai to refer an inquiry from an Argentine diplomat to a specialist in that country's affairs "so I can reply to the writer as requested." And ten days later she wrote asking for a meeting to discuss the feasibility of establishing a new position of "communications officer" at the UN, its responsibility described as publicizing "what [all departments of] the government [presumably the U.S. government] is doing in different parts of the world." The public, she felt, needed to be "better informed than it is today." She would be gone "on a lecture tour till December 1, then off again for a few days on the 11th."

For all the obligations—and social events, of which there were a pleth-ora—that filled his calendar, Adlai would not forget her seventy-seventh birthday. He sent her flowers accompanied by a brief note:[31]

> Dear Mrs. R.—Among the blessings I count daily, and never more than on your birthday, is the honor of calling such a great lady my colleague and dear friend. As always I send you devoted love, Adlai

It would be his last such communication; a year hence she would be too ill to see him.

CHAPTER 2

CODA

ON DECEMBER 7, Adlai sent Eleanor a check for $1,000, proceeds, he said, from an article he had written for a popular magazine. (Walter Johnson thought it was "probably 'United Nations: Capital of the Family of Man,'" which Stevenson had written for the *National Geographic*'s September 1961 issue.) He wanted ER to forward it "to any cause which you designate." The note ended with a revealing sentence: "I think especially of the AAUN and wonder if it still has a priority among your concerns."[1] Revealing because it shows beyond any doubt just how truly out of touch he had allowed himself to become with the woman who for fifteen years had been his guide, his mentor, his confidante, and, she thought, his close friend. Six weeks earlier he had called her "his conscience" when he inscribed her copy of Stuart Gerry Brown's book *Conscience in Politics: Adlai E. Stevenson in the 1950's.* (Eleanor, thanking him, had written back in a jocular, big-sisterly tone: "I am sorry you consider me your conscience because I am not at all sure that a conscience is always pleasant to have around!")[2] Was she chiding him gently for being inattentive?

He wrote her a few days later. He had sent AAUN's executive director, Clark Eichelberger, a check and regretted that he was unable to have dinner on the 14th: "I seem to be engaged all the time these days, and that night is no exception. Maybe when the General Assembly is over we can have an evening together. I hope so."

But such meetings seemed inordinately difficult to arrange. That difficulty's roots were many...and tangled. We have encountered some of them in previous chapters. Adlai's new position had added significant external pressures to those that had begun to disturb him inwardly. His first priority had to be the organization of the USUN Mission headquarters. Securing staff and security clearances for the top echelon of new hires, reconfiguring communication channels with not just the State Department but also a dozen governmental agencies, Congress, and the White House was a Herculean logistical task. Then came establishing relations with the ninety-seven-member state delegations. Simultaneously with both those priorities he was dealing with the emergent agendas of the various UN agencies themselves, the Security Council and General Assembly first and foremost. Small wonder that, from the time of his arrival to the end of the year, when he was in New York, everyone of the new U.S. ambassador's lunches was a working session.

Creating a serviceable relationship with the new president had to be an early priority if life was to be bearable over the next four years, and there was some fence mending to do. Following their initial sparring over the post in November 1960,[3] Kennedy had promised Adlai direct and unmediated access to the Oval Office. Though at first he made frequent trips to Washington, Stevenson used the privilege discreetly, preferring written communication to the occasional face-to-face audience. Martin says Kennedy "worked hard to improve their relationship," and Schlesinger notes that Kennedy recognized Adlai's value to his administration, that he "had an essential respect and liking for Stevenson,...admired his public presence and wit, valued his skills as diplomat and orator,"[4] but was baffled by Stevenson's demeanor whenever the two of them were together. On the latter such occasions there was a tenseness, largely on Adlai's part, that seemed hard to account for. It was as though he couldn't dismiss the thought that he could (or should) have been the Oval Office occupant instead of this sharp-elbowed, debonair but ruthless young politician. Returning from a Cabinet meeting in the Capital, he sputtered to an associate: "That young man in the White House, he never says please and he never says thank you."[5] Their styles and temperaments were different, as Eleanor had noted in her column the previous August after Kennedy's visit to Val-Kill, Kennedy's crisp and inclined to be impulsive, Adlai's more reflective and judicious. "I never felt so keenly," Schlesinger wrote, "the way these two men, so united in their objectives, could so inadvertently arrive at cross purposes."

There was nothing unclear, however, about Stevenson's value to the young president's new administration. In a series of diplomatic performances during one crisis after another that presented itself almost as soon as Kennedy had moved into 1600, Pennsylvania Avenue—the Soviet "troika" proposal and the Soviet blockade of West Berlin, a bloodbath in the former Belgian colony of Congo that turned into a civil war, the proposed seating of Communist China, and the Bay of Pigs disaster, to mention only the most difficult—Stevenson proved time and again in his first six months at the UN his value to John Kennedy's presidency. (He was fond of saying that diplomacy was "composed of equal parts of protocol, alcohol, and geritol.") A telegram from the White House to the ambassador following his diplomatic maneuvering on the China question bespoke the president's appreciation: "Today's votes...are further evidence of your outstanding skill and leadership in the UN and I am grateful for your eloquent and active support on this issue. With esteem & warm regards."[6]

Such sentiments make all the more puzzling a comment recorded by Joseph Lash about a relaxed New Year's Eve at Val-Kill at year's end:

> F[DR] jr and Sue were there full of tales about the Kennedy White House. Stevenson had spent several hours with President Kennedy and Jacqueline at Glen Ora [the Kennedy retreat] outside Washington.... Just before the champagne was offered around at midnight, Mrs. R. asked how the President and Stevenson got on.... Jackie had replied Jack can't bear being in the same room with him.[7]

Another obstacle to an occasional quiet visit with Eleanor was the inherent complexity (bordering on unworkability) of Adlai's position relative to the State Department. Foreign policy, after all, was made in Washington D.C., not in New York, however much Stevenson wished it otherwise. His being granted a seat in the president's Cabinet also turned out to be more liability than asset. He complained numerous times that agreement at the Cabinet level would within hours be contradicted by an interoffice directive from Washington. This led to an almost plaintive memorandum to the president urging "changes in the relations between the U.S. Mission to the United Nations and the State Department in two principal respects: (a) The instructions from the Department should be more generalized and permit greater flexibility and independence of action by the Mission; (b) There should be more advance planning on large and enduring issues that affect U.S. influence and 'image.'"[8] But the State Department jealously guarded its prerogative of making policy that the USUN Mission was supposed to carry out, and it had thousands of employees on staff compared with the USUN's 125.

His letters, fewer now, to friends throughout 1961 and 1962 complain about the "relentless" pace of his life: "Keeping up with my speaking and writing commitments here is more than I have been able to do," he told Clara Urquhart.[9] His deputy representative at the Security Council, Charles W. Yost, said Adlai led "an appallingly busy life"; Marietta Tree, longtime friend and Stevenson's advisor at the UN, agreed: "His calendar was nearly always hopelessly crowded."

He had written Philip Noel-Baker shortly after the painful press conference at Kennedy's Georgetown home: "I note with interest what you say about the U.N....I must also add in candor that I would go back to those precincts and trials only with reluctance."[10] Marietta Tree, one of the few who knew him best, told Carol Evans that after Adlai had accepted the UN ambassadorship, "I think he felt in a strong position because *at that point he did not care desperately about it* [italics added], but knew that Kennedy needed him for domestic as well as global political reasons."[11] In other words, Adlai threw himself into the UN job, but his heart wasn't entirely in it. The world had rejected his most strenuous efforts and frustrated his fondest hopes; he would live out the remainder of his life still "giving it his all," but now persuaded that in the end even his best showing would fall short of what he *could* have accomplished had he been granted larger responsibility. His was the attitude of every winner of the consolation prize.

Furthermore, having disappointed ER's hopes as well as his own and been the cause of her extraordinary expenditures of energy and concern on his behalf, in not one, not two, but three political campaigns for the highest office in the nation, but to no avail, how could he avoid a twinge of guilt whenever the prospect of a visit with her presented itself? Try as he might, he could not outgrow the feeling that ER was not just his admired and admiring older sibling but also his conscience. Furthermore, although a visit with her was always pleasant and informative, there was seldom an occasion when something serious was not on ER's mind that Adlai could help straighten out. He was overextending himself already in just such activity fourteen to sixteen hours every day; relief from the role of "mender and fixer" was what he needed. Who would sit in judgment, then, if a visit with Eleanor were deferred for a ball at the Waldorf, a reception at Sardi's, or an evening at the theater? (Francis Plimpton said, "Adlai loved to go to first nights and go backstage and be greeted by the lady star."[12])

There was, however, another important, perhaps defining reason for Stevenson's failure to maintain a closer relationship with Eleanor Roosevelt toward the end of her life. For him, an emotional divide had been present from the beginning of their relationship and it persisted up to the end, while for Eleanor it had long since dissolved. She had moved in her relationship with him from what psychotherapist Lillian Rubin calls "the secular" to "the sacred" realm where friendship is defined not in terms of choice but rather of obligation.[13] For her, he was still her witty, urbane, and talented younger brother for whom her warm affection could never be extinguished. She could, therefore, be excused for feeling that a doting and respectful younger brother should have *made* the occasion for a visit more often than Adlai had done. As for him, throughout the intertwining of their lives he had been either unwilling or incapable of allowing himself that depth of commitment. Though he regarded theirs as one of the most precious relationships of his life, he somehow never allowed it to cross the threshold of what Rubin calls the "secular" dimension.

*   *   *

Her commitments to the AAUN, her advisory role for the Peace Corps, and her chairmanship of the Status of Women Commission required three trips to Washington in January. In February she flew with Maureen Corr to London and Paris, followed by a quick visit to Israel. In the French capital she taped a program with Jules Moch, France's UN ambassador, for her Brandeis "Prospects of Mankind" program, and then flew to Jerusalem with Edna Gurewitsch for an hour's interview on Israeli radio before flying back to London. There she had meals with Lady Reading and Lord Elibank, dined "with 6 ladies in policy making government positions"—(ammunition, perhaps, for her next meeting with the Status of Women Commission back home?). She was "working hard," she told Joe and Trude Lash, but otherwise "I did nothing else but rest." A week in St. Moritz with David and Edna after a strenuous fortnight drew her pronouncement "I have never had such a good rest."

Back in the United States she traveled twice to Washington in March for the Status of Women Commission, twice again in April, during the second visit recording an hour's conversation with President Kennedy on her commission's work. She wrote Adlai in April, enclosing an appeal from the South Moluccas: "I seem to be swamping you with letters & I apologize for taking your time."[14] (Was there a slight edge to that apology?)

At the end of June, David volunteered his services for three weeks aboard the hospital ship *Hope* in Peru. ER tried to disguise her anxiety. In a letter for him to read "On the Plane—Not Before," she acknowledged, "All goodbyes are poignant now, I like less and less to be long separated from those few whom I deeply love. Above all others you are the one to whom my heart is tied and I shall miss you every moment till we meet again."[15] She would try to help Edna but knew that "this separation will be hard for her to bear."

She had not forgotten her plan to resolve the problems caused by the seeming duplication of effort between the U.S. Committee for the UN and the AAUN. Robert S. Benjamin, the committee's former chairman, told an interviewer in 1977 that about this time ER said to him, "To facilitate the merger, now that you're continuing to be chairman of the U.S. Committee, why don't you succeed me as chairman of the AAUN?"

And for about a year I was chairman of the AAUN and the US Committee. . . . That made [merger] easier because then I wasn't an advocate for one or the other.

[It took a little over four years, but merger was finally accomplished in 1965.]

A related matter was on her mind this summer, for which ER made another luncheon date with Benjamin, this time inviting him to her apartment on East 74th Street.

They exchanged pleasantries, ER commenting on a tremor that made it impossible for her to cut the "very thin meat" on her plate. Benjamin did it for her. Finally, "after a lot of idle and light conversation," ER came to the point. "'I wanted to talk to you about one person,' she said. 'Nothing else would have prompted me to be so firm. What about Clark Eichelberger's future?'" Benjamin responded: "'Well, it does look, Mrs. Roosevelt, like the merger will go through. But I want to assure you that...Clark Eichelberger will be on the payroll of the organization until the day he's seventy-two. And I don't know now what his age is.' She told it to me, but it doesn't matter. And she said, 'I'm glad to hear that. I'm glad I didn't have to ask it.'"

He went on: "So that was uppermost in her mind, and answers your question how did she feel about Clark. Though she wanted merger, *against his instincts* [italics added], so much so that she was willing to override him, she never overrode her feeling about him. And it was mostly in compliance with that promise that Mr. Clark Eichelberger stayed with us until he withdrew to head the CSOP [Committee to Study the Organization of Peace], and stayed there for a number of years before he retired."[16]

The annual picnic for the aberrant boys of Wiltwyck School was held at Val-Kill on July 6 and ER carried off her customary role as hostess with flair. But two days later she was feeling weak and unsteady. Dr Hyman ordered a transfusion. She required "two full bags," she wrote David, "I should need nothing more for a long time." She was working on her book *Tomorrow Is Now*, with Elinore Denniston, keeping up with her column, and fulfilling her other responsibilities with what seemed to outsiders her usual vigor, though now her exertions exhausted her. "Home to bed" was Maureen's calendar entry after ER had spent a day in New York City campaigning for the reform group Committee for Democratic Voters. On August 4, she had to go to the hospital again. Adlai wrote, "Please get out of there quickly! And *please please* let me know if there is anything I can do." He appended a postscript: "I'm hoping you can come to dinner with Martha Gellhorn and Tom Mathews on the 12th [of September]."[17]

In mid-August, against David's strong advice, ER traveled by car to Campobello Island for the dedication of the Franklin Roosevelt Memorial Bridge linking the Island with the U.S. mainland. On the return journey she stopped off (twice) to visit friends but by Belfast was too weak to get out of the car to enjoy seeing the stuffed animals in Perry's Nuthouse, a tradition in the Roosevelt family when they drove to the Island from Hyde Park. A momentary reprieve in September enabled her to attend a reception for the U.S. delegation to the 17th General Assembly session. Joe Lash reported, "She sat on the dais for two hours and was miserable throughout." From then on, her descent was steady and, tragically, protracted. On the 26th of September she returned to Columbia Presbyterian Hospital in Manhattan. Adlai heard the news and rushed to the hospital where David barred the way to her room. He gave the excuse that ER was too weak to see anyone.

Joe Lash says, "Privately he told me she had not wanted to see him."[18] Adlai penned a note:

> Dearest Eleanor: I have been getting regular bulletins from Maureen and *pray* it won't be long before I can come to see you—and what a long deferred visit it will be! How I wish that preparations for the General Assembly and all these trips to Washington had not interfered with the visit to Hyde Park we had planned before I went abroad!
>
> The General Assembly is off to a better start than usual. I love you dearly—and so does the whole world! But they can't *all* come to see you and perhaps I can when David gives me permission.
>
> Devotedly, Adlai

On her birthday, October 11, she was seventy-eight. Hundreds of cards and letters arrived from all over the world, wishing her a speedy recovery. Maureen helped sort them. Conflicting emotions, anger, and hurt feelings riled nearly the entire period of ER's illness till her final release in death. Trude Lash wrote Paul Tillich, the noted Protestant theologian who had presided at the Lashes' wedding:

> There was only suffering for Mrs. Roosevelt from the first day in July when she was taken to the hospital for the first time. There was no moment of serenity. There was only anger, helpless anger at the doctors and nurses and the world who tried to keep her alive. [She felt] betrayed and persecuted by all of us.
>
> She was not afraid of death at all. She was...so infinitely exhausted, it seemed as though she had to suffer every human indignity, every weakness, every failure that she had resisted and conquered so daringly during her whole life—as though she were being punished for being too strong and too powerful and disciplined and almost immune to human frailty.[19]

Joe Lash, in a journal entry, recorded how on October 31, the New York *World-Telegram* complicated the situation of ER's caregivers by running a story quoting James Roosevelt that on October 25 ER had asked for Stevenson and he had left the Cuban crisis debate to see her in the hospital.[20] Asked about the story, Anna said that "her only reason for doing this [letting Stevenson come] was that David had been so terribly rude to Adlai." Lash's account continues, quoting Anna:

> I called [Stevenson] to bring him up to date....He sounded like a rather irate gentleman who felt he had been close enough to mother and should have been treated better. Come if you would like to, I said, but I don't think she will recognize you. He dropped everything and came within the hour. I warned him not to tell anybody and I also warned the boys.

James Roosevelt described the scene:

> Adlai Stevenson came in the day before Eleanor died. I was there.... He came in, and just stood by her for a minute and gave her a kiss on the forehead and left.[21]

Lash again:

> When I went up to 74th Street at 4, Maureen's version was that Mrs. R. had tried six or seven times to see Stevenson and he wasn't able to find the time. When it was discovered she had gone to the hospital, it must have bothered his conscience and he came up to the hospital and ran into David who wouldn't let him see her. He went away furious and has been repeating the story around New York.... She would not have wanted Stevenson to come. She doesn't do these things by the "importance" of the people involved.[22]

It is not entirely clear whether Lash is describing this last sentiment as Ms. Corr's or his own, though we assume it is Ms. Corr's. Of all ER's close associates, she had been closer than even David Gurewitsch on a daily and often hourly basis for over nine years. It must be accepted that, regardless of his UN obligations, Adlai's conduct during ER's last two years had unquestionably widened the gap between them. Not until her health had begun to decline did his inattention begin to rankle in her breast. It was an inexpressibly sad note on which to end a friendship that for sixteen tumultuous and vibrantly creative years had enriched and sustained them both, challenged them both, and across the globe lifted the spirits of a generation.

She breathed her last on the 7th of November. Instantly the world was told the news and the world's press gave her story the prominence it deserved. On November 17, Adlai gave the memorial address at New York's St. John the Divine Cathedral:

> One week ago this afternoon, in the Rose Garden at Hyde Park, Eleanor Roosevelt came home for the last time. Her journeys are over. The remembrance now begins....
>
> What other single human being has touched and transformed the existence of so many others?... She walked in the slums and ghettos of the world, not on a tour of inspection, not as a condescending patron, but as one who could not feel complacent while others were hungry, and who could not find contentment while others were in distress...
>
> Eleanor Roosevelt's childhood was unhappy—miserably unhappy, she sometimes said. But it was Eleanor Roosevelt who also said that "One must never, for whatever reason, turn his back on life." She did not mean that duty should compel us. She meant that life should. "Life," she said, "was meant to be lived." A simple statement. An obvious statement. But a statement that

by its obviousness and its simplicity challenges the most intricate of all the philosophies of despair....

What we have lost in Eleanor Roosevelt is not her life. She lived that out to the full. What we have lost, what we wish to recall for ourselves, to remember, is what she was herself. And who can name it? But she left "a name to shine on the entablatures of truth, forever".

We pray that she has found peace, and a glimpse of sunset. But today we weep for ourselves. We are lonelier, someone has gone from one's own life who was like the certainty of refuge, and someone has gone from the world who was like a certainty of honor.[23]

CHAPTER 3

THE SUMMING-UP

THERE IS MORE THAN A LITTLE PRESUMPTION behind any effort of one human being to evaluate the life of another. In one of her novels May Sarton has a character say, "We cannot know what is occurring inside someone else's marriage. In fact, we probably aren't wholly clear about what's happening in our own." This study cannot claim immunity from similar criticism. But both Eleanor Roosevelt and Adlai Stevenson possessed qualities so rare in their breadth and depth in woman or man in any age in human history, we may safely predict that generations hence there will be others eager to explore the sources of their strength and the power of their example.

Each possessed an unusual capacity to stir deep and motivating emotions in the psyches of their hearers/readers. Martha Gellhorn described it as ER's *attendrissante,* a French term for the ability to awaken feelings of tenderness in others.[1] Lillian Smith spoke of a somewhat different kind of awakening in a speech she gave at the A.D.A. dinner honoring Eleanor Roosevelt on February 28, 1957:

> In the early thirties, down in the South, ... as millions of us everywhere were waking up, Mrs. Roosevelt was a symbol to me of the new, uncreated world that must be made. She was standing there—I remember her no other way—nudging us awake, saying: <u>Come, come, you have slept long enough now; it is time to wake up! The old world has gone, haven't you heard? We have a whole new world to make and we must get to work.</u>* Quite a few of us had not heard that the old world had gone, some didn't believe it. ... and too many, of course, after working a few years, have gone back to sleep. But Mrs. Roosevelt has never stopped shaking the sleepy-heads awake—nor has she ever failed to encourage those who kept going when the going was rough ...[2]

*Underlining in original manuscript

A year later, Ms. Smith wrote on a Christmas card to ER: "I think of you with so much gladness. What a wonderful thing it is for the world that you exist...In a sense you have created a new kind of woman, you have shown feminine possibilities that did not exist before—they inherently existed but had not found their way into the personality of a woman before."

By common consent of his peers, Adlai awakened in a somnolent and self-satisfied electorate a rebirth of confidence in themselves as citizens of a democratic republic whose health is entirely dependent upon their participation and initiative. "He lighted up the sky," said George Ball, "like a flaming arrow, lifting political discussion to a level of literacy and eloquence, candor and humor that tapped unsuspected responses in the American electorate."[3]

He too touched deeper springs. Testimony to that effect came from, among others, CBS commentator Eric Sevareid: "He was intensely aware of his friends. That was, I think, the real reason his friends loved him so much....Adlai made me feel importantly alive, and he made me feel trusted....He was what the French call 'a friend of the heart' because he saw through to your heart."[4]

It should be clear from such testimonials (which are legion) that the greatness of both these extraordinary people, though it was immediately palpable even to a casual observer, had its roots in a quality rare in the experience of most of us. Adlai's friend Barbara Ward (Lady Barbara Jackson) described it best, writing about him in words equally applicable to Eleanor Roosevelt:

> He had that quality for which the Africans...have found a special word. "Nommo" is the Bantu word for the gift of making life rather larger and more vivid for everyone else. One might say "life enhancement" if it did not sound so dreary...Any group of people would be likely to feel a lift when he appeared, with his...quick look of interest, the smile that was never a formality and the whole manner that seemed to say: "Now, I really am delighted to be just here just now." Perhaps this suggests the practiced bonhomie of a good mixer. It was the opposite: The Governor never had to practice curiosity or zest. If anything, he had to repress them.[5]

He and Eleanor shared a view of politics as a moral enterprise, one in which the fulfillment of its "mission" was the betterment of the human condition, especially for the most vulnerable of a nation's citizens. Stevenson's companions on trips abroad sometimes complained about his insistence on poking about in the back alleys of the barrios and shantytowns where the least privileged members of a nation eked out their marginal existence. When he spoke of Eleanor Roosevelt's doing so, he was describing his own as well as her first-hand acquaintance with poverty and despair. Such curiosity was the foundation upon which their legislative initiatives were constructed, hers primarily on the domestic front, his more inclined to the international. Empirical evidence, more than theory, grounded their initiatives.

Uncommon courage marked them both: Recall Adlai's choice of audiences and/or timing for his most controversial addresses: the American Legion for his proposal to substitute for the draft an all-volunteer, professional army, ignoring the advice of his advisors about the cost of speaking out against Joseph McCarthy; his retort, when told his nuclear testing moratorium initiative would lose him the election: "It is more important to tell the American people the truth than it is to win an election." Recall, too, his affidavit testifying to the reputation of Alger Hiss insofar as he knew of it in 1946–47:

> I said his reputation was "good" so far as I had heard from others, and that was the simple, exact, whole truth, and all I could say of what I knew. . . . It will be a sorry day for American justice when a man, particularly one in public life, is too timid to state what he knows or what he has heard about a defendant in a criminal trial for fear that the defendant might be later convicted.[6]

Recall Eleanor Roosevelt's similarly ringing pronouncement at an A.D.A. dinner at the height of McCarthy's vicious "anti-Communism" campaign:

> The day I'm afraid to sit down with people I do not know because five years from now someone will say five of those people were Communists and therefore you are a Communist—that will be a very bad day. . . . In a democracy you must be able to meet with people and argue your point of view—people whom you have not screened beforehand. That must be part of the freedom of people in the United States.

When Theodore H. White called the election of 1956 in effect the last hurrah of the "patrician élite" members of American society, he was raising the issue of class. It is true that both Eleanor Roosevelt and Adlai Stevenson were born to privilege, a fact most notably evident in the patrician manner and tone of their speech. Adlai's speeches were always more polished than Eleanor's—a wag once complained that too many of her *My Day* columns read as though they'd been composed on a bicycle; he was notorious for perfecting his remarks while being introduced to an audience. It sometimes seemed he thought the flow and cadence of his prose to be of nearly equal importance to its content, while Eleanor's chief concern was to be understood by the least "lettered" of her hearers. (Her Hyde Park archive has a note on the stationery of *The Nation* magazine, written by editor Frida Kirchwey to another staffer, attaching a letter from Eleanor Roosevelt. Kirchwey writes, "She says so much when it appears she's saying nothing.")

White did not explain what he meant in his reference to the decline in influence of the "patrician élite" segment of this nation's powerful men and women. At least part of what he implied referred to a tension that has existed among foreign policymakers of all political parties since the Republic was born: namely, the proper balance between U.S. economic and military interests, that is, between "security" and trade. A deep divide along this fault line separated career State Department officers within the Eisenhower administration, on the one hand, and those who shared the views of Eleanor Roosevelt and Adlai Stevenson, on the other.[7] Because they knew that desperate people will eventually turn on the society that ignores them, Eleanor Roosevelt and Adlai Stevenson urged administration operatives and the country—*as a matter of strategic policy*—to invest a significant portion of U.S. aid funds in projects and programs designed to rid the world of illiteracy, poverty, fear, and despair, while still keeping one's powder dry. (Eisenhower warned of the dangers of an overemphasis on the military side of the equation in his famous farewell address.)

Our two protagonists in this story knew well that they were operating in a world where power and national self-interest were at the core of the "game." Nor did they pretend otherwise. Yet in memo after memo, in magazine articles and in speeches, as well as in the inner circle of U.S. policymakers, Stevenson decried the preponderance of military over economic assistance in U.S. foreign policy. He argued the case for programs that could close the gap between the have and the have-not portions of humanity, not out of sentimental "softness" but hard-headed self-interest. He frequently aired those same concerns in the United Nations. His efforts did not always succeed, but even when he failed he earned respect for the United States and an enviable reputation for personal integrity. Associates remarked on his ability to listen and absorb the views of those who disagreed with him. Venezuela's UN ambassador expressed the gratitude of his fellow delegates when he said that Stevenson was "a liberal in the true sense of the word. He was a man free of extremism, ever respectful of the opinions and viewpoints of others, but always convinced of the force of reason, not the reason of force."[8]

In her books, her columns, her speeches, as well as in her personal involvement Eleanor Roosevelt earned a similarly humane reputation both internationally and domestically. On frequent occasions she not only supported but also extended and enlarged the causes her protégé initiated. Among her vast personal contributions to the public sphere, her forging of the global agreement on a Universal Declaration of Human Rights would head every list.

This account has traced the evolution of a friendship from its beginning in postwar London to ER's death a brief sixteen years later. Like all friendships, theirs knew ebb and flow, peaks and valleys, while historic events in one of the most dangerous periods in American and world history tried the resilience, the patience, and the wisdom of both, bringing them periodically to a point of near-despair and sometimes desperation. The choices each made in such circumstances did not always prove as wise as the conditions required—or so it seemed at the time. Hindsight, however, has far more often vindicated those choices than condemned them.

Sixty years after our two principals' years of transformative public service, their words—still fresh, prescient, and relevant—still stir and challenge the reader of their speeches and other writings. They move us to examine our own first principles and assumptions, to ask, with Immanuel Kant: Would my action—or my passivity—if universalized, improve or subvert the public welfare, enhance or diminish the possibility of a more sustainable and humane existence for the seventh generation—not just in our land but across the world? Unhappily the past half century has been a period in which "the reason of force" has too often dominated U.S. foreign policy. In a world of nuclear bombs and the missiles to deliver them to GPS-determined targets, a different perspective might promise greater longevity for the human project.

* * *

We are left to wonder: Would Adlai Stevenson have been a "good," even superior president of the United States? That Eleanor Roosevelt thought he would is testimony enough for many. George Ball, a practical statesman of the "realist" school, had no doubt whatever that Stevenson "could have been a great President....He would have given dignity to America, improved the moral and intellectual tone, and, in my view, led the country steadily and well."[9] United Nations Secretary General U Thant wrote, "Ambassador Stevenson demonstrated with rare distinction how it was possible to combine the highest form of patriotism with loyalty to the idea of international peace and cooperation. His eloquence expressed the hopes and aspirations of the common man the world over."

For this writer, a note that David Lilienthal, former chairman of the Tennessee Valley Authority and later chairman of the Atomic Energy Commission, confided to his diary on February 15, 1953, may serve as a final verdict for this story:

> To a Jefferson-Jackson Day dinner at the Waldorf last evening...to meet and hear Governor Stevenson. As in his campaign, he made an impression of greatness with his uncanny way of expressing those things that one _feels_ about this country, and about her proper relation to the rest of the world. I was so "low" when he had finished, almost lower than election night itself, because of a feeling that we had suffered a disaster, for a great figure had come across the stage and we had missed him.[10]

ACKNOWLEDGMENTS

My first thanks must go to the Elderhostel organization (now Exploritas) for their unwitting inspiration of this project, which was conceived during a course that institution sponsored at Hyde Park, New York in November 2002. Five people who knew Eleanor Roosevelt explored the variety of roles she played in the lives of her neighbors and on the world stage. Reflecting on the contrast in national mood in our cynical time with the "can do" one of the "Roosevelt era" (1932–1962), I decided to inquire at the FDR Library whether it held documents that might illuminate the relationship between Mrs. Roosevelt and Adlai Stevenson. They were two Americans who, despite contrary evidence, exuded a hardheaded optimism about the human prospect that enlivened an entire generation. Perhaps, if the record showed they indeed shared more than a casual acquaintance, their story would bear retelling. At the time I had no inkling about either a possible relationship or what that record might reveal.

The Roosevelt Library turned out to possess a veritable gold mine of primary materials—manuscripts, correspondence, photographs—that seemed to justify further exploration. Thanks to Christopher Breiseth, CEO at the Franklin and Eleanor Roosevelt Institute at Hyde Park, an Arthur M. Schlesinger, Jr. grant, matching one by an anonymous donor, underwrote several week-long visits over the next three years. From each I returned with bundles of photocopies. My gratitude is boundless for the kindly—and extensive—ministrations of the FDR Library staff: Virginia Lewick, Karen Anson, Robert Clark, and Alycia Vivona. A week's exploration at the Seeley G. Mudd Manuscript Library at Princeton University, repository of the Stevenson archive, was richly enhanced by Carl Haag's extraordinary hospitality. University archivist Dan Linke and his able staff, Kristin Turner, Jennifer Cole, Christine Kitto, and Dan Santamaria, gracefully unraveled several Gordian knots on my behalf. At the Dag Hammarskjöld Library of the United Nations in New York, Marleen Buelinckx was particularly helpful.

In Washington D.C., as guest of cherished friends Lily and Ruel Eskelsen, a week at the Eleanor Roosevelt Papers Project at George Washington University led by Eleanor Roosevelt authority Allida M. Black produced a couple of nuggets that might otherwise have been missed. Ruel's sleuthing has subsequently resolved several seemingly intransigent dilemmas. Getting the historical context right, together with the large cast of characters who played varying roles on the domestic and global stages where both principals were leading figures, proved challenging but exhilarating. The book was finished in October 2007.

While simultaneously steadying my periodic quavers about its fate, John Morton Blum has been extraordinarily helpful on behalf of the book's publication. Grateful thanks go to Nancy Smith Fichter for permission to use quotations from her writer-aunt Lillian Smith's speeches and letters to Mrs. Roosevelt. Leonard and Carmen Friedman gave warm encouragement at the project's inception and since, as have my two siblings, Phyllis H. Stevens and David D. Henry. Nan Bentley kindly introduced me to her brother, Christopher Breiseth. He and David Woolner, president of the Roosevelt Institute at Hyde Park, have endured my far too many queries throughout the months since the manuscript was completed; their sound guidance and charitableness are exceeded only by their endless patience and I salute them here as men of rare quality, indeed. Low bows to the Palgrave team captained by Chris Chappel. Samantha Hasey and Matt Robinson were both particularly patient, tolerant and accommodating as were Rohini Krishnan and Maran Elancheran at Palgrave's production line partner, Newgen Imaging Systems.

Finally I doff my hat to Denver, Colorado's First Unitarian Church and its longtime member Robert Allen. In 1960 Allen was the Democratic majority leader in Colorado's House of Representatives when Stevenson came stumping for John F. Kennedy. Allen's telephone overture won Stevenson's cordial agreement to address a dinner launching our campaign for a new church building. The text of Stevenson's memorable impromptu remarks is among the papers in the church's archive.

My deepest thanks are for Patricia for her encouragement throughout the birthing of this project. Appropriately enough, she has been my severest critic as well as warmest enthusiast for the work. I trust she will find the finished product worth the emotional capital she has expended on its behalf; it would not have crossed the finish line without her.

Notes

Part I

Chapter 1   The United Nations, Crucible of the Alliance

1. *No Ordinary Time,* Doris Kearns Goodwin, 213.
2. Ibid., 214.
3. Ibid.
4. *Papers of Adlai E. Stevenson,* II, 10ff.
5. *Adlai Stevenson of Illinois,* 229.
6. *Adlai Stevenson: His Life and Legacy,* 95.
7. *Papers of Adlai E. Stevenson,* II, 241.
8. *Witness to History,* 1929–1969, 245.
9. Verbatim Minutes of Preparatory Commission, November 24, 1946. UN Archives, New York City.
10. Brian Urquhart, then private secretary to Sir Gladwyn Jebb, executive secretary of the Preparatory Commission, and later under-secretary-general of the UN. *A Life in Peace and War,* 94.
11. *Papers of Adlai E. Stevenson,* II, 272.
12. *Autobiography,* 280.
13. *Act of Creation: The Founding of the United Nations,* 71.
14. Ibid., 72.
15. See Jason Berger's seminal study, *A New Deal for the World: Eleanor Roosevelt and American Foreign Policy.* Social Science Monographs, 1981.
16. *Eleanor and Franklin,* 927.
17. Members of the delegation, in addition to Byrnes and Mrs. Roosevelt, were Edward R. Stettinius, Jr. U.S. representative to the UN; Senator Tom Connally; and Senator Arthur H. Vandenberg. Stevenson was named senior adviser to the delegation and first deputy to Stettinius.
18. *My Day,* January 3, 1946.
19. *Autobiography,* 303.
20. *Papers of Adlai E. Stevenson,* II, 338. Ms. Fosdick, daughter of the Protestant minister Harry Emerson Fosdick, was a State Department official, member of the Dumbarton Oaks working committee, later served with Stevenson in London and later New York. She provided material for Stevenson speeches and later became a Stevenson intimate.

21. FDRL, Eleanor Roosevelt Correspondence, Oral History Project, Durward V. Sandifer file.

22. Refugees who were resettled after World War I by the Nansen Commission of the League of Nations, precursor of the United Nations Office of the High Commissioner for Refugees. According to Vladimir Nabokov, authorities throughout Europe regarded holders of Nansen passports as "intrinsically despicable since [they] existed outside a national administration" and were consequently viewed with "preposterous disapproval." *Speak Memory: An Autobiography Revisited,* 277.

23. FDRL, Eleanor Roosevelt Papers, Box 4575a, USGA/Ia/SHCom/Del Min/3.

24. The rigors of negotiation were illustrated in a later diary entry, February 6: "At 3:10 we sat down in the sub-committee at Church House and we got up at 6 having agreed on 25 lines!"

25. Verbatim Record of First General Assembly, United Nations Archive, New York.

26. *The Private Papers of Arthur H. Vandenberg,* 240.

27. *Eleanor: The Years Alone,* 54.

28. *Autobiography,* 305.

29. *A Life in Peace and War,* 94.

30. *Papers of Adlai E. Stevenson,* II, 304.

31. Ibid., 191.

32. *Papers of Adlai E. Stevenson,* II, 339f.

33. A month later he had turned down invitations to head the Securities and Exchange Commission, the Foreign Policy Association, and the Carnegie Endowment for Peace.

34. *Papers of Adlai E. Stevenson,* II 338.

35. The General Assembly's final vote at the London meetings selected the United States as the agency's world headquarters, but New York City wasn't agreed upon until March, 1947. Land on Manhattan was then donated by John D. Rockefeller; the buildings were not ready for occupancy until 1952.

36. Since renamed Herbert Lehman College.

37. FDRL Small Collections, FER:SC:GUREW;ER;'47-'48, File 04144. ER to Edna Gurewitsch, January 20, 1948.

38. Personal communication, February 6, 2007. Following two terms as a Democratic member of Congress, in 1979 Mikva was appointed by President Jimmy Carter to the U.S. Court of Appeals for the District of Columbia Circuit. He served that circuit as chief justice until his retirement in 1994, was White House counsel, 1994–95, then returned to the University of Chicago Law School where he is currently Schwarz Lecturer and senior director of the Mandel Legal Aid Clinic.

39. A similar tribute appears in Mrs. Roosevelt's *Autobiography,* 354.

40. *Autobiography,* 320.

41. FDRL Joseph Lash Papers, Box 44, Lash interview with James Hendrick, New York City, May 5, 1970.

42. *A Brief Biography of Adlai Stevenson,* by Deb Myers and Ralph Martin, 12f.

PART II

CHAPTER 1   THE 1952 CAMPAIGN

1. *Adlai Stevenson: His Life and Legacy*, 253f; *Adlai Stevenson and the World*, 401.
2. *Papers of Adlai E. Stevenson*, III, 531.
3. *Portrait: Adlai E. Stevenson*, 55.
4. *Adlai Stevenson of Illinois*, 566.
5. *The Sower's Seed: A Tribute to Adlai Stevenson*, 12f.
6. He did eventually endorse Eisenhower, telling Mrs. Roosevelt: "I do not like the gang around Stevenson one bit." *Eleanor: The Years Alone*, 212.
7. Original in FDRL.
8. *Autobiography*, 353.
9. Original in FDRL.
10. Original in FDRL.
11. *My Brother Adlai*, 293.
12. *Adlai Stevenson of Illinois*, 606.
13. See John Bartlow Martin's *Adlai Stevenson of Illinois*; Walter Johnson's *How We Drafted Adlai Stevenson*; Stuart Gerry Brown's *Conscience in Politics;* George W. Ball's *The Past Has Another Pattern*.
14. "With AES in War and Politics," in *As We Knew Adlai*, 148.
15. *Adlai Stevenson: His Life and Legacy*, 250.
16. Ibid., 444f.
17. *Adlai Stevenson of Illinois*, 759.
18. *Papers of Adlai E. Stevenson*, IV, 223–229.

CHAPTER 2   ON THE WORLD STAGE

1. Johnson would later serve as editor of *Papers of Adlai E. Stevenson*.
2. New York, Harper & Co., 1954. It contained his Godkin Lectures delivered at Harvard University.
3. *Papers of Adlai E. Stevenson*, IV, 43.
4. Ibid., IV, 218.
5. Ibid., IV, 223.
6. Ibid., footnote 229.
7. *LOOK*, April 18, 1953.
8. *Papers of Adlai E. Stevenson*, V, 184.
9. Ibid., 317.
10. His blistering critique of the Communist regimes of Eastern Europe in *The New Class,* published in the United States in 1957, earned Djilas four years in jail; his *Conversations with Stalin*, a five-year jail term from which he was released in 1967.
11. D.J. Jerkovic, "Stevenson—Rome and Belgrade," *New Republic*, July 27, 1953, 15f.

12. *Autobiography*, 334.
13. Ibid., 334.
14. FDRL, ER Personal Correspondence, 1953–56, Box 3452.
15. Ibid.
16. *Adlai Stevenson: His Life and Legacy*, Porter McKeever, 309.
17. Sir Winston Churchill had proposed that representatives from the West should sit down with the new leaders of the U.S.S.R. to discuss "the wicked futility of war, because I must in good conscience make sure, if I can, that nothing is overlooked needlessly."
18. October 5, 1954 issue, 80, 82.
19. *Eleanor: The Years Alone*, Joseph P. Lash, 234.
20. *Truman*, David McCulloch, 891.
21. *Adlai Stevenson and the World*, J.B. Martin, 83f.
22. Despite its roster of distinguished sponsors—Arthur Altmeyer, Alan Barth, Mary McLeod Bethune, Charles I. Brannan, Frank Graham, A.J. Hayes, Murray Lincoln, James Patton, Leon Keyserling, Robert R. Nathan, Walter Reuther, Harry Schacter, Stephen Spingarn, and Telford Taylor—there was no overlap between this group and the "Finletter Group."
23. Nucleus members were Tom Finletter, John Kenneth Galbraith, Roy Blough (University of Chicago economist and member of Truman's Council of Economic Advisers), Seymour Harris (Harvard economist), Richard Bissell (MIT economist who had been Harriman's aide in administering the Marshall Plan), Clayton Fritchey (former Truman aide), Paul Appleby (Syracuse University economist and former member of FDR's Agriculture Department), Richard Musgrave (University of Michigan economist), and Arthur Schlesinger, Jr.
24. FDRL, Joseph P. Lash Papers, Box 44.
25. *A World of Love*, Joseph P. Lash, 401.
26. *What I Think*, Adlai E. Stevenson, ix and x.
27. In September 1955 the Civil Service Commission admitted that under the program "only 1016 employees had been charged and of these only 342 were dismissed," but the devastation wreaked on those accused was incalculable and the citizenry was seriously traumatized.
28. *New York Times*, March 14, 1954.
29. *Adlai Stevenson and the World*, J.B. Martin, 126.

CHAPTER 3   RACE AS AN ISSUE

1. *Hearts and Minds*, 92f. Ashmore reports that at the opening of the first school term following *Brown I*, "moderate leaders of the Upper South fell silent. Governor Stanley of Virginia reversed himself, announcing 'I shall use every legal means at my command to continue segregated schools in Virginia.' He did so at the direction of the state's venerated political boss, Harry Flood Byrd . . . who sent a signal to neo-Confederates everywhere when he proclaimed: 'We have a right to resist.'" Ibid., 218.

2. From his *The Court Years,* quoted in Ashmore *Civil Rights and Wrongs,* 103.
3. Lorena Hickok called it "the damnedest cesspool of human misery...in America." *Eleanor Roosevelt, Vol. 2, 1933–38.* Blanche Wiesen Cook, 13.
4. Mordecai Johnson, president of Howard University; John Hope, president of Atlanta University; Robert R. Moton, president of Tuskegee Institute; Charles S. Johnson, chair of social sciences at Fisk University; Charles C. Spalding, president of the North Carolina Mutual Life Insurance Company; and Walter W. White, executive director of the NAACP.
5. *Eleanor Roosevelt, Vol. 2, 1933–38,* Cook, 153.
6. *Adlai Stevenson and the World,* J.B. Martin, 122.
7. "Japan...is declaring in the Philippines, in China, in India, Malaya, and even Russia that there is no basis for hope that colored peoples can expect any justice from the people who rule in the United States, namely, the white people. For specific proof the Japanese point to our treatment of our own colored people, citizens of generations in the United States." *American Unity and Asia,* Pearl S. Buck, 29.
8. *Conscience in Politics: Adlai E. Stevenson in the 1950's,* Stuart Gerry Brown, 82.
9. FDRL, Eleanor Roosevelt Personal Correspondence, NAACP, 1952–54, Minutes of NAACP Board of Directors, September 22, 1952.
10. pp. 1013–1020. Sponsored by the Carnegie Corporation, the study was seven years in the making and involved more than a thousand contributors from all walks of life. Nobel Prize-winning Swedish sociologist Gunnar Myrdal headed the research team. He was given complete freedom to travel anywhere in the United States, to interview anyone he wished, and publish his conclusions without any editorial direction (save one very minor one) or interference from Carnegie. Nikhil Pal Singh notes that "the two published volumes bore the sole name of their Swedish author, even though black intellectuals...provided much of its substantive intellectual content.... [Ralph] Bunche, for example, penned four memoranda, comprising well over one thousand pages of prose, whose major findings were silently incorporated into the final report." *Race Is a Country,* 143.
11. *An American Dilemma,* II, 1021.
12. *When Affirmative Action Was White,* 131, 143. See also Justice William O. Douglas, concurring opinion in U.S. Supreme Court, Reitman v. Mulkey, 387 U.S. 369 (1967) at footnote 8, p. 397. On Web at http://supreme.justia.com/us/387/369/case.html#TTT1: "Realtors and mortgage lenders are largely dedicated to the maintenance of segregated communities. 1 Realtors commonly believe it is unethical to sell or rent to a Negro in a predominantly white or all-white neighborhood 7 and mortgage lenders throw their weight alongside."
13. Ibid.
14. FDRL, Eleanor Roosevelt Personal Correspondence, Box 3461, 1953.
15. FDRL, Eleanor Roosevelt Personal Correspondence, Box 3338, NAACP.
16. *Adlai Stevenson and the World,* 187.
17. Though it became known as "the Powell amendment," referring to Rep. Adam Clayton Powell, Jr., the only African American member of Congress who was

also minister of the Abyssinian Baptist Church of Harlem, New York, the legislation was actually authored by attorneys of the NAACP. That organization's board decided in 1950 to work through Powell for adoption of its goals of racial justice. [See Hamilton, 226–235]. Powell's mercurial temperament and cavalier regard for truth made him periodically a difficult person to work with. Sociologist Kenneth Clark called him "the most honest corrupt human being I have ever met," *New York Times,* May 2, 2005, A-23.

18. *Papers of Adlai E. Stevenson,* IV, 528, AES to Hubert H. Humphrey, July 15, 1955.

19. J.B. Martin reports that Stevenson had originally written but decided not to use a paragraph in his May 27 statement on the *Brown* decision: "I don't believe the ultimate solution is going to be either as difficult, explosive, or dangerous as some of the highly colorful reports of an embattled South would indicate. And I do know that the responsible leaders of the Negro communities want to see this new legal principle worked out in harmony." *Adlai Stevenson and the World,* footnote 122.

20. *Adlai Stevenson of Illinois,* 158.

CHAPTER 4   A SECOND RUN FOR THE PRESIDENCY

1. *The Worlds of Herman Kahn, 185.*

2. Ibid., 21.

3. Ibid., 84.

4. January 16, 1956 issue. Authored by James Shepley, *Time-Life* Washington Bureau Chief, the piece trumpeted "How Dulles Averted War—Three Times, New Disclosures Show He Brought U.S. back from the Brink" [in Korea, Vietnam, and Quemoy-Matsu].

5. *Papers of Adlai E. Stevenson,* IV, 468ff.

6. *Papers of Adlai E. Stevenson,* VI, 182.

7. *Archibald MacLeish Papers,* Library of Congress, Speeches and Lectures File, 1939–78, Box 49.

8. Stevenson died in London on July 14.

9. *Papers of Adlai E. Stevenson,* VI, 182.

10. *Autobiography,* 354.

11. *Hearts and Minds,* 218.

12. *New York Times,* August 13, 1956.

13. *Rosa Parks, A Life,* 100.

14. In 2004 the U.S. Justice Department, citing new evidence, announced it would reopen the case, but as this book goes to press the plan has not yet been acted upon.

15. *New York Times,* October 19, 1956.

16. *Adlai Stevenson and the World,* 211.

17. Manuscript in Mudd Library, Princeton, N.J.

18. Text in *What I Think,* 105–113.

19. *Rosa Parks, A Life,* 100.

20. *Hearts and Minds,* 245.

21. *Journals, 1950–2000,* 78.
22. *Papers of Adlai E. Stevenson,* VI, 292.
23. *Rosa Parks, A Life,* 100.
24. *Hearts and Minds,* 245.
25. *Journals, 1980–2000,* 78.

CHAPTER 5   CIVIL RIGHTS AGAIN

1. *Adlai Stevenson and the World,* 250. In a position later assumed by the U.S. Supreme Court, Stevenson consistently argued for federal control of offshore oil lands. The 1952 Republican platform promised "restoration to the States of their rights to all lands and resources beneath navigable inland and offshore waters within their historical boundaries."
2. *The Papers of Adlai Ewing Stevenson,* VI, 61f.
3. FDRL, Eleanor Roosevelt Personal Correspondence File, NAACP 1954–56, Box 3461, Minutes of NAACP Board of Directors Meeting, February 13, 1956.
4. *New York Times,* February 15, 1956, p. 1.
5. FDRL, Eleanor Roosevelt Personal Correspondence File, 1953–56, Box 3461, NAACP, 1954–56.
6. FDRL, Eleanor Roosevelt Personal Correspondence File, Box 3461, NAACP, 1954–56.
7. Princeton University Mudd Library, Stevenson Papers, Box 50, fl. 8, Herbert H. Lehman, 1952–1964.
8. FDRL, Eleanor Roosevelt Personal Correspondence File, 1953–56, Box 3461, NAACP, 1054–56. In 1934, Joseph Lash had accounted concisely for ER's inability to keep racial issues on her husband's agenda: "FDR was a political broker. Eleanor was a moralist." Quoted in Ashmore, *Civil Rights and Wrongs,* 23. Ten years later she was well on her way to becoming both.
9. Ibid.
10. Ibid.
11. Ibid.
12. Ibid.
13. *Papers of Adlai E. Stevenson,* VI, 73. Stevenson to Mrs. Robert Kintner, February 20, 1956.
14. FDRL, Eleanor Roosevelt Personal Correspondence File, Box 3461, 1954–56.

CHAPTER 6   STRAINS IN THE ALLIANCE

1. *Hearts and Minds,* 232f.
2. *Papers of Adlai E. Stevenson,* VI, 94.
3. *Politics of Honor,* 325.
4. *Papers of Adlai E. Stevenson,* VI, 98.
5. Ibid., VI, 99f.

6. Original in Mudd Library, Princeton University.

7. Ibid., VI, 109.

8. *FDRL, Eleanor Roosevelt Personal Correspondence 1954–56*, Stevenson file.

9. *Papers of Adlai E. Stevenson*, VI, 109.

10. *FDRL, Eleanor Roosevelt Correspondence, 1954–56, Stevenson file.*

11. *America in Search of Itself*, 73.

12. *Adlai Stevenson: His Life and Legacy*, 369f. Marietta Tree and her British husband, Ronald, had befriended Adlai's family during his work in London with the Preparatory Commission of the United Nations. Tree had been a member of Parliament and of Churchill's cabinet. Marietta, former vice-chair of the CIO's Political Action Committee and a *LIFE* magazine staff member, was active in the national Stevenson-for-President Committee. Stevenson had visited the Trees at their Barbados estate on several occasions.

13. *Adlai Stevenson: His Life and Legacy*, 369.

14. Ibid., 372.

15. Ibid., 381.

16. Ibid., 402.

CHAPTER 7   CROSSCURRENTS ON RACE

1. FDRL, Eleanor Roosevelt Correspondence File, NAACP 1954–56.

2. Ibid.

3. *Adlai Stevenson: Patrician among the Politicians*, 170.

4. FDRL, Eleanor Roosevelt Correspondence, 1954–56.

5. FDRL, Eleanor Roosevelt Correspondence, 1954–56, NAACP file.

6. NAACP Papers, Supplement 1, Reel 1, Minutes of Board of Directors and Secretary's Monthly Reports, May–December, 1956 University Microfilms, Bethesda, MD. By November 1956, Secretary Wilkins reported that NAACP's "Texas lawyers are gravely concerned for their licenses lest they be taken away because of the pronouncements of the NAACP itself." Minutes of Board of Directors, November 1956.

7. *Papers of Adlai E. Stevenson*, VI, 136. AES to Mary Bancroft, May 14, 1956

8. In mid-summer Aubrey Williams, newspaper editor, Alabama-born progressive who held numerous positions throughout the Roosevelt administrations, wrote Mrs. Roosevelt from Montgomery, Alabama:

> Maybe it isn't important that time and attention be spent on the few whites in the South that are still fighting. The Negroes down here are doing such a magnificent job, and that is what was needed, that it does not make too much difference what happens to these few brave souls. Don't worry too much about it.... I just came back last night from Orangeburg, S.C. where the Negro State College students refused to attend classes until the Governor removed the troops he— police—had riding the campus, and he removed them. The student leader was fired, but he is not really hurt, and I have not talked with a finer spirit in many a year. Tomorrow I go to Florida to get the

story of the boycott down there....It is really a wonderful thing to see, this coming alive of a whole race of people and fighting to gain their freedom.

9. Original in Mudd Library, Princeton University, Princeton, N.J. Eleanor Roosevelt file, AER to AES, June 13, 1956.
10. FDRL, Joseph P. Lash Papers, Box 44
11. FDRL, Eleanor Roosevelt Correspondence File, 1954–56, ER to AES, June 20, 1956
12. Original in Mudd Library, Princeton University, Princeton, N.J. Eleanor Roosevelt file, AER to AES, June 13, 1956.

CHAPTER 8   THE 1956 DEMOCRATIC
NATIONAL CONVENTION

1. FDRL, Joseph P. Lash Papers, Box 54.
2. *Adlai Stevenson: His Life and Legacy,* 374.
3. FDRL, Eleanor Roosevelt Correspondence, 1954–56, Gurewitsch file.
4. See above page 49.
5. Obviously as of this date Stevenson and Mrs. Roosevelt had not discussed civil rights in any depth.
6. The Democratic and Republican Civil Rights planks' direct references to the Supreme Court *Brown* opinions read:

Democrat	Republican
Recent decisions of the U.S. Supreme Court, relating to segregation in publicly supported schools and elsewhere have brought consequences of vast importance to our Nation as a whole and especially to communities directly affected. We reject all proposals for the use of force to interfere with the orderly determination of these matters by the courts	The Republican Party accepts the decision of the U.S. Supreme Court that racial discrimination in publicly supported schools must be progressively eliminated. We concur in the conclusion of the Supreme Court that decision directing school desegregation should be accomplished with "all deliberate speed" locally through Federal District Courts. .... Use of force or violence by any group or agency will tend only to worsen...the situation.

7. *World of Love,* 447.
8. *Eleanor: The Years Alone,* 253.
9. *New York Times,* August 7, 1956, p.1.
10. Ibid., August 8, 1956, p.1.
11. *New York Times,* August 11, 1956, p.1. Doris Kearns [Goodwin] sheds a defining light on the differing styles of Johnson and Stevenson in her study of the political genius from Texas, *Lyndon Johnson and the American Dream:* In the

1950s his style, not that of Stevensonian confrontation,... matched the belief and temper of the times. "Just look at the election results," Johnson said, "and you've got the perfect way to measure the success of my leadership against that of all those intellectual liberals who supported Paul Butler and Adlai Stevenson. After all, their method of campaigning—with their search for big issues and big fights with the Republicans—was tried twice and it failed twice, producing the greatest defeat ever suffered by the Democratic Party. Now you put that dismal record beside my method of campaigning for a Democratic Congress on the basis of the positive achievement of the Democratic Party, striving all the time to work out solutions rather than merely creating electoral issues, and what do you see but an unbroken string of successes for me and an unbroken string of failures for them? I was winning Democratic seats in the Congress while they were losing the Presidency." 152f.

12. *Mother R.,* 232.
13. *New York Times,* August 12, 1956, p.1.
14. Ibid., 61.
15. *The Years of Lyndon Johnson,* Volume 3, *Master of the Senate,* 801–809.
16. *Rendezvous with Destiny,* 237.
17. *New York Times,* August 13, 1956, p.1.
18. *Eleanor: The Years Alone,* 256.
19. *Official Report of the Proceedings of the 1956 Democratic National Convention,* 494.
20. *Adlai Stevenson: His Life and Legacy,* 377.

CHAPTER 9   THE CAMPAIGN TRAIL AGAIN

1. FDRL, Eleanor Roosevelt Personal Correspondence File, Box 3485; Stevenson (1953–56). Kennedy appeared on "Face the Nation" July 1, 1956 and gave evasive answers to interviewers who asked whether he would have voted with his senatorial colleagues in December 1954 to censure Joseph McCarthy. (Kennedy was in a hospital recovering from back surgery at the time.) The executive chairman of the New York State Stevenson-for-President Committee sent Mrs. Roosevelt the relevant paragraphs from the broadcast. She commented, "I think Mr. Kennedy's answers on the McCarthy censure were far from satisfactory." She maintained that bias until Stevenson's third bid (1960) for the presidency was rejected.
2. Original in Mudd Library, Princeton University, Stevenson Collection, Box 262, fl.7.
3. *World of Love,* 448.
4. Ibid., 449.
5. *Eleanor: The Years Alone,* 260.
6. *Adlai Stevenson: His Life and Legacy,* 379.
7. *Eleanor Roosevelt: Without Precedent,* 255.
8. *Eleanor: The Years Alone,* 261.
9. Ibid., 261f.
10. *World of Love,* 451 and *Eleanor: The Years Alone,* 260.

11. Original in Mudd Library, Princeton University, Princeton, N.J.
12. FDRL, Eleanor Roosevelt Personal Correspondence, Stevenson file.
13. Ibid.
14. *Papers of Adlai E. Stevenson*, VI, 261.
15. FDRL Eleanor Roosevelt Personal Correspondence, Stevenson file.
16. FDRL Eleanor Roosevelt Correspondence, Pauli Murray file.
17. Ibid.
18. FDRL Eleanor Roosevelt Personal Correspondence file, 1953–56.

CHAPTER 10   AFTERMATH: TIME FOR REFLECTION

1. *My Day*, October 27, 1956.
2. *My Day*, October 29, 1956.
3. *As We Knew Adlai*, 186f.
4. *Adlai Stevenson: His Life and Legacy*, 381.
5. *My Day*, November 2, 1956.
6. By November 1, "National estimates...generally agreed that the boiling tensions in the Middle East were worth from 3 to 5 per cent to Eisenhower in the final election outcome." Arthur Schlesinger, Jr., *History of American Presidential Elections*, 3352.
7. As we saw in Section II, Chapter 6, the substance of both Stevenson's proposals was adopted by subsequent administrations.
8. *World of Love*, 453.
9. *American Presidential Elections*, 3352.
10. *Eleanor: The Years Alone*, 264.
11. Ibid., 265.
12. *World of Love*, 116.
13. Ibid., 436.
14. Ibid., 243.
15. Ibid., 461. Unfortunately most of David's letters to ER, including the one to which this responds, are lost.
16. FDRL, Eleanor Roosevelt Personal Correspondence, 1957–60, Agnes Meyer file.
17. *Papers*, VI, 404, AES to AER, January 10, 1957.
18. FDRL, Eleanor Roosevelt Personal Correspondence, 1957–60, Agnes Meyer file.
19. The editors of Stevenson's *Papers* were unable to find the column in question, but see *Adlai Stevenson of Illinois*, 574, for Stevenson's comment on the subject.
20. *Papers*, VI, 437, AES to Mrs. Ernest L. Ives, January 28, 1957.
21. Ibid., VI, 454, AES to Karl Menninger, February 7, 1954.
22. *Papers*, VI, 532f., AES to Agnes Meyer, n.d.
23. *Adlai Stevenson: His Life and Legacy*, 398.
24. *Adlai Stevenson of Illinois*, 478.
25. Ibid., 478.
26. *Adlai Stevenson: His Life and Legacy*, 397.
27. Much of the material in this section is derived from J.B. Martin's 1966 interview with Mrs. Meyer. Princeton University's Mudd Library, John Bartlow Martin files, Box 1, folder 52.

28. *Adlai Stevenson and the World*, 200.
29. J.B. Martin files, Box 1, folder 52, Mudd Library, Princeton University.

CHAPTER 11   THE 1957 CIVIL RIGHTS BILL

1. *Papers of Adlai E. Stevenson*, VI, 458.
2. Ibid., VII, 4ff.
3. Ibid., VII, 23.
4. Ibid., VII, 98.
5. *Papers of Adlai E. Stevenson*, VII, 107.
6. *Autobiography*, 366f.
7. Ibid., 289f.
8. FDRL, Eleanor Roosevelt Papers, Oral History Project. Interview of Abram Sachar by Emily Williams, Nov. 10, 1978.
9. *Master of the Senate*, 850.
10. Ibid., 909.
11. *Lyndon Johnson and the American Dream*, 150.
12. *World of Love*, 469.
13. *My Day*, August 9, 1957.
14. *Master of the Senate*, 909.
15. Lyndon Johnson and the American Dream, 159.
16. *Papers of Adlai E. Stevenson*, VII, 73.

CHAPTER 12   THE ALLIANCE LOOSENS

1. *New York Times Magazine*, December 22, 1957.
2. See above Chapter 8, 107.
3. *Adlai Stevenson and the World*, 417.
4. *Papers of Adlai E. Stevenson*, VII, 140.
5. Ibid., VII, 152.
6. Ibid., VII, 160ff, 160ff.
7. *Friends and Enemies: What I Learned in Russia*. N.Y., Harper Bros., 1959.
8. *A World of Love*, 481.
9. Ibid., 507.
10. *Autobiography of Eleanor Roosevelt*, 60.
11. *On My Own* (1958), 190f.
12. Ibid., 195f.
13. *A World of Love*, 481.

CHAPTER 13   END OF THE ALLIANCE

1. *Papers of Adlai E. Stevenson*, VII, 306–310.
2. Ibid., 321ff. A native of Yorkshire, Davies was minister of the capital's All Souls Church (Unitarian) from September 1944 until his death at age 55 on September 26, 1957. During those thirteen years he wielded significant

influence among the District's liberal community. Supreme Court Associate Justice William O. Douglas, who edited a volume of Davies' writings, *The Mind and Faith of A. Powell Davies,* quoted him as saying that "Religion grows not by walking alone in a subtly self-gratifying mist of ego- cosmic melancholy, but in a dedicated personality, actively devoted to the great claims and causes of the age."

3. FDRL, Eleanor Roosevelt Personal Correspondence, Stevenson file, 1956–62.
4. *Eleanor: The Years Alone,* 280.
5. Ibid., 282.
6. *Adlai Stevenson: His Life and Legacy,* 426f.
7. *New York Times,* December 8, 1959.
8. *Papers of Adlai E. Stevenson,* VII, 379.
9. Ibid., VII, 376f.

CHAPTER 14 TRANSITION

1. *Eleanor: The Years Alone,* 284.
2. *Papers of Adlai E. Stevenson,* VII, 558.
3. James Jerome Wadsworth was U.S. Ambassador to the UN, as such a U.S. member of the UN "Peace Observation Commission," and later President John F. Kennedy's science adviser.
4. "Putting First Things First," *Foreign Affairs,* January 1960 issue, pages 191–208.
5. Mudd Library, Princeton University, Box 15, folder 2.
6. Mudd Library, Princeton University, Box 57, folder 1.
7. *World of Love,* 513.
8. Ibid., 517.
9. Mudd Library, Princeton University, Box 57, Folder 1.
10. *Papers of Adlai E. Stevenson,* VII, 521f. Mrs. Roosevelt apparently departed from her written statement, which read: "He [Stevenson] has the humility, courage and flexibility of mind which makes it possible for a great man to recognize a mistake if he makes one and turn to another solution."
11. *Adlai Stevenson: His Life and Legacy,* 451.
12. FDRL, Joseph Lash Papers, Correspondence with Eleanor Roosevelt, Box 43.
13. *Papers of Adlai E. Stevenson,* VII, 515.
14. *World of Love,* 522.
15. See *Adlai Stevenson: His Life and Legacy,* 437–464; and *Adlai Stevenson and the World,* 517–528 for play-by-play accounts of the Convention week.
16. *Adlai Stevenson: His Life and Legacy,* 456.
17. Mudd Library, Princeton University. John Bartlow Martin files, Box 1, Folder 52, 1966. Interview with Agnes Meyer.
18. FDRL, Eleanor Roosevelt Papers, Oral History Project, Thomas F. Soapes interview with Anna Rosenberg Hoffman, October 13, 1977, 23f.
19. *Rendezvous with Destiny,* 260.

20. *A Thousand Days*, 24.
21. *Papers of Adlai E. Stevenson*, VII, 507.
22. *JFK: The Presidency of John F. Kennedy*, 191.
23. Mudd Library, Princeton University, Box 797.
24. *Readers Digest*, April 2003.

PART III

CHAPTER 1 ELEANOR, ADLAI AND J.F.K

1. *World of Love*, 529.
2. *Papers of Adlai E. Stevenson*, VII, 558. AES to AER, August 15, 1960.
3. *Adlai Stevenson and the World*, 549.
4. Ibid., 563.
5. Ibid., 554.
6. Ibid., 562.
7. Ibid., 562.
8. Ibid., 591.
9. *World of Love*, 531. AER to Lorena Hickok, December 4, 1960.
10. FDRL, Eleanor Roosevelt Personal Correspondence, 1960–62, Stevenson file.
11. *World of Love*, 534.
12. Dorothy B. Robins' *Experiment in Democracy: The Story of U.S. Citizen Organizations in Forging the Charter of the United Nations*, is an illuminating study of the proliferation of organizations for international justice and world peace between 1900 and 1946.
13. FDRL, Eleanor Roosevelt Personal Correspondence, Oral History Project, Robert S. Benjamin file, December 13, 1977. Thomas Soapes, interviewer.
14. Original in Mudd Library, Princeton University.
15. FDRL, Eleanor Roosevelt Personal Correspondence, 1960–62, Stevenson file.
16. *Bay of Pigs*, 73f.
17. *A Thousand Days*, 271.
18. *Papers of Adlai E. Stevenson*, VIII, 54.
19. Ibid., VIII, 59, AES to Agnes Meyer, May 14, 1961.
20. *World of Love*, 316. Eleanor Roosevelt to Adlai Stevenson, April 19, 1961.
21. Ibid., Eleanor Roosevelt to Adlai Stevenson, April 21, 1961.
22. Original in Mudd Library, Princeton University.
23. *Papers of Adlai E. Stevenson*, VIII, 70.
24. Ibid., VIII, 81. Report to the President on the South American Mission, June 4–22, 1961.
25. Ibid., VIII, 79.
26. Ibid., VIII, 89.
27. *My Day* July 12, 1961.
28. *World of Love*, 540.
29. *Mother and Daughter*, 343.
30. FOIA released file, Part 2 of 4, FBI BUFILE 62–62734.
31. *Papers of Adlai E. Stevenson*, VIII, 126.

CHAPTER 2   CODA

1. *Papers of Adlai E. Stevenson.*, VIII, 170. AES to ER, December 7, 1961.
2. FDRL, Eleanor Roosevelt Correspondence, 1960–62, Stevenson file.
3. See preceding Section III, Chapter 1, p.168f.
4. *A Thousand Days*, 462.
5. *Remnants of Power* , 205.
6. *Adlai Stevenson: His Life and Legacy*, 500. Schlesinger to interviewer: "I've been told that [Kennedy] had no use for Stevenson.... I have never seen him show this. Kennedy always made allowances for Stevenson. He thought the values were worth it." Mudd Library, Princeton University, J.B. Martin file, Oral History interviews January 14, 1967.
7. *World of Love*, 541.
8. *Papers of Adlai E. Stevenson*, VIII, 173.
9. Ibid., 189. AES to Clara Urquhart, December 7, 1961.
10. Ibid., VII, 593. AES to Philip Noel-Baker, December 6, 1960.
11. Ibid., VIII, xiii. Marietta Tree to Carol Evans, May 8, 1973.
12. *Adlai Stevenson and the World*, 583.
13. *Just Friends*, 194f.
14. *World of Love*, 545.
15. Ibid., 545.
16. FDRL Eleanor Roosevelt Correspondence, Oral History Project, Thomas Soapes interview with Robert S. Benjamin, December 13, 1977.
17. *Papers of Adlai E. Stevenson*, VIII, 286. Martha Gellhorn, a friend of ER's since New Deal days, was a glamorous and fearless journalist whom David Gurewitsch had considered marrying after his divorce. She later married T.S. Mathews. Like her, he was an author and had formerly been an editor at *Time* Magazine.
18. *World of Love*, 561.
19. Ibid., 574.
20. October 25 was the "tipping point" in the U.S.-U.S.S.R. confrontation over the Soviets' installation of offensive missiles on Cuban soil. It was a day when the world confronted the abyss of a global nuclear war, and Stevenson was carrying the U.S. case before the bar of world opinion.
21. FDRL, Eleanor Roosevelt Papers, Oral History Project, Emily Williams interview with James A. Roosevelt, May 17, 1979.
22. *World of Love*, 570.
23. *Papers of Adlai E. Stevenson*, VIII, 342–346.

CHAPTER 3   THE SUMMING-UP

1. FDRL Eleanor Roosevelt Oral History Project. Interview with Martha Gellhorn, conducted by Emily Williams, February 20, 1980.
2. From a manuscript copy at the University of Georgia Hargett Library, Athens, GA. (Underlining in original). Speech at the Americans for Democratic Action Roosevelt Dinner, New York, February 28, 1957.

Lillian Smith Collection, Manuscript No. 1283A, Box 42, Speeches: Folder Heading: "The Creative Task of Our Time." Used by permission of Nancy Smith Fichter, Executrix of the Lillian Smith Estate.

3. *As We Knew Adlai*, 148.

4. *Look* magazine, November 20, 1965 issue.

5. *As We Knew Adlai*, 212.

6. *Papers of Adlai E. Stevenson*, IV, 166.

7. The division was present among as well as between both Republican- and Democratic-leaning policy makers in the State Department. McKeever reports a conversation between Adlai and John J. McCloy, one of his advisors, during the Berlin Wall and Soviet nuclear testing crises. Stevenson had argued for a decent respect for world opinion, to which McCloy responded tartly: "World opinion? I don't believe in world opinion. The only thing that matters is power." *Adlai Stevenson: His Life and Legacy*, 499.

8. *Papers of Adlai E. Stevenson*, VIII, viii.

9. *The Past Has Another Pattern*, 152.

10. *Journals of David E. Lilienthal*, Volume III, 369.

BIBLIOGRAPHY

Asbell, Bernard (ed.), *Mother and Daughter: Letters of Eleanor and Anna Roosevelt*, Coward, McCann & Geohagan, 1982.

Ashmore, Harry S., *Civil Rights and Wrongs*, New York, Pantheon Books/Random House, 1994.

————— *Hearts and Minds: The Anatomy of Racism from Roosevelt to Reagan*, New York, McGraw-Hill, 1982.

Baker, Jean H., *The Stevensons: A Biography of an American Family*, New York, W.W. Norton, 1996.

Ball, George W., *The Past Has Another Pattern*, New York, W.W. Norton, 1982.

Beasley, Maurine H. (ed. with Henry R. Beasley and Holly Cowan Shulman), *The Eleanor Roosevelt Encyclopedia*, Westport, Greenwood Press, 2001.

Berger, Jason, *A New Deal for the World: Eleanor Roosevelt and American Foreign Policy*, New York, Social Science Monographs, 1981.

Black, Allida M. (ed.), *Casting Her Own Shadow*, New York, Columbia University Press, 1996.

————— *Courage in a Dangerous World: The Political Writings of Eleanor Roosevelt*, New York, Columbia University Press, 1999.

Bohlen, Charles E., *Witness to History, 1929–1969*, New York, W.W. Norton, 1973.

Bradlee, Benjamin C., *Conversations with Kennedy*, New York, W.W. Norton, 1975.

Brinkley, Douglas, *Rosa Parks, A Life*, New York, Viking, 2005.

Brown, Stuart Gerry, *Conscience in Politics: Adlai E. Stevenson in the 1950's*, New York, Syracuse University Press, 1961.

————— *Adlai E. Stevenson*, New York, Barron's Woodbury Press, 1965.

Caro, Robert, *The Years of Lyndon Baynes Johnson, II, Master of the Senate*, New York, Knopf, 1982.

Cochran, Bert, *Adlai Stevenson: Patrician among the Politicians*, New York, Funk & Wagnalls, 1969.

Cook, Blanche Wiesen, *Eleanor Roosevelt: Vol. 1—1884–1933; Vol. 2—1933–1938*, New York, Viking, 1992 and 1999.

Cooke, Robert J., *The Political Career of Anna Eleanor Roosevelt: A Study of the Public Conscience*, unpublished PhD. thesis, New York, Syracuse University, 1965.

Davis, Kenneth S., *The Politics of Honor: A Biography of Adlai E. Stevenson*, New York, G. P. Putnam, 1957, 1967.

Doyle, Edward P., *As We Knew Adlai*, New York, Harper & Row, 1966.

Emblidge, David, *Eleanor Roosevelt's My Day*, 3 vols., New York, Pharos Books, 1991.

Fasulo, Linda M., *Representing America: Experiences of U.S. Diplomats at the U.N.*, New York, Praeger, 1964.

Flemion, Jess, and O'Connor, Colleen, *Eleanor Roosevelt, An American Journey*, San Diego, CA, San Diego State University Press, 1987.

Ghamari-Tabrizi, Sharon, *The Worlds of Herman Kahn*, Cambridge, MA, Harvard University Press, 2005.

Goodwin, Doris Kearns, *Lyndon Baynes Johnson and the American Dream*, New York, Harper & Row, 1976.

———, *No Ordinary Time*, New York, Simon and Schuster, 1994.

Goodwin, Richard N., *The Sower's Seed*, New York, New American Library, 1965.

Halberstam, David, *The Fifties*, New York, Villard Books, 1993.

Hamilton, Charles W., *Adam Clayton Powell, Jr.*, New York & Toronto, Athenaeum, 1991.

Hareven, Tamara K., *Eleanor Roosevelt: An American Conscience*, Chicago, Quadrangle Books, 1968.

Ives, Elizabeth S., *My Brother, Adlai*, New York, Morrow, 1956.

Johnson, Haynes, *The Bay of Pigs*, New York, Dell, 1973.

Johnson, Walter (ed.), *The Papers of Adlai Ewing Stevenson*, 8 volumes, Boston, Little Brown, 1973–77.

——— *How We Drafted Adlai Stevenson*, New York, Knopf, 1955.

Jonas, Gilbert, *Freedom's Sword: The NAACP and the Struggle against Racism in America, 1909–1960*, New York & London, Routledge, 2005.

Katznelson, Ira, *When Affirmative Action Was White*, New York, W.W. Norton, 2005.

Kearney, James R., *Anna Eleanor Roosevelt: The Evolution of a Reformer*, Boston, Houghton Mifflin, 1968.

Lash, Joseph P., *Eleanor Roosevelt: A Friend's Memoir*, New York, Doubleday, 1964.

——— *Eleanor and Franklin*, New York, W.W. Norton, 1971.

——— *Eleanor: The Years Alone*, New York, W.W. Norton, 1972.

——— *Life Was Meant to Be Lived: A Centenary Portrait*, W.W. Norton, 1984.

Lilienthal, David E., *The Journals of David E. Lilienthal,* 3 vols., New York, Harper & Row, 1964–83.

Martin, John Bartlow, *Adlai Stevenson of Illinois*, New York, Doubleday & Co., 1976.

——— *Adlai Stevenson and the World,* New York, Doubleday & Co., 1977.

MacLeish, Archibald, *Archibald MacLeish Papers* (1907–1981, bulk 1925–1970), LC control number mm82030932, Washington, DC, Library of Congress.

McCullough, David, *Truman,* New York, Simon and Schuster, 1992.

McKeever, Porter, *Adlai Stevenson: His Life and Legacy*, New York, William Morrow, 1989.

Myers, Deb, and Martin, Ralph, *A Brief Biography of Adlai Stevenson*, Foreword to *The Speeches of Adlai Ewing Stevenson,* New York, Random House, 1952.

Myrdal, Gunnar, *An American Dilemma: The Negro Problem and American Democracy,* 2 volumes, New York, Harper Brothers, 1944.

Nabokov, Vladimir, *Speak Memory Official Records of the United Nations General Assembly, 1946–52,* United Nations, New York.

Official Report of the Proceedings of the [1956] Democratic National Convention, Boston, Beacon Press, 1957.

Parmet, Herbert S., *JFK: The Presidency of John F. Kennedy,* New York, Dial, 1983.

Robins, Dorothy B., *Experiment in Democracy: The Story of U.S. Citizen Organizations in Forging the Charter of the United Nations.* New York, Parkside Press, 1971.

Roosevelt, Eleanor, *Autobiography,* Cambridge, MA, Da Capo Press, 1992.

——— *You Learn by Living,* New York, Harper, 1960.

——— *Tomorrow Is Now,* London, Hutchinson, 1964.

Roosevelt, Elliott, and Brough, James, *Rendezvous with Destiny: The Roosevelts of the White House,* New York, Putnam, 1975.

——— *Mother R: Eleanor Roosevelt's Untold Story,* New York, Putnam, 1977.

Rubin, Lillian B., *Just Friends: The Role of Friendship in Our Lives,* New York, Harper & Row, 1985.

Sachar, Abraham, *The Many Lives of Eleanor Roosevelt,* Waltham, MA, Brandeis University pamphlet, 1963.

Scammon, Richard M., *America at the Polls: Handbook of American Presidential Elections, 1920–1964.* Pittsburgh, Pittsburgh University Press, 1965.

Schlesinger, Arthur M. Jr. *A Thousand Days,* Boston, Houghton Mifflin, 1965.

Schlesinger, Arthur M., Jr. (ed.), and Israel, Fred R. (Assoc. ed.), *History of American Presidential Elections, 1789–1968; Vol. IV.* New York, Chelsea House/McGraw-Hill, 1971.

Schlesinger, Stephen C., *Act of Creation: The Founding of the United Nations,* Boulder, CO, Westview, 2003.

Schlup, Leonard, and Whisenhunt, Donald (ed.), *"It Seems to Me": Selected Letters of Eleanor Roosevelt,* Lexington, KY, University of Kentucky Press, 2001.

Sherwood, Robert E., *The White House Papers of Harry L. Hopkins,* 2 vols., London, Eyre & Spottiswoode, 1949.

Singh, Nikhil Pal, *Black Is a Country,* Cambridge, MA, Harvard University Press, 2004.

Sorensen, Theodore, *Kennedy,* New York, Harper & Row, 1965.

Steinberg, Alfred, *Mrs. R: The Life of Eleanor Roosevelt.* New York, Putnam, 1958.

Stettinius, Edward R., *The Diaries of Edward R. Stettinius, 1943–46,* Thomas M. Campbell and George C. Herring (eds.), New York, New Viewpoints, 1975.

Urquhart, Brian, *A Life in Peace and War,* New York, Harper & Row, 1997.

Vandenbergh, Arthur H., *The Private Papers of Arthur H. Vandenberg,* Boston, Houghton Mifflin, 1952.

Walton, Richard J., *The Remnants of Power: The Tragic Last Years of Adlai Stevenson,* New York, Coward-McCann, 1968.

White, Theodore H., *America in Search of Itself: The Making of the President, 1956–1980,* New York, Harper & Row, 1982.

Whitman, Alden, and *The New York Times, Portrait: Adlai E. Stevenson,* New York, Harper & Row, 1965.

Wilson, Joan Hoff, and Lightman, Marjorie (eds.), *Without Precedent,* Bloomington, IN, Indiana University Press, 1984.

Zangrando, Joanna S., and Robert L., *ER and Black Civil Rights,* in Wilson, Joan Hoff and Lightman, Marjorie, *Without Precedent,* Bloomington, IN, Indiana University Press, 1984.

INDEX